Camaro!
From Challenger to Champion:
The Complete History

An Automobile Quarterly Marque History Book

Cam

aro!

From Challenger to Champion: The Complete History

BY GARY L. WITZENBURG

PRODUCED BY THE STAFF OF AUTOMOBILE QUARTERLY

AUTOMOBILE QUARTERLY PUBLICATIONS

Publisher and Editor-in-Chief: L. Scott Bailey
Associate Editors: John J. Keebler III, Marguerite Kelly
Art Directors: Thomas C. Houtz, Michael Pardo
Editorial Assistant: Alan Coon
Production Editor: Mary B. Williams
Vice-President: Margaret Bailey
Business Manager: Kevin Bitz

Typesetting and printing by Kutztown Publishing Company, Kutztown, Pennsylvania;
color separations by Lincoln Graphics Incorporated, Cherry Hill, New Jersey;
binding by National Publishing Company, Philadelphia, Pennsylvania

Library of Congress Catalog Number: 81-70135

ISBN 0-915038-33-1   Princeton Publishing Inc.

Contents

Foreword

It was mid-summer, 1964.

Ford's Mustang had opened in April to rave reviews and was standing room only on the sales charts. It was the hottest subject at Chevrolet Engineering, where I was working prior to my senior year in college.

Would it continue to thrive or ultimately fizzle? Was it any good as a sporting car or just a rebodied Falcon? Would Chevrolet have something to go up against it? How soon?

I attended an orientation meeting for summer students where Design vice president Bill Mitchell was one of the key speakers. "When will Chevy have an answer to the Mustang?" he was asked.

"We already have," Mitchell bellowed. "It's called the Corvair."

True enough, there was a sharp, new '65 Corvair coming in the fall. But it was a six, and even turbocharged it would never quite cut the mustard.

Chevrolet finally got the corporate go-ahead in August, not long after Mustang sales had hit a hundred thousand, and work began in earnest on what would become the first Camaro.

I went back to school, finished my final year and returned to Chevy Engineering as a College Graduate in Training. I never worked on the new ponycar, but bits and pieces of it were coming together all around me.

That fall, 1966, the '67 Camaro was introduced. Though pretty, it lacked its rival's aggressiveness and fell a tad short in performance. It got off to a mediocre start but gained momentum as improvements were quickly made.

I left again, this time on military leave. In 1968 I ordered a new Nova—same as a Camaro under the body, I reasoned, but cheaper and more roomy inside.

Fall of '69 found me back at Chevy Engineering. The Nova had been stolen, and I needed a car. "Wait'll you see the new Camaro," said the personnel guy. "Wait'll you see the new Camaro," echoed everyone I met in the hallways.

So I ordered one, sight unseen: Rally Sport (sounds good on paper), F-41 suspension, four-speed, 250-hp (regular gas) 350 V-8, positraction, full instrumentation, console, harvest gold with black custom interior. . . . (Didn't want any cop-baiting, premium fuel-swilling Z-28).

I waited. . . . And waited. . . . And waited.

Public Introduction was Thursday, February 26th, 1970. My car arrived at the dealership a week before that. I went over to see it, sat in it, and drooled all over it, but they wouldn't let me have it.

God, it was gorgeous!

On Monday, the Camaro engineers started driving home their new company cars, but the dealer wouldn't deliver mine. I was going nuts.

The week ground by.

When Thursday finally came, I rushed over after work, signed the papers and took it home. I parked it in front of my apartment and couldn't stop looking at it. God, it was gorgeous!

Next day I left for a ski trip to Northern Michigan. I tried to break it in carefully, but it was too smooth and quiet. I kept catching myself going ninety on the two-lane roads. My brother, a terrific skier but no hot-shot driver, was trying to follow me in a '68 Camaro convertible and scaring himself and his passengers senseless. It created quite a sensation at the ski lodge.

A couple of weeks later, I drove it east on the Pennsylvania Turnpike. One man pulled in behind me at a gas stop and asked if it was the new Corvette.

The next year it was pressed into tow-car duty when I resumed racing. It moved west with me in 1973 when I left GM to try my luck as

Autoweek's *engineering editor, then back to Detroit the following year for another writing job.*

Many years and many cars later, I still have that '70-½ Camaro. I haven't driven it much since 1975, but I still love it when I do. It's the only car I've owned that I've never tired of.

You'll find it in the Color Portfolio section of this book, as photographed in late 1980 by my friend, Roy Query.

God, it's gorgeous!

Chevrolet's initial entry into the galloping ponycar market was unveiled on September 12th, 1966—a very fast reaction to a strong market need. Car and Driver *called it "a pleasant little car" that should sell "phenomenally well" and "ought to give Ford a helluva good run for its money." Just over 201,000 '67's were sold, less than half of Mustang's 443,000. But Camaro was off to a running start.*

Sales improved slightly in '68 but sagged in '69 as safety fever and insurance costs cut into the youth-car market. Camaro was still second to Mustang, but a strong second in an increasingly competitive field.

Tired of following, Chevrolet moved boldly into the styling and technological lead with its stunning '70-½ Camaro. Road & Track *called it "the best American car we've ever driven," but its sales impact was dulled by regulation, recession and strikes—the second of which nearly killed it in 1972.*

Then followed a decade of evolutionary change with four-year facelifts. While Camaro's reputation strengthened, the rival Mustang's ebbed as it grew first too big and then too small. Camaro thrived during the first fuel crisis but lost its high-performance Z-28 version; it finally topped the Mustang's sales in '77—the same year the Z-28 was re-introduced to an excitement-starved market.

I am most grateful for the opportunity to author this work, and for the kind assistance of publisher L. Scott Bailey and the staff of Automobile Quarterly Publications. I am also indebted to Jim Bradley, longtime curator of the Detroit Public Library's Auto History Collection, who passed away as the book was in progress.

The project could not have been completed without the willing and effective assistance of Jim Williams, Ralph Kramer, Jim Crellin and especially Suzanne Kane (who did most of the legwork) of Chevrolet Public Relations; Cliff Merriott, Bill Knight, Colleen Belli and Bruce MacDonald of GM Corporate PR, Floyd Joliet and Jim Brady of GM Design Staff and Bob Norwood of Campbell Ewald Co. Also thanks to Tom Blattler of the Sports Car Club of America, Dan Luginbuhl of Penske Corp., Al Binder of Ward's Communications and Dave Arnold of Mid-Ohio. And very special thanks to my fiancée and best friend Jill for her able help and tolerance.

Past and present Camaro designers and Chevrolet executives and engineers who granted interviews and aided the considerable research job include, in alphabetical order: George Angersbach, John DeLorean, Bob Dorn, Pete Estes, Hank Haga, Dave Holls, Chuck Jordan, Paul King, Bob Knickerbocker, Bunkie Knudsen, Bob Lund, Alex Mair, Don McPherson, Bill Mitchell, Jerry Palmer, Vince Piggins, Bill Porter, Lloyd Reuss, Irv Rybicki, Fred Schaafsma, John Schinella, Bill Scott, John Shetler, Ed Taylor and Tom Zimmer.

About the time this book appears, the remarkable third-generation Camaro will be ready for market, fully up to its task of continuing the legend.

It enters the era of the Eighties leaner, meaner and loaded for bear. It will be another all-time classic, an affordable American exotic. In a couple of years it will also be, along with Corvette, one of two remaining rear-drive Chevrolets. And by mid-decade it will begin to look pretty large again as everything else continues to shrink down around it.

Chances are, the fourth-generation Camaro will come soon after—much smaller and lighter, with space-saving front-wheel drive and supercharged four-cylinder engines instead of V-8's and sixes. It will surely be an exciting car in the long Camaro tradition. But it will never be the same.

—Gary Witzenburg

Troy, Michigan

CHAPTER ONE

Preludes

When American auto workers returned to passenger car production after World War II, the business was much simpler than it is today. Essentially, there were Chevrolets, Fords, Plymouths and Nashes at the bottom; Cadillacs, Lincolns, Chryslers and Packards at the top; and a fair selection of intermediate material in-between. A hard-working, car-starved public lined up at the dealerships for nearly anything that moved on four wheels. Almost no one but returning servicemen had heard of Volkswagen or Renault or MG.

But Americans gradually began to covet the smaller, sportier and more fuel-efficient European cars. In 1950 Nash countered with the first domestic "compact" car, the Rambler. Three years later, Chevrolet was first to answer the small but growing demand for sports cars by introducing the Corvette. Ford followed in 1955 with its two-seat Thunderbird.

In 1956, dealers sold nearly 100,000 imported cars in the United States. A year later that figure more than doubled, accounting for 3.4 percent of total U.S. sales. While sports car demand had leveled off, it became clear that the major domestic automakers would have to work seriously to combat the swelling economy car market, led by Germany's Volkswagen.

Crash programs at Detroit's Big Three led to fall 1959 introductions of the 1960 Chevrolet Corvair, Ford Falcon and Plymouth Valiant. These new small cars beat back the import invasion for a time, from a high of over 600,000 units (10.1 percent of the market) in 1959 to about 340,000 (4.8 percent) in 1962. But they also opened a new competitive can of worms for Detroit.

Chevy's Corvair was by far the most sophisticated of the three. Conceived under engineer/general manager Ed Cole and inspired by VW's highly successful "Beetle," it boasted independent rear suspen-

XP-836 anti-Mustang concepts began where Rybicki's "warehouse" project ended, had general theme embodied in Camaro.

sion and a rear-mounted, air-cooled flat six-cylinder engine. Nevertheless, it was a sales disappointment. Ford's dirt-simple—and cheap—Falcon set first-year sales records for its maker and killed Corvair in the marketplace, while even Plymouth's plain-vanilla Valiant gave the little Chevy some serious competition.

Then late in 1961 in a flash of marketing genius, Chevy dressed up a special version of its lackluster Corvair with bucket seats, wire wheel covers and a four-speed floor shift, called it "Monza," and watched it become an instant hit. "I think Ed Cole deserves the credit for creating the sporty Corvair," recalls Paul King, then a Chevrolet development engineer. "It took off like gangbusters, and soon we were selling more Monzas than we had sold Corvairs in total before that time."

It was the industry's first really youthful, exciting and yet affordable small car. Its success did not go unnoticed by Lee Iacocca, the aggressive young Ford Division manager who was looking for a way into the hearts of America's youth to steal them away from arch-rival Chevrolet. The youth-oriented Corvair Monza provided just the inspiration he needed, and two years later led to the creation of America's first ponycar, the hugely successful Ford Mustang.

Meanwhile, the GM car divisions were bidding for the right to produce and market what would become the corporation's first luxury specialty car, competition for the four-seat Thunderbird, another Ford success story. Buick Division emerged the lucky winner, and the handsome new car, fashioned in a special studio under GM styling vice president Bill Mitchell, was soon being groomed for a 1963-model debut as the Buick Riviera.

This gave then-Chevrolet chief designer Irv Rybicki an idea. Why not do a similar, but smaller and less expensive "personal" coupe based on a Chevrolet? Rybicki recalls sitting with Mitchell in his office in 1962, kicking the idea around. "By God," Mitchell said, "that's not a bad idea! But let's do it outside the building where no one in the corporation can see what we're up to."

"So," Rybicki continues, "we went across the street to our warehouse, created a little room there and started a program. We did a car based on the new-for-'62 conventional compact Chevy II that was so close to the Mustang in length, width and height, it was astounding . . . and we didn't even know those devils at Ford were doing one!" Five months later, when the clay version was completed, Mitchell was so impressed that he invited Bunkie Knudsen, who had succeeded Cole as Chevrolet general manager in 1961, to have a look.

Rybicki reports that Knudsen liked the car, but said " 'I'll tell you, fellows, the one thing we don't need right now is another car.' The

mid-sized Chevelle, readied for a '64-model introduction, would be the fifth distinct Chevrolet line. There wasn't a Mustang around at that time and, had I been in his position, I guess I would have said the same thing. He was pretty adamant that we couldn't sell a sixth car line, so we abandoned the project all together after that."

Combined, the Corvair and Chevy II did a pretty fair job of combating Ford's Falcon for the next year and a half, while rumors flew about the new Ford sports car to be launched early in 1964. But with the Corvette alone and thriving in the domestic sports car market and the Corvair Monza covering the low-cost sporty field, the upcoming Ford aroused little concern at Chevrolet.

Late in 1963 Rybicki's Chevrolet Number Two Studio under studio chief Hank Haga whipped up a Chevy II-based concept car called "Super Nova," a sporty coupe with long hood, short rear deck, low roofline and very little chrome. When they showed it to Mitchell and his predecessor, retired design vice president Harley Earl, both liked it. Thereafter, the design was translated from clay into fiberglass and thence into a running car. During the winter of 1964 it appeared at the New York Auto Show several weeks before the similarly proportioned Ford Mustang's debut at the World's Fair, also in New York.

The Super Nova created a lot of excitement at the show, and Chevrolet general manager Bunkie Knudsen was one who especially liked it. "It was an idea car," he says, "but not so exotic that you couldn't produce it. I recall some of the Ford people coming over while I was standing there and asking whether we were going to build the car, and I remarked, 'If they'll let us, we'll build it.' I think that shook 'em up a bit, because it was a pretty good looking little car."

"It was just a concept piece," says Rybicki, "to see what reaction we'd get from the public, and the reaction was fairly good. I remember Knudsen came back talking about it and wondering how he could sell it [to GM upper management]." But management wasn't biting yet.

"At that time," Knudsen relates, "Jack Gordon was president of the corporation, and he was not very excited about sporty cars. He turned us down on the Super Nova, and that left us with nothing but the Corvair." Because the Corvair was due for a very nice major redesign for the 1965 model year, and there was an optional tur-bocharger for those who wanted extra power, the corporation believed that it would hold the fort just fine against any small sporty car from Ford.

Even when rumor became reality in April and Ford unveiled its small, inexpensive and very sporty Mustang, GM brass didn't take it seriously at first. There's a tendency to look critically at the other guy's product, pick over its weak points and minimize its strengths. It's a natural prejudice even when people try to be objective, and the Mustang's case is a classic example.

"I remember walking in to view the Mustang the first time we got hold of one," recalls Bob Lund, then a Chevy assistant general sales manager, "and I looked at it and said it would never sell. It seemed too boxy and square, unappealing." Rybicki thought it was "a funny looking little coupe." Styling vice president Mitchell tells of seeing one for the first time at the posh Bloomfield Hills, Michigan Country Club in the company of famous Italian designer Sergio Pininfarina. "He looked it all over," Mitchell relates, "and in his Italian way said, 'This is not a sports car. . . . It has no flavor. . . . It has nothing.' "

Opposite page, left to right: S.E. Knudsen was Chevrolet general manager during Camaro's conception, Irv Rybicki was chief designer; Alex Mair was engineering director, Pete Estes general manager when car was launched. This page: Rybicki's small-car project in mid-1962.

Mitchell himself called it the "Hamtramck Ferrari" (after a largely Polish community near Detroit) which Ford General Manager Lee Iacocca didn't appreciate at all.

But some at GM were not so sanguine. "I happened to be at Design Staff when the first Mustang rolled into the garage," relates E.M. "Pete" Estes, who was then Pontiac Division general manager. "Everybody was standing around saying what a disaster it was and how market research showed there was no market for it, and so on. I didn't say anything, but I had a feeling that this thing was going to backfire on us sure as Sam Hill."

While top GM management kept its collective head in the sand throughout much of that first summer of Mustang Mania, it became increasingly obvious to those below that something would have to be done. Even while design chief Mitchell was saying publicly that the '65 Corvair *was* Chevy's answer to the Mustang, he was promoting his Corvair Super Spyder concept car to the top brass as a production sporty-car candidate. Rybicki had Haga's studio already working on some new sporty concepts in clay, and Knudsen kept trying to sell the idea at monthly Engineering Policy Committee meetings.

It took just four months for the Mustang to top 100,000 sales on its way to the biggest first-year success of any new car in history. And it took that first 100,000 sold and delivered Mustangs to awaken conservative GM corporate management. "Some of those people up at the top had some information that the Mustang wasn't selling very well," says Knudsen. "They were shocked to pieces when they found out how many had been sold in such short order."

But a sleeping giant, once aroused, can run pretty fast. It was already August of 1964 when Knudsen was given the go-ahead—less

11

than two years before his potential Mustang-killer would have to be in production for a fall 1966 introduction. Code-named XP-836, the program was already underway and awaiting approval in Hank Haga's design studio. "We had a lot of artwork on the wall," says Haga. "We knew it was going to happen someday because those Mustangs were out there creating a lot of excitement in the market-place. It was hot-and-heavy in our studio once we got the word. We were really flying, did a lot of renderings and put in a lot of over-time!"

Different people recall "getting the word" differently, depending upon where they were and what they were doing. Assistant general sales manager Bob Lund remembers when he heard about the go-ahead. "We were all highly elated because we just didn't feel that the Monza could cope with that kind of competition. I remember how we rushed it every chance we got to bring it to market as fast as we could." But Alex Mair, who was at that time an executive engineer in the Chevrolet Truck Group, says, "All I remember is hearing that we had decided to do it, and that we were calling it the 'F' car. We were all amused at that, see, because of the relationship to Ford."

When the order *was* given, the mandate was clear. Despite the short gestation period, Chevrolet's ponycar would have to be superior to the Mustang in every way. In other words, do it fast, but do it right—and better. Better styling, better performance, better ride, better handling, longer, lower, wider and more roomy inside.

"We were looking for a vehicle that would compete with the Mustang," says Irv Rybicki, who by then had been promoted to group chief designer over the Chevrolet studios. "As I remember, the word came down that we would have to beat it in every dimension. More torso room, more rear legroom. I don't know if we talked about fuel efficiency at that time, but I'm sure we talked about per-formance. We talked about the degree of interchangeability with another program, and ground rules were set down."

Adds development engineer Paul King: "We were aiming for the appearance aspects, the personal attraction, the image aspects, so the Design Staff participation was very important. From the function standpoint, we were interested in a car that was better in perform-ance, better in handling and so forth, than the cars [Chevy II] that we were springing from at the time. It had to look sportier and more special than the products we had been doing, and it had to have per-formance to match its image."

According to Rybicki, it was common to have a competition of sorts among two or more studios to determine the design of a new product that would be shared by more than one division. "You start with a variety of themes," he explains, "and let each room run. However, the '67 car was largely done in the Chevrolet studio because Pontiac was in and out of the program during the course of its development." It wasn't until very late in the program, in fact, that Pontiac was given the go-ahead to do its own F-car version, which became the Firebird, and it was too late to change it much for divisional identity.

Dave Holls, who became Chevrolet group chief designer when Rybicki was promoted in 1966, explained the design process in detail in a 1967 Camaro promotional film:

Since automobiles are designed around people, one of the first steps is to design a seating package ... the best height and seating angle ... legroom, hiproom, shoulder room, headroom.... How well can [the driver] see? In front, at the sides and in the rear?

As the basic seating package takes shape, exterior styling begins. Initially, stylists are given free reign. Each stylist's interpretation is considered. Eventually, a styling concept begins to emerge. The byword becomes: don't just try to be different, try to be right. Come up with an honest look—clean, sleek, no tinsel or gingerbread, nothing contrived. A direct approach to design that will be in style for years, look right in any setting and have its own distinct personality.

While one group works on exterior design, another concentrates on interiors. Appearance inside must be in keeping with appearance outside. Instruments must be clustered for quick reference, easy to read, nicely recessed and set against a black background to minimize glare; controls located close at hand, no unnecessary reaching.

Hank Haga's studio, which had been doing sporty four-seater concepts all along, was given the assignment of bringing this new design along toward production. "The people in the studio—designers, modelers and engineers alike—were all enthusiasts," says Haga, "and they were pretty excited when they found they had a chance to design an all-new four-place sports car which would eventually compete directly with the Ford Mustang."

Starting with concepts similar to what had evolved from Rybicki's short-lived "warehouse" sporty coupe project of two years before, Haga and assistant studio chief John Schinella soon had their own ideas molded in clay for three-dimensional viewing. The theme was "fluid," looking like canvas stretched over wire, the dominant GM design concept at that time.

"We felt very strongly about reducing design to its simplest form, using only one peak down the body side interrupted by accented wheel arches," explains Haga, who also had presided over the similarly-themed '65 Corvair. "It really evolved from that Corvair, which was very much evolved from the Italian school of design. This gave the Camaro its own character and set it apart from the Mustang approach, which was much stiffer and more angular, like a big car scaled down. They [Ford] had proportion working for them in the

Opposite page: early '64 Super Nova show car; above left: Henry Haga, head of Chevy #2 Studio; right: George Angersbach, assistant chief designer in charge of first interior; below: refined XP-836 clay model.

This page: highly refined design with Italian-inspired look of "canvass stretched over wire." Page opposite: three new concept drawings from October '64, all with fastback roofline that was soon incorporated into clay model resembling finished product.

side view, but every big-car cliché in the book was in that car. That wasn't what we were after."

A new series of full-size drawings was done in late September and early October with swoopier lines, fastback roof treatments and more prominent peaks over the wheel arches. These ideas were then incorporated into the clay model, which was beginning to take on the now-familiar look of the eventual finished product. As it turned out, the "coke bottle" fender shapes stayed, but the fastback roofline didn't.

"The profile of the car also was very simple," Haga continues, "using the classic approach of crowned fenderlines with their high points directly above the accented wheel arches. We purposely avoided any contrived design lines or superfluous detail. Even the execution of the wide, horizontal-loop front end, with its hidden headlamp RS variant, was as pure in content as we could make it."

How did they come up with the odd "bumble bee" striping around the SS-model's nose? "We started looking at some fighter planes, and they had the black, non-reflective panel on top of the nose so the pilot wouldn't get reflections off the bare aluminum, and some of those also had a sort of bumblebee stripe around the air intake. So we applied that to our nose. One reason was that it tended to visually shorten the nose and made it look a little tougher."

As for the rear end, "We did a million different taillights," says Schinella. Among many others, the traditional Chevrolet round lamps were tried, "but they didn't locate right," according to Haga. "We wanted to get a bigger lens area on that car. It still looked too much like a sedan, and round taillights looked a little out of place. Also, we were trying to stay away from the Corvair look at that point."

Meanwhile, the Number Two Interior Studio under assistant chief designer George Angersbach was struggling with an instrument panel that had to look better and more sporty than the Chevy II's but could not cost much more to produce. Angersbach mounted a four-speed shift handle on the side of his office chair to remind himself that he was working on a performance-oriented car and developed a very attractive concept similar to that used in the Super Nova show car. It featured three separate round pods housing a speedometer and tachometer on either side of a large clock, with smaller auxiliary gauges at eye level high in a large center console extension that swept up from floor to crash-pad. The panel sloped away from top to bottom to give a feeling of spaciousness, and the console extended well back into the rear-seat area.

Unfortunately, this idea was watered down to a less interesting,

Refined models, one of them compared with '65 Mustang in December 1964.

less expensive design with two large portholes for speedo and tach and three small, optional gauges low on a shorter, plainer console. "It had some of the flavor of the Corvair," says Angersbach, "and also some flavor from the Corvette design. We were doing a new Corvette instrument panel at the time, which didn't fly, so we used part of that design on the Camaro. At first the gauges were on the instrument panel and located high, but they slipped down onto the console when they became optional."

Like their Design Staff counterparts, the Camaro development engineers were faced with the task of creating a car based upon, but very different from, the compact Chevy II economy car. But they did have one big advantage: the Chevy II was due for replacement by an all-new version for 1968, so they could spin their '67 sporty car off a much-improved body/chassis platform. Provided they could get it done in time.

As Don McPherson, then-chief engineer for engines and passenger car transmissions, axles and drivelines, pointed out in the previously mentioned introductory film, newly emerging computer technology played a large role in improving efficiency and speeding the development process:

Still on paper, computers evaluate the engineering approach of the new car ... such basic information as the

Early instrument panel had triple round pods, full console with high-mounted auxiliary gauges and protruding switches.

height of the car, its weight distribution, center of gravity and wheelbase dimensions. The computer comes up with the best combination of such factors as roll axis, roll distribution, roll stiffness, ride rate, front-end geometry and so on. . . .

Another use for computers is to produce prototype parts. Design information is fed into the computer, which in turn operates a machine that produces the part. Any changes are programmed into the computer and incorporated into the finished product.

"We had a rather aggressive development group at the time, stationed at the Proving Ground," relates then-development engineer Paul King. "We had lots of facilities, and we did a lot of investigating of different kinds of structural concepts, arrangement concepts, suspension concepts. This was the environment where a lot of the background work was done on the first Camaros.

"We had a lot of freedom, so when a development engineer had an idea, he had the facilities and machinery and so forth to try it out. The bad ones we didn't say much about, and the good ones we took a step further to the demonstration phase and showed them to management.

"Two of the things we were unhappy with on the first Chevy II

were some of its driving characteristics and its lack of isolation. We had ten zillion programs going on the Chevy II to improve these things. We were not thrilled with the front springing arrangement up on top of the upper control arm, and we were not thrilled with the front structure.

"The construction was unibody, but there was a bolted joint right at the cowl. It was built in two pieces, the front structure and the rear structure, and bolted together. Looking for improvement, we did a lot of things with different types of mounting arrangements between the two. As we studied further, we had all kinds of stub frame arrangements built; some reached back to the front eyes of the rear springs. Once we got the word to go, a lot of that was used as the platform on which the Camaro was based."

This work ultimately evolved into a clever combination of the two basic types of automobile construction, body-frame integral ("unibody") and separate frame. A partial frame, looking like the front portion of a conventional ladder frame, became the platform on which the entire front structure—inner and outer sheetmetal, engine, transmission, suspension, brakes, steering—was assembled. This unit extended under the rear unibody section as far as the front-seat area, and was bolted to it through tuned rubber mounts.

The front suspension used short upper and long, wide, "wishbone-

type" lower control arms with tube shocks inside coil springs mounted between the lower arms and a structural suspension crossmember. Steering was a parallel relay "recirculating ball" design mounted behind the suspension. Standard brakes were 9.5 inch drums with 2.5 inch wide linings front and 2.0 inch rear. The Hotchkiss rear suspension was Chevy II based, with a Salisbury solid rear axle suspended on single-leaf ("mono-plate") rear springs, which were shorter than the Chevy II's and splayed outward front-to-rear to make room for the 18 gallon gas tank. Rear tube shocks were outboard of the springs, near-vertical in base cars, and staggered in the SS-350 performance version. Later, this simple and inexpensive arrangement would prove to be the most controversial feature of the 1967-1969 Camaro.

The 1967 Camaro promotional film described the testing process in this way:

> Mockups of parts and components are fitted into a wooden framework of the F-car. Meanwhile actual components are studied. Will they go together properly? Will they work together? Concealed in the familiar bodies of current models, these components are subjected to thousands upon thousands of driving miles, both on the Proving Grounds

Winter 1964-65 renderings; looking for the right taillamp configuration.

and around the country. Then they are torn down and examined carefully. Then they are subjected to exhaustive testing, sometimes put through millions of cycles, more than they will ever be called upon to operate during the life of the car.

On July 1st, 1965, about halfway through the Camaro program, Bunkie Knudsen was promoted into GM's corporate management and Pete Estes came over from Pontiac Division to take his place as Chevrolet general manager. "The interior design was pretty well set by the time I got there," he recalls, "but we were still working on the front end and the rear end at that time. I remember when we took it off the Proving Grounds for test rides. We had the whole thing camouflaged, all blacked out with cardboard on the quarter panels and everything. But even then the fact that it was low and sleek and slender in the body prompted lots of questions. If a prototype car causes a big commotion, even looking like that, when you pull into a gas station or something, you really know you've got something. That was a hot car right from the start."

As a new product nears production, efforts to camouflage it on test trips taper off in the last minute rush to find and fix all remaining problems. Paul King recalls a trip that led to the discovery, late in the program, of the rear axle hop that would plague the Camaro throughout its first three years.

"We had a fleet of Camaros on a Western trip, and I had the first Super Sport. We went down to a restaurant in L.A. for dinner. This was getting fairly close to production, and these may have been pilot-line cars. They were good-looking, they looked different, people knew they were different, and they attracted attention. The parking lot guys took the cars, and when we came out from dinner they were oohing and ahhing over this Super Sport. I obviously wanted to make a good show of leaving, so I peeled out onto Sunset Boulevard. It was a manual transmission job, which we hadn't had many of until then, and I got into the damnedest power hop. I didn't back off, and it was really bad. That got us busy working to fix the problem and led to the staggered shocks.

"That's why we like the road trips, because you have a certain set of roads and you do certain things, but sometimes you drive around under unplanned, random circumstances, and every once in a while you'll discover something . . . some combination of cornering, road surface and a limited-slip differential, for example, that creates a problem. We had not been aware of this problem until then."

Alex Mair, who was promoted in October 1965 to chief engineer,

Clay-modeler fine-tunes Rally Sport front end while instrument panel design nears completion in interior studio.

Don McPherson, chief engineer engines and passenger car transmissions, axles and drivelines during Camaro's development; Paul King, passenger car development engineer at the Proving Ground; experiments with Rally Sport and nose-striped performance version.

passenger cars, tells of torsional shake problems with the Camaro convertible, and his unusual solution: "When we first got the development convertible, because it was not a full integral body and because it had the stub frame, it was one of the shakiest cars ever."

When Pete Estes took a ride in it, Mair relates, "it had this torsional shake, just constantly torsionally vibrated. If you hit one or two bumps on a smooth road, it would shake about eight or ten cycles. Estes said, 'you'll have to get rid of that.' He viewed the Chevrolet engineering department as the biggest in the world, an outstanding place that could solve everything.

"We tried everything that had worked in the past," Mair continues, "stiffening the underbody, putting in pillar reinforcements and Mercedes-type door strikers, everything—and nothing seemed to influence it at all. Finally we decided to do it with harmonic damping. We put some 'cocktail shakers,' as we called them, big iron bobweights mounted on springs in steel cylinders, clear in the corners of the car—up near the headlights in front and by the taillights in the rear—and tuned them to get the car squared away. That did a super job.

"One day we proudly invited Estes out to the Proving Ground to show him, and he was just unbelievably pleased, the car was so good—until he found out how we did it. I think it added about sixty pounds, maybe seventy, and it looked to him like a non-inventive way to do it. He announced to everyone that in his whole life in engineering, it was the biggest disappointment he'd ever had that a good group of engineers like us had to resort to cocktail shakers in the corners of a car. We worked on it from then until the convertible was dropped in 1970, and we never did get them out. The cars went into production that way, and they were super convertibles, but they did have those bob-weights in the corners."

The philosophical baselines from which both design and engineering groups started were defined in a Society of Automotive Engineers (SAE) paper on the first Camaro by Chevrolet engineers Don McPherson, Charles Rubly and Victor Valade in the following terms: "distinctively modern aerodynamic styling . . .; small, highly maneuverable size with packaging for four . . .; broad range of available performance capability; quick, sharply defined roadability with a firm, yet comfortable ride; 'cockpit-type' interiors . . .; an evolutionary . . . design approach to maintain maximum value . . .; wide selection of mechanical and appearance equipment to allow customer tailoring to his needs and desires."

These objectives were then translated into three specific design parameters: "four-passenger packaging in a low silhouette where

tunnel requirements do not impose severe spatial restrictions; long-hood, short-deck styling on a short wheelbase with the passenger envelope placed more to the rear; use of conventionally arranged and readily available powerplants and drivelines."

The new Camaro was designed both to ride better than the stiff-legged Mustang, and thanks to its computer-tuned suspension, to outhandle the Ford pony, beginning with the base, six-cylinder version on "average" tires. "Handling" here means not only ultimate cornering capability but also safe, stable and predictable response to both normal and emergency inputs.

Several new safety features, most of them required by law on 1967 models, were incorporated into the design. These included a mesh-type collapsible steering column, dual hydraulic braking circuits divided front and rear, a brake system warning light, four-way hazard flashers, front seat backrest latches and built-in attachments for optional front-seat shoulder harnesses. One innovative convenience feature was a new lane-change signal activated by moving the turn signal lever to a position just short of the detent in either direction.

"Readily available powerplants" translated into selections from the Chevy engine supermarket shelf (140 hp base 230 cubic-inch six, 210 hp base 327 V-8, 155 hp optional 250 six, 275 hp optional 327 4-bbl. V-8), and one new engine exclusive to Camaro, a 295 hp 4-bbl. 350 V-8 to go with the high-performance SS option. All offered a choice of three-speed (column- or floor-shift), floor-mounted four-speed or Powerglide automatic transmissions. Soon after introduction a 325 hp 396 became available with Turbo Hydra-matic transmission.

Single exhausts were used with the six-cylinder and 327 engines, duals with the 350 and 396 V-8's, all with a single transverse-mounted muffler between the rear axle and the fuel tank. The dual system would be an option with the 327's, and a "deep-tone" dual system without resonators would be optionally available with any of the V-8 engines.

There was considerable controversy over base tires and wheels. Although standard Chevrolet procedure was to start with small, inexpensive, barely adequate rubber and work from there to optional tire/wheel combinations, both the designers and the engineers wanted more substantial equipment for Camaro. "When you start any kind of passenger car program," says Camaro studio chief Hank Haga, "you put together the tire and wheel sizes that the final car will run on, and this car was treated just like any sedan. It had to have that wide variety of tire sizes like any ordinary car. But when you put

the smallest tire into the wheel opening necessary for the biggest tire, it looked horrible.

"One day we had our fiberglass model together and reviewed it out at the Proving Grounds, and it looked like a car on roller skates. It looked so bad we were just sick about it, and the implication was that we had designed it that way. Well, we had designed it the best we could with the objectives we had. If we could have dropped that little tire and had a larger standard tire and wheel, it would have worked out much better."

Explains development engineer Paul King: "In the engineering department, we, too, were promoting wider rims and more rubber for better handling. The designers always liked the appearance of bigger wheels and tires, but that's a fairly expensive way to buy appearance if you don't need it from the engineering standpoint. I guess economics was a very significant factor. This was ahead of the time when we were upgrading the whole concept of tire life and capability. We were in a transition stage, when a lot of Chevrolet people, marketing people included, were not really fascinated with the importance of Chevrolet's being in the performance market."

Unfortunately, the cost accountants won out, and the base tires were ridiculous looking 7.35x14's on five-inch rims. A "high performance" tire option was a same-size white-stripe, while more appropriate D70x14 wide-oval red-stripes on six-inch wheels were specified as standard on SS models and optional on all other Camaros.

Other than that weakness, most agreed that the styling turned out well. Early in 1965 the rounded, coke bottle shape was wind tunnel tested for drag, lift, side forces and pitching, rolling and yawing, and minor changes resulted. The front fender and lower valence shapes, for example, were altered slightly for better aerodynamic flow, improved directional stability and reduced wind drag.

Chevy characterized the finished result as a "clean, straightforward piece of sculpture" with "curved contours" giving it a "feeling of motion achieved by light reflections while the car is stationary as well as moving." The base car featured what the company described as a "jet engine" nose opening with a fine eggcrate-pattern grille and round park lamps inboard of larger round headlamps. The optional Rally Sport front had pivoting headlamp covers blending into a larger-mesh, blacked-out grille and rectangular park lamps in the valence below the bumper. Specific side trim and taillamp treatments and RS identification were included in the package.

The electrically powered RS headlamp covers were interesting in themselves, opening sideways toward the vehicle's center and hiding

Technicians check engines and computer-generated prototype parts for fit.

completely behind the grille when the lights were turned on. Pushing the light switch to "off" with the ignition key in the "on" position closed them again, but shutting off the ignition first would leave them open so the headlamps could be cleaned. Since it took electrical power to close the doors, they would not suddenly shut if power to their relays failed while driving at night. They also could be manually pushed or pulled to the desired position with the ignition off.

With the SS (Super Sport) option came the more powerful engine, "bumblebee" nose stripe, heavy-duty chassis components, a raised-center hood with simulated chrome louvers, and various "SS" emblems. Still another variation was a combination of the RS and SS options. Inside the car were standard and custom interiors from which to choose and "Strato-bucket" seats or a bucket-styled front bench with a fold-down center armrest. A "deluxe-styled" oval steering wheel, molded luggage compartment mat and hood sound insulation were part of the deluxe interior, while any Camaro could be ordered with an optional fold-down rear seatback for additional carpeted storage.

Almost from the time of the Mustang's introduction in April 1964, rumors that Chevrolet was preparing a rebuttal flew hot and heavy around the industry. From August on, of course, these rumors were true, and Chevrolet did little to discourage them. In an April 8th, 1965 article, *Detroit News* writer Jack Crellin described a "crash program" at Chevrolet to launch a "Mustang-type" car as a 1966-½ or 1967 model. He mentioned "Panther," "Colt" and "Chevette" as potential names and speculated that both Pontiac and Buick Divisions would also have versions of the car. "Its styling," said Crellin, "is expected to generally follow that of the Chevy II Super Nova," the design concept car that was shown a year earlier at the New York Auto Show. "GM's Answer to Mustang?" was the caption given to a photo of the Super Nova.

The December 1965 issue of *Popular Science* contained a "Sneak Preview" story by auto editor Jan Norbye on "Chevrolet's New Rival for the Mustang." "Chevy is getting ready to pitch its Panther against Ford's Mustang in Detroit's biggest dogfight since they threw the 'stovebolt six' against old Henry's Model A," it declared on the first page, alongside an artist's not-too-accurate interpretation of the forthcoming Chevy ponycar. But Norbye did accurately report the Camaro's wheelbase, its Chevy II heritage, most of its engineering details and the fact that it would be slightly larger and rounder than its Ford rival.

About a year into the program, in July and August 1965, Chevrolet Public Relations began to shoot pictures of everything from

Above: technical cutaway of '67 Camaro; below: Chevy II-derived solid-axle rear suspension with single-leaf spring.

drawing board to clay model to finished prototypes in preparation for a potential *Life* magazine story, "Birth of the Camaro." Although that article never materialized, the photos proved useful to countless other publications, and many appear on these pages.

The car was first shown to sales, advertising and PR executives in November, and most of them were extremely enthusiastic. Though its internal code name remained "F-car" in accordance with GM practice, it was universally known as "Panther" both inside and outside the company. At about the same time, the PR team began planning its July 1966 magazine introduction, while advertising and marketing groups started preliminary work on catalogs, direct mail and sales promotion materials as well as ads for outdoor, print and electronic media. The real PR build-up began early in 1966 with a program of close contact with high-circulation magazines to work out fall-issue features and cover illustrations. Prototypes and finished styling models were photographed extensively, while Chevrolet Engineering contributed detailed technical illustrations.

But only so much promotional and advertising material could be prepared before the car had a name. While the press and public seemed to be settled on Panther, there was concern within the cor-

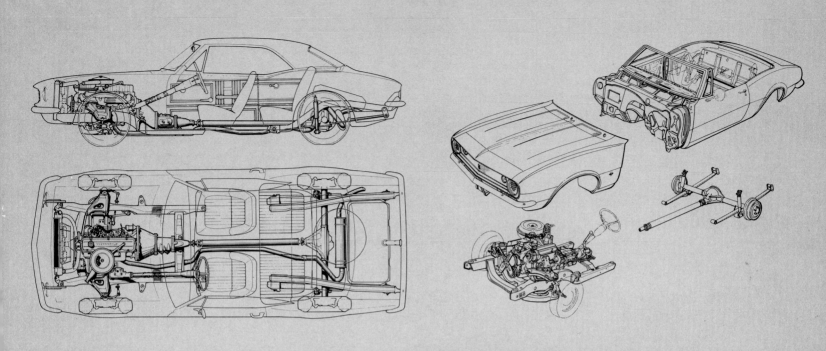

Above: '67 Camaro body, chassis and driveline.

poration about using such an aggressive, macho-sounding name in the face of growing criticism from Ralph Nader and others who were then riding the safety bandwagon.

"Picking the name was an ordeal," Estes recalls. "We had a terrible time with that. Bob Lund was the merchandising manager, and he had a bookful of names for the darned thing, and none of them would sell with the corporation. It was 'G-Mini' to start with. When we found we couldn't sell that, we changed it to 'GeMini' with a big 'G,' a big 'M' and an 'e' in the middle. Then we said we won't make the 'M' big, just "Gemini," but by that time we'd ruined everything completely. The theory for not calling it that was that you couldn't put 'GM' on any car because you never knew when it might be a failure. That's a terrible thing to say, but that was the thought."

"We were in the process of tooling, and we nearly completed the car with four different names," relates Alex Mair. "We had a whole bunch of names, and it was almost the start of production when we decided to name it 'Camaro.' With the Ford name being 'Mustang,' I think we had at least a couple of animal names. 'Panther' was one of them; I think we tooled that. 'Wildcat' was another. But there was pressure at Chevrolet to use something starting with 'C.' 'Corvette,'

'Corvair,' 'Chevy II,' 'Chevelle'—almost all of our names did at the time, and that policy had been very successful. Also, even though it was a sporty car, Chevrolet thought that names should have a good, soft, even feminine sound, not harsh. As it turned out, Camaro didn't have much meaning to anybody, which was OK, and it sounded good and didn't exist anywhere."

Chevrolet employees suggested some five thousand names, none of which seemed suitable, before Bob Lund and GM Car and Truck Group vice president Ed Rollert came up with "Camaro." "I wanted to name it 'Chaparral,' " says Lund [after the famous Chaparral Chevy-powered race cars], "but I wasn't able to do so. I submitted a lot of names and couldn't get any approved. Finally it got to the point where we were desperate. We *had* to have a name to make the tools to cut the damned name.

"One morning Ed Rollert and I got together and went over all the names that had been submitted for consideration. We had an English-French and an English-Spanish dictionary and a copy of *Roget's Thesaurus*. Finally I found this word 'Camaro' which had kind of a ring, a dramatic sound to it, and I said, 'Here's a hell of a name!' . . . I read him the various definitions of it, one of which was

25

very appropriate for the car—'friend,' 'warm friend,' or something of that nature. There were also some other definitions that weren't quite so complimentary. One, if I recall correctly, described 'Camaro' as a crawfish of some kind."

In March 1966 PR decided to make about twenty well-equipped Camaros available for selected daily press people to drive home from

Chevy development engineers leave for on-road test in winter of 1965-66. Prototype cars have disguised Camaro fronts grafted to Chevy II bodies.

the September new-car preview, and began preparing a list of writers in key locations who would be invited to participate. A "Panther" review story appeared in *Car Life*, this one sounding a negative note. "It probably should be called the Reluctant Dragon," groused the author. "It has been reluctant to arrive, its creators seem reluctant to build it, and the parent division is reluctant to admit its own two-year delay in recognizing this spectacular segment of the automotive market." He also speculated that the car would be positioned "right on top of both Chevy II and Corvair, making it only a matter of time before one or the other is killed off." The article was accompanied by some attractive but inaccurate drawings and equally inaccurate predictions about the car's styling and other features.

Estes already had admitted at February's Chicago Auto Show press breakfast that a "new car" was in the works, and confirmed at a similar meeting at the New York Show in April that it would be "in the Corvair/Chevy II range." Advertising and promotional creative work was progressing even though there was still no decision on the name. May brought the first formal presentation by Campbell-Ewald, Chevy's ad agency, but it was still the "F-car" as far as anyone knew.

The June *Mechanix Illustrated* ran a preview story using the Panther name, inaccurate photos and little correct information. Then sneak photos taken with a long lens over the back fence of GM's

Michigan Proving Ground hit the UPI wire service and were picked up by newspapers and magazines all over the country. One of these was the June 17th issue of *Time*, which ran photos and brief descriptions of both of Mustang's upcoming rivals for 1967, the Chevrolet "Panther" and the Mercury "Cougar."

Then on June 29th, 1966, Chevrolet took a very unusual step to announce the Camaro name, bury "Panther" once and for all, and reveal some information about the car. A huge conference call was arranged through the Bell System linking simultaneous press meetings in fourteen different cities. Amplifiers and microphones allowed reporters to hear Estes' Detroit-based presentation and each other, and to direct questions back to Detroit.

Calling it a "four-passenger package of excitement," Estes declared that "the Camaro is aimed at the fast-growing personal sports-type market that was pioneered by Chevrolet's Corvette in 1953 and further defined by the Corvair Monza in the 1960's." Because of its computer-aided design and development and its wind-tunnel-tested shape, he claimed that the new car was "perhaps more than any other automobile, a true product of the space age."

He jabbed the reporters about their persistent speculation, saying, "You've conceived it, sketched it, merchandised it, priced it and, above all, you've named it. In fact, you've made 'Panther' a household word. You've inspired a surge of mail, ranging from an animal trainer who wanted to lease us a live panther to a chemical company of the same name that wanted to order a fleet of cars. Regardless of our protestations about 'what Panther?' we've gotten mail praising and criticizing the name . . . and we've gotten a flood of substitute suggestions. One Detroit newsman even suggested, with tongue in cheek, calling it the Chicken."

Quarter-scale model tested in jet-aircraft wind tunnel in February 1965. Ink streaks show air-flow direction on the body's surface.

Lightweight plastic structural scale model aided computer body design process.

With that, a group of six Michigan State University cheerleaders bounced into the room carrying huge letters and arranged themselves to spell "CAMARO" while a narrator described the scene for those in the other cities. Unmentioned over the communications linkup was the fact that a couple of the coeds lined up out of order at first, spelling "CAMAOR." That didn't sound as good but to most people would have had as much meaning as the corrected version did.

Estes told the two hundred-odd reporters assembled nationwide that Camaro meant "comrade or pal" in French, and "thus it suggests the real mission of our new automobile . . . to be a close companion to its owner, tailored to reflect his or her individual tastes and at the same time provide exciting personal transportation." Asked how he had come up with the name, he joked that he had locked himself in a closet just that morning and had come out with "Camaro." Later he would quip that a Camaro was a little-known animal "that lives on Mustangs."

Just so no one would miss the point, French-English dictionaries were distributed and huge blow-ups of the proper definition accompanied the press releases so the audience "wouldn't have the wrong interpretation and use that crawfish or shrimp definition," says Lund. "We were very conscious of the potential problem." But that was just the beginning of a long-winded controversy over the car's name, which drew barbs from some writers and chuckles from the competition over at Ford, who quickly picked up on the Spanish definition, "a shrimp-like creature with many legs found in salt or fresh water."

As a result of the unique media event, the Camaro's christening received a tremendous amount of print coverage, much of it commenting on the name as well as reporting it. Even the lofty *Wall Street Journal* took up the controversy in a June 30th article by staff reporter Ronald G. Shafer. "Camaro," he said, "rhymes with bolero and it doesn't mean anything in English. . . . The Camaro resembles

Sextet of Michigan State cheerleaders helped Chevy general manager Pete Estes introduce Camaro's name during telephone-linked press conference.

the successful Mustang, and it already has been irreverently dubbed the Parrot by some Ford officials."

Shafer went on to discuss the agonizing car-naming process in general, using interesting examples from the past. "The current controversy over auto safety," he pointed out, "is making auto manufacturers shy from any name that has a connotation of speed or recklessness. Some critics of the auto companies contend many car names subtly encourage a heavy foot on the accelerator by exciting images of power and violence." Adding that recent Mustang ads had depicted a panther chasing a Mustang with the not-so-subtle message "you're ahead in a Ford," he said that Chevy had abandoned "Panther," "Cheetah" and other "vicious animal" names, "possibly to appease advocates of greater auto safety."

Camaro was misspelled as "Camero" in the *Detroit Free Press'* coverage, the first known incidence of a mistake that continues to this day. Letters and articles started to appear in newspapers and

magazines arguing the name's pros and cons, and one *Time* writer went so far as to dig up a Spanish variation of the word that meant "loose bowels" and worse, prompting some serious defensive research and counter-publicity from GM. Nevertheless, the July magazine preview came off as scheduled and included representatives from most major publications, who drove and photographed prototypes and interviewed key executives, engineers and designers for September and October articles. Distribution of press kits containing photos and specifications of the Camaro and other 1967 models to radio and TV representatives also began in July in preparation for the September introduction.

Camaro starred at a Chevrolet sales convention in late August, and then the first "teaser" ad appeared in the September 5th *Life*. Press conferences for daily print and radio/TV media and more advertising followed in late September. The sporty little Chevy was on its way into young America's hearts and driveways.

CHAPTER TWO

Act One

Chevrolet's entry into the galloping ponycar market was unveiled at a GM Proving Ground press conference on September 12th, 1966.

Announcing forty-eight models in six separate car lines for 1967, Chevy general manager Pete Estes boasted, "we've filled every bin in our store with an outstanding product." He described the restyled "regular car" and intermediate Chevelle and their respective SS-427 and SS-396 high-performance versions, and then followed with the little-changed Chevy II, Corvair and Corvette. Then Estes introduced the all-new Camaro.

"Over the years," he said, "there has been a shift within the small car market from the family small car to the small sports-type car. It is in the expanding sports car portion of the small-car market that our sales position has been weak, and that's where Chevrolet's newest line of small cars—the Camaro—comes in.

"But before we talk about what we hope the Camaro will do, let me show you why I think it will be a success . . . and that begins with its looks. So here is the 1967 Camaro."

Curtains opened center stage. There, in full dress, was an SS-350 convertible. Estes paused for effect and then mentioned Chevrolet's belief that this car would set a new standard in small car beauty. "Now perhaps you can understand why we couldn't give it the name of a stealthy, vicious animal," he remarked, "any more than one of you would have named an excitingly beautiful woman 'Panther.' "

As the car began rotating slowly on a turntable, Estes resumed. "To continue the feminine analogy, there are plenty of curves to the Camaro. In fact, its entire aerodynamic body is molded of curved contours that were polished to perfection in a jet-age wind tunnel. The upper body has curved side glass. The pronounced roll-under styling of the lower body accentuates the wide tread of the wheels and

Presenting the Mustang-killer: early promotional shot shows encounter between '67 Camaro convertible and SS-350 coupe.

adds to the sports car look."

Estes went on to describe the Camaro's two different grille and headlamp treatments, the Rally Sport and SS-350 options, the special stub frame body/chassis construction and its competitive advantages over the Mustang: longer, lower, wider, wider tread, more passenger room, fully synchronized base three-speed transmission, larger standard engines (230 cubic-inch six versus 200; 327 V-8 versus 289), more available rear axle ratios and greater overall braking area.

After the curtains closed, Estes described GM's high hopes for the new car. "We expect it to restore Chevrolet's penetration of the small-car field . . . We don't expect the Camaro to outsell the Mustang immediately, but eventually, it will! We have plenty of respect for the Mustang as an established competitor which expanded a market pioneered by Corvette and Corvair. However, we do expect the Camaro to cut substantially into Mustang sales in the 1967 model year."

Estes said that Camaro production was planned for nearly 300,000 for the first year and hinted that more could be built if needed. "As a first car, it will go largely to a youth market . . . persons under 35 with emphasis upon women customers as well as men. In two-car families, it should appeal to men and women of every age who want exciting, personal transportation.

"Of our Camaro sales, perhaps one-third will come from buyers who choose Camaro instead of our other lines, primarily Chevy II and Corvair. However, we expect that two-thirds of the sales should be plus business for Chevrolet. This plus business will be divided in two ways.

"First, there will be the Chevrolet owners who, in 1967, will decide to try a personal size car. If there were not a Camaro, they might buy a Mustang or Barracuda. So, in effect, a sale saved for Chevrolet will be a sale gained.

"Secondly, this plus business for Camaro will be made up of conquest sales from a variety of competitors. And when aging cow ponies begin arriving in large numbers on Chevrolet used car lots, I'm sure our dealers will do the kindly thing—feed 'em and retire 'em to somebody's pasture."

Estes concluded his presentation with a brief discussion of the new safety features on all 1967 GM products—energy-absorbing steering column, dual-master-cylinder brake system, front seatback latches, passenger-guard door locks, four-way hazard warning flasher—and the corporation's new five-year, 50,000 mile warranty on powertrain components over and above the standard two-year, 24,000 mile

coverage.

A press release issued the same day contained some more Estes enthusiasm over his division's latest products, claiming that "Camaro offers the greatest choice of engines, trims, options and accessories Chevrolet has ever introduced with a new line of cars. The buyer can literally tailor his own automobile." Footnoted at the bottom of the page was the proper phonetic pronunciation: "ca-*mair*-o."

News representatives were suitably impressed. John Teahen of *Automotive News* noted the friendly but serious rivalry between Estes and his neighbor, Ford Division head Don Frey, and wrote that the new car should help Chevy fend off Ford's strong challenge for sales leadership. He said that Camaro "rhymes with arrow and it's aimed right at Mustang, the sporty little Ford that has been giving Chevrolet fits the last two-and-a-half years."

Under the headline "Camaro Could Hurt '67 Mustang Sales," *Columbus Dispatch* business writer Mardo Williams called it "Chevrolet's glamorous new entry into the sports car field." He raved about the SS-350's looks, comfort, handling and performance. Emphasizing that Ford had improved its Mustang and the Lincoln-Mercury Division had introduced its slightly larger, plusher and more expensive Cougar, Williams concluded that "the result may well be the most interesting sales race in automotive history."

On September 26th Chevrolet announced the Camaro's base price at $2466 as opposed to Mustang's $2510; six-cylinder convertible versions would start at $2704 compared to Mustang's $2747, while V-8 hardtops would list for $2572 for Camaro, $2616 for Mustang and $2881 for Mercury's Cougar.

Well before the Camaro's public introduction, Chevy's marketing people had been sharpening their pencils gleefully in preparation for the coming battle. An internal memo listed several pages of competitive comparisons and every imaginable advantage that Camaro held over its rivals. It was lower and wider, with a wider tread for better handling, and longer and heavier than the Cougar, at a time when weight was considered an advantage. There were also more safety features: softer, more vibration-free ride due to the unique stub-frame construction; wider choice of power teams; "flush and dry" rocker panels for better corrosion resistance; and bonded brake linings rather than Ford products' riveted shoes. Camaro offered more external appearance variations and better interior comfort and trim level than Mustang and Barracuda, and also had an acrylic lacquer finish instead of the usual enamel. Finally, there were options such as power windows, speed warning indicator and fold-down rear seats—the latter available only on the more expensive Mustang and Barra-

Chevy general manager Pete Estes launching Camaro sales campaign.

cuda fastbacks. All this, plus slightly lower prices for comparably equipped models, offered substantial advertising ammunition for Chevy.

Manufacturers typically staged elaborate extravaganzas in those days to introduce each year's new products to dealers throughout the country. Chevy's '67 model dealer show was no exception. Twenty-five performances in as many cities used four different road companies to play to an estimated thirty thousand people.

Beginning in late September, some lucky reporters received extended test drives.

"Chevy's Camaro Proves a Joy," crowed Frank Tolbert of the *Dallas Morning News* after putting a thousand miles on an SS-350. He said that it was more like a Corvette than a Mustang and "as much fun to drive." He praised the car's "rattle and squeak-free" body, its "very comfortable" front bucket seats and its "lovely, long, low, aerodynamically functional shape—lean-looking yet muscular." "Lights reflect on the rounded surfaces," he enthused, "making this automotive creature seem to be moving when it is parked."

The Washington Star's automotive writer Charles Yarborough also compared the SS-350 Camaro to a Corvette. "The quality was

Camaro and other 1967 new products await press review reception, while on dealer lots, new car sparks interest among young and not-so-young consumers.

excellent," he wrote, "the ride slightly choppy and quiet, the cornering superb and the acceleration sensational. Chevrolet's answer to the phenomenal Ford Mustang, however belated, is coming in loud, clear, attractive and agile. It may be a late start, but it's going to be a most interesting race."

Magazine reports, which began rolling in with October issues, were less ecstatic but generally positive. *Motor Trend* writers John Ethridge and Steven Kelly conducted a three-car comparison of Camaro, Mustang and Cougar. Listening hard for squeaks and rattles on rough surfaces and hearing none, they concluded that "the rubber-isolated modular construction is highly successful, and is one of the outstanding features of the Camaro." They also were happy with the standard suspension's "inherently good traction when cornering hard on irregular surfaces .... Camaro offers the best compromise between ride and handling."

On the negative side, Ethridge and Kelly complained that the car's two-speed Powerglide optional automatic transmission was outdated, and that the "suspension-packaged Mustang covertible seems to have [an] edge on the like-equipped Camaro when driven near [the] limit." Mustang also offered three body styles, coupe, converti-

ble and fastback, to Camaro's two. The writers also pointed out that the Ford product was "ahead in the power race." Still, the article concluded, "the Camaro is a well-engineered, carefully thought-out car and a worthwhile addition to a class of machines that, in appreciative hands, yield far more than mere transportation."

"Though a follower in a field pioneered by others," said *Car Life,* "the Camaro nonetheless seems exciting in looks and performance, is particularly well-suited to its intended market and will be sold and serviced by the world's largest dealer body .... The speculators (*CL* included) who said the Camaro was to be a 'modified Chevy II' were wrong. It isn't. It's virtually a new car."

Popular Mechanics called it "a tidy, handsome and spirited little car that should warm the hearts of all Chevy enthusiasts .... In the SS-350 version, it's a true dazzler." But *PM's* tester noted, as would others later, that the sport steering wheel's chrome spokes sometimes reflected light that could be "blinding."

Rival *Popular Science* recruited racer Mario Andretti to test a couple of Camaros at GM's Milford, Michigan Proving Ground. Somewhat disappointed at first, Mario upped the tire pressures to 30 p.s.i. and then pronounced the handling "terrific." "There was next

33

Front and rear views highlighting the subtle but significant differences between standard Camaro for '67 and SS-350 with RS option.

to no body lean in the tight turns, or front-end dive on hard braking." He called the 350 V-8 "peppy but nothing exceptional," and compared it favorably to a 289 V-8 Mustang. Andretti also liked the overall styling and especially the hidden-headlamp RS front end, control layout, sport steering wheel, interior finish and the four-speed transmission and clutch. He did gripe about the balky two-speed Powerglide automatic, the inconvenient console-mounted auxiliary gauges, and the car's rear appearance, which he called an "economy design."

Not to be outdone, *Popular Mechanics* countered in November with an exclusive Dan Gurney test of an SS-350 convertible. Gurney called it "a good-looking, outstanding performer that immediately convinced me Mustang has a worthy competitor." Like Andretti, he added air to the tires, "ten pounds all around," and it "made a big difference in how the SS handled. I gradually worked up speed, going through the bends as fast as possible, and discovered the Camaro to be a most forgiving car. It's not the least bit vicious, even as you approach its limit." Gurney also commended the car's optional disc brakes and its front seat room. He managed a 7.3 second 0-60 time despite "a slight bit of rear end hop." Top speed was reported as 118 mph.

Mechanix Illustrated's Tom McCahill also tested an SS-350 convertible, pronouncing it "a handsome-looking buzzard." He recorded a 0-60 run of eight seconds, a quarter-mile time of 15.9 seconds and a top speed of "118-plus."

But the first full road test by a major car enthusiast magazine reported mixed findings. After praising the Camaro's styling—"a tasteful American interpretation of a European *Gran Turismo*"— and its cornering and braking traction, the November *Car and Driver* criticized its lack of rear axle control, relatively mild performance, and two-speed Powerglide automatic.

"The Mustang's equivalent to the SS-350 is the 390-GT," said the article, "which boasts an engine some 40 cubic inches larger and 25 horsepower more powerful . . . . With the combination of the SS-350 engine and the four-speed manual transmission, drag racing starts are impossible. The rear axle judders almost uncontrollably, with the car hopping sideways almost as far as it is making headway . . . . Although the Camaro's power steering is as light as a plucked feather, it still doesn't seem fast enough, and there is virtually no road feel through the wheel rim . . . . All told, Chevrolet's Camaro does not offer the extremes of performance that the Mustang does. GM's eggs are in a softer, more middle-of-the-road basket."

Despite these complaints, the author called Camaro "a pleasant little car, with several characteristics that won't go unnoticed by the taste-making enthusiasts." Although he predicted that it should sell "phenomenally well" and "ought to give Ford a helluva good run for its money," he lamented that "we—and some other enthusiasts— don't think it is yet the kind of success that we'd been hoping for." Performance figures were 7.8 seconds 0-60, 16.1 seconds at 86.5 mph in the quarter-mile and 120 mph top speed.

What did Ford think of this new competition? Predictably, not much. In mid-November, Ford Division assistant general sales manager M.S. McLaughlin told *Automotive News* that Chevy's new ponycar was "expanding the specialty-car market," not taking any Mustang sales away. October figures showed Mustang outselling its combined competitors by almost two-and-a-half to one and Ford Division as a whole outselling Chevy that month for the first time in years. The public had seen the Camaro and was buying more Mustangs than ever, scoffed McLaughlin. He also hinted that model year '67 could see the end of Chevrolet's long-time sales leadership. "We've been improving at a substantial rate," he boasted, "and Chevrolet has been declining at a substantial rate. I think we're doing

more of the right things than anyone in this business, and we'll eventually be the leader. It may be this year."

What this rather smug Ford executive didn't know, indeed, no one outside of General Motors could have known, was that Chevy had not yet begun to fight. Recognizing that the Camaro's reputation—and through it Chevrolet's image with the fast-growing youth market—needed serious polishing, Estes and his top lieutenants were soon to spring some significant surprises.

Although GM corporate management was not about to defy the 1957 AMA (Automobile Manufacturers Association) ban on factory racing as Henry Ford II had done in 1962, Chevrolet Division had been helping its better competitors under the table for some time. This help included development of "heavy-duty" engines and parts, and occasionally shipping some out the back door to deserving drag, stock and road-racers to help them compete against the openly-backed Ford and Chrysler teams. The parts resulting from this development were catalogued and sold through Chevrolet dealers to anyone who wanted them, which tended to legitimize the program and make it at least partially self-supporting.

Since the ban, Chevy's racing involvement had ebbed and flowed depending upon certain factors: who was the division's general manager and how far he was willing to go, public and government sentiment, and what was going on in the new-car market and in the various forms of competition. In the late Fifties and early Sixties while Ford had followed the AMA ban and stayed away from racing completely, Chevrolet, Oldsmobile and especially Pontiac Division had participated covertly by supporting dealer-sponsored stock cars. Chevy also had built the reputation of its Corvette sports car with heavy, although not open, support for competitive road-racing teams. As a result, the excitement value of Ford and its products had sagged while these GM divisions had prospered.

This situation reversed about midway through 1962 when Ford came out of the closet. The company began pouring millions into all types of racing, successfully promoting the results and using them to spur sales. GM, on the other hand, cracked down on its divisions and at one point—according to John DeLorean, who was chief engineer at Pontiac when Pete Estes was general manager there—told the general managers that the next one caught racing would be fired.

The new youth car called Mustang emerged from this atmosphere of heavy competition at Ford and virtual absence of same at GM. By 1965, factory-backed Shelby Mustangs were winning Sports Car Club of America (SCCA) amateur road racing events against essentially independent, small-block Corvettes. The following year

Advertising photos featuring '67 Camaro Sport Coupe, convertible and SS-350 coupe direct their message to youthful market.

Personal style and convenience: '67 SS-350's instrument panel and interior. Page opposite: model demonstrates SS-350's RS hidden headlamp.

SCCA instituted a professional Trans-American sedan series for small, four-seat sporty cars. Ford's Mustang won it handily.

Vince Piggins, Chevy product promotion (which really meant "competition parts development") manager knew that SCCA would expand this new form of racing and that the other three U.S. manufacturers planned to compete. So in August 1966 he recommended creating a special option package for the soon-to-be-introduced Camaro to make it a viable Trans-Am competitor. Most importantly, since the Camaro's smallest planned production V-8 was to be a 327, a new engine close to the Trans-Am's 5.0 liter (305 cubic-inch) maximum displacement would have to be developed and released as an option.

As a performance-oriented general manager who understood the importance of such a project to his new car's future success, Estes tentatively agreed and work began on what was to become the famous Z-28 Camaro. Piggins' group built the first prototype with a high-performance 283 V-8 engine and numerous chassis and driveline modifications for better acceleration and handling. In mid-October they arranged a test drive for the general manager at GM's Michigan Proving Ground.

"When I was demonstrating it to Estes," Piggins recalls, "it was a pretty hot little job even with the 283. But as we were driving back

from the straightaway I suggested that we could go with our 327 block and a 283 crankshaft, which would make a perfect four-inch bore, three-inch stroke combination for 302 cubic inches. We had all the parts in production, and that would just fit inside the Trans-Am displacement rule.

"He agreed, and when we got back to the launching pad where everyone was gathered, he walked over to [then-chief passenger-car engineer] Don McPherson and said, 'let's build this thing and put a 302 cubic-inch engine in it.' Mac thought it was a great idea, and that was really the birth of the Z-28. From there on, we started working on the job as a Trans-Am competitor."

This became option package number twenty-eight in the Camaro line, eventually to be designated the "Z-28" option. "We already had a Z-28 option at the time," explains Estes, "a handling package or something on the regular car, but we never made much of it. Chevrolet options all had letters and numbers. Then we said, damn, that's a good name, so we pulled it out of the bag and put it on just the Camaro."

The Trans-Am series was based on international rules controlled by a French organization called FIA, which required that a car and all modifications be "homologated" by its maker to be eligible for competition. A minimum of one thousand copies had to be produced

Six car lines for '67: Corvair Monza, Corvette Sting Ray, Chevy II Nova, Chevelle Malibu and Chevrolet Impala joined by Camaro in SS version.

before it could race, and all special parts had to be approved by FIA and offered for sale to the public. Naturally, this involved considerable paperwork and difficulty for the manufacturer and greatly complicated the development process.

But homologation papers were drawn up, submitted and eventually approved, and an early prototype mysteriously appeared on display under a tent at a November 26th race at Riverside, California, near Los Angeles. Local Chevrolet officials expressed surprise at first, but later confirmed that the Z-28 would indeed go into production soon after the beginning of the new year. Chevrolet representatives from Detroit who were at the Riverside race denied that Chevy was getting back into racing. They did allow, however, that if someone wanted to go racing with a Camaro, they would have "something to go racing with."

A brief fact sheet was available under the tent. "Displayed today," it said, "was a Camaro coupe that incorporates the latest in a list of factory option packages—the Z-28." It described the special 302 engine with mechanical lifters, "tuned runner" intake manifold, 800 CFM Holley four-barrel carburetor with "closed positive ventilation," five-blade fan with viscous fan clutch and dual drive pulleys for both the fan and water pump, 2.02 inch intake and 1.60 inch exhaust valves, high-output coil and high-rpm distributor points, and

dual exhausts with "low-tone" mufflers. It detailed the suspension's heavy-duty springs and shocks, shot-peened ball studs and rear-axle radius rod; the drivetrain's close-ratio four-speed with 2.2:1 low gear, 3.73:1 rear axle; the brakes' power-assisted front discs; and the steering's 24:1 manual ratio.

On the display car were 7.35x15 NF nylon white-stripe tires on 15x6 inch wheels, though red-stripe tires were listed with the Z-28 package. It was painted a light cream with dual wide black stripes over the hood and rear deck and sported a rear aerodynamic spoiler and a black vinyl top, both listed as options.

"An unusual feature," the sheet pointed out, "is the plenum air feed to the carburetor. A plastic duct takes high-pressure air from the plenum or chamber in front of the windshield directly into the Holley four-barrel carburetor." It listed no less than six other available axle ratios—3.07, 3.31, 3.55, 4.10, 4.56 and 4.88, the first three with or without positraction, the latter trio positraction-only. Also mentioned were such extra-cost options as heavy-duty front brake pads, sintered metallic rear shoes and power or fast-ratio (20:1) manual steering. On the display car, but not part of the Z-28 option, were a custom interior, Rally Sport (RS) package, console, instrument cluster and radio. Horsepower and torque were described as "not available yet," and the price was not yet established.

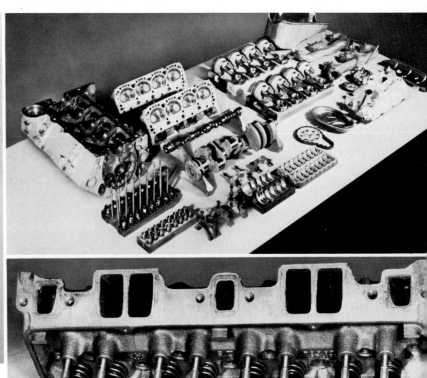

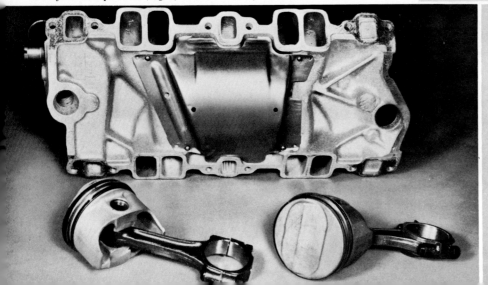

Above (left): assembled Z-28 Camaro 302 cubic-inch V-8 engine; (right): collection of major parts and cylinder head assembly. Below (left): inlet manifold and pistons; (right) 4-barrel Holley carburetor 800 CFM.

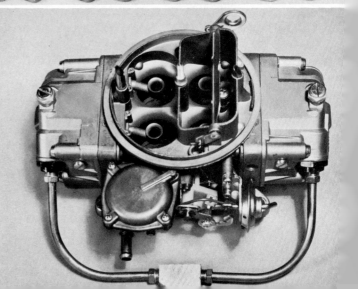

"According to a company spokesman," the Chevrolet handout concluded, "the Z-28 package was developed to make the Camaro an exceptional touring machine having relatively light weight, a smaller but highly responsive V-8 engine with four-speed transmission, and suspension refinements that result in excellent stability and handling characteristics."

Of course, the racing community and its followers immediately concluded that Chevy was about to start building factory Trans-Am race cars. One person who picked up on this not-too-subtle message and beat a hasty path to Pete Estes' door was Chevy dealer, racing team organizer and ex-champion driver Roger Penske. "He came in to see me," Estes relates, "and he brought in Sunoco [his money sponsor] to sell me on the idea that we should go into this Trans-Am. We had a session, and Rog gave us a big sell.

"I recognized that the exposure we got in stock-car racing used to do a lot for Pontiac when I was there. So I said, well, we won't advertise it, but we've got to have an appearance out there. I didn't argue with the [GM anti-racing] policy, but I tried to interpret it as being primarily anti-advertising. Granted that the safety pressure was coming on, but I said we've still got to have the exposure. Somebody is going to be on the track, so we've got to be there too. We didn't support the program in dollars and cents, but we made parts available, released them and sold them as spare parts."

Then-engineering director Alex Mair remembers: "We decided to enter the Trans-Am, or at least be a part of it. Penske ran the team, and we offered guidance from the ride and handling group and from the Chevrolet performance group on engines. The Z-28 was really developed to meet that need."

Meanwhile, the advertising and marketing teams were pulling some other significant rabbits out of their hats to boost Camaro's performance reputation. Ads in December hot-rod and sports-car magazines showed a mean-looking SS-350 with the RS front end. "Meet the Masked Marvel," teased the headline. "Domed hood, rally stripe and Camaro's biggest V-8 . . . four fat red-stripe tires . . . high-rate springs . . . stiffer shocks. It's a ball and a half."

But no sooner did this advertisement appear than it became obsolete, because in went Chevy's 325-hp 396 big-block V-8 to top Camaro's engine option list. Now there would be two high-excitement Camaros to suit any taste: an agile, high-revving Z-28 for sports car fans and a thundering, pavement-pounding SS-396 to challenge Ford Mustang's 390 on the streets and strips. No more complaints about mild performance, thank you.

There were occasional complaints from the press, some justified and others not. Someone with the improbable moniker of Joe Gutts wrote a critical report for the December *Science and Mechanics* that was almost amusing in its bias. He called Camaro a "copy cat version of the Mustang . . . as close to the Mustang as GM could build without being sued for patent infringements . . . a disappointment. With all the big brains at Chevy," he scoffed, "we would have expected more than a warmed-over (and second-rate) Mustang made up, it almost seems, from old surplus parts that were laying [sic] around the shop. Nothing radical, nothing really new, nothing exciting. Just nothing."

Gutts did have some more legitimate beefs: that the Powerglide transmission "still features an obsolete two-speed torque converter that the rest of the industry abandoned to the Flintstones and other Neanderthal types"; the near-useless trunk—"Just the thing for taking along a six-pack of beer on your vacation"; the base model's stripped-down looks and glare from the cone-shaped plastic covers over the tach and speedometer. "If you were to take a Corvair body and weld it to the platform chassis of the Chevy II, stoke the engine a bit and put it up front, you would have the long-awaited Camaro," he grumped.

By contrast, December's *Motor Trend* reported testing two new Camaros, an SS-350 four-speed and an RS with the 327/Powerglide combination, both coupes. It concluded that "the Camaro is one of the most pleasurable cars of its size—or any other size—we've driven. . . . Enthusiasm for the Camaro comes easy." The article showed 8.0 seconds 0-60 for the SS and a respectable 10.7 seconds for the automatic 327 RS, with quarter-mile times of 15.4 seconds at 90 mph and 18.2 seconds at 77 mph, respectively.

One interesting TV ad of the time showed an SS-350 convertible rising monster-like from a volcano. To create it, Chevy went to Columbia Pictures' ranch at Burbank, California and adapted the same stage set that had been used for the famous typhoon scene in *The Caine Mutiny.* According to a *Detroit News* report, fluorescent paint and live steam were used to simulate boiling lava; smoke sticks, black powder and burnt cork made up the volcanic ash, and the "rocks" that rolled away from the volcano's mouth as the Camaro emerged were lightweight pyroseal. The effect was certainly spectacular, whether or not it sold many cars.

January magazine test reports, conducted before the twin performance surprises, were still mostly favorable. Referring to Camaro as the "new kid on the block," *Hot Rod* gushed: "There is a certain fascination that just oozes from all the flowing lines and a 350 cube engine that's got to be one of this year's treats." The magazine tested

an SS-350 with quick steering, disc/drum brakes and heavy-duty suspension, including an anti-wheel-hop traction bar on the right rear. There were raves about its styling, performance, handling and braking: "No one we encountered in many miles of driving had anything but favorable comments about the way our car looked . . . . The Camaro went like blue blazes—around corners or in the straight . . . pure sweetness to negotiate a bend at twice the normal velocity and still be master of the situation . . . comes to a halt like nothing short of a Sting Ray."

With some tweaking and much experimentation, *Hot Rod* managed an amazing 14.9 second quarter-mile at 95.7 mph. The coming 396 engine option was mentioned ("Good grief, B/Stock!"), and on the fairly short complaint list were the base, low-priced Camaro's "Plain Jane" looks—"too fat through the midsection and a little humpbacked"—the balky Muncie four-speed shifter, the lack of luggage room, the old Powerglide automatic and the light-reflecting chrome-spoked steering wheel.

John Hearst Jr. gave a decidedly mixed review in the January 15th *World Journal Tribune* newspaper. After praising the SS-350's looks, calling it "a candidate for a speeding ticket based on appearance alone" and reporting a 0-60 performance of 7.5 seconds, he criticized the car's rear axle hop under both acceleration and braking, its lack of front seat adjustment—no rake adjuster, insufficient fore/aft travel—the four-speed shifter's stiffness and the lack of standard instrumentation. Hearst also complained of too many squeaks and groans from the bodywork: "Our test car had but 3,000 miles on it, yet sounded like a '46 station wagon."

The nation's racing writers by now were into heavy speculation about the Z-28 and Chevy's apparent return to competition. "Although it's yet to run a race, Chevrolet's new Z-28 Camaro is being touted as the one to beat in the Trans-American sedan series this season," wrote Ev Gardner of the *Washington Daily News*. "The Z-28 option package transforms the Camaro from a tractable street carriage into a full-bore competitor."

It wasn't quite that simple, though. At Chevrolet Engineering, and out at the Michigan Proving Ground, engineers were working like mad to get the necessary special parts designed, developed and released, while Piggins labored to get them FIA-homologated in time for the February 2nd season-opener at Daytona. Over and above the street Z-28 equipment, the racers would need heavy-duty spindles, axles and shafts, bushings, special 37 gallon racing fuel tanks, and considerably more. Once available in sufficient quantity, all these pieces had to be rush-shipped to the appropriate dealers where the teams preparing cars could pick them up. Given the short time available, it was a monumental task.

The first production Z-28 rolled off the Norwood, Ohio Camaro assembly line on December 29th, 1966. It was delivered to Aero Chevrolet in Alexandria, Virginia to be prepared for the Daytona race on January 30th. Penske picked up Z-28 number twelve on January 10th and immediately took it to Smokey Yunick's Daytona race shop for preparation.

"We had the material down there at the dealership," says Piggins, "heavy-duty rear axles, springs and everything, and it was being sold to Camaro competitors right there at the track. Penske brought his car down to Smokey's garage, and they practically rebuilt it there."

Back in Detroit, Piggins was pushing an accelerated and comprehensive development program. "During the '67 season," he pointed out in a memo to engineering director Alex Mair, "we can expect heavy emphasis to be placed on Group II Trans-Am sedan racing by our competitors . . . . With the Mustang firmly entrenched in the compact sports sedan market we must, with the Camaro, create a superior performance image to augment our market penetration." His recommendations included working with Yunick on "evaluation and development of Camaro heavy-duty chassis components and high-speed vehicle dynamics" and passing the results through him to Penske.

Three days before Daytona, Mair received a memo from Piggins' boss Walter Burwell. It outlined Burwell's own proposals for parts development for drag, stock car and sports car racing, as well as the Trans-Am series. In addition to work on the L-88 427 engine for use in SCCA's professional sports car series, which later became the Can-Am, Burwell recommended development of the 302 engine "for high-speed durability," and the Camaro chassis "to provide the best handling and durability within the limitations of Group II regulations."

Burwell's memo also specified methods for establishing sources for parts and insuring top quality, both from GM sources and outside suppliers. And he emphasized that "this program is to provide information to those who choose to compete with the Camaro and also to establish the requirements for heavy-duty chassis items . . . . Our past experience indicates that there is a ready market for the special high-performance parts; in fact, in many cases, it has been difficult to keep up with the demand. Our objective in this would be to furnish those parts which are not readily available from outside sources."

Four Camaros showed up at Daytona in various states of preparation and competitiveness. Penske was best equipped, thanks to his

Sunoco sponsorship and connections at the "factory," closely followed by a Canadian car entered and driven by Craig Fisher. Soft-spoken engineer/driver Mark Donohue started the Penske Camaro third, behind the factory Cougars of Dan Gurney and Parnelli Jones, and led the first three laps of the Trans-Am event before its engine went sour with rocker ball problems. He dropped out after fourteen laps to prepare for the 24-Hour race which started later that same day. Fisher finished second behind Bob Tullius' factory Dodge Dart, Jones' Cougar wound up third, and Jerry Titus' factory Mustang was fourth.

Three of the four Camaros entered the 24-Hour, but none finished. Donohue ran with the class leaders until his transmission failed early Sunday morning; he returned with a new gearbox only to have the engine blow two hours from the end. Fisher blew at about half distance, and the third car, which was essentially stock and not competitive, retired with suspension problems after 186 laps. An independent Mustang took the class win, but the Camaro's competitive potential had definitely been proven. There were numerous teething problems, including severe rear wheel lockup under braking, but nothing that couldn't be dealt with. Top speed on the Daytona back straight had been an incredible 162 mph.

After the race, Penske shipped his failed and badly worn parts to Piggins for engineering evaluation. He also requested expeditious shipment of new developmental pieces for the next event. Most of these parts were heavy-duty brake and suspension components still not readily available elsewhere. One interesting item on the list was a Corvette-type adjustable rear brake pressure regulator, which Penske hoped would cure the rear lockup problem.

Less than a month later Chevrolet announced that a Camaro would pace the Memorial Day Indianapolis 500 race, touching off further speculation about a full-scale GM return to racing. "The 1957 AMA resolution, which GM has clung to publicly, specifically forbids a member firm from providing a pace car at any performance event," wrote *Detroit News* sportswriter Ben Dunn. "Thus the Camaro-Indy tie-in is in direct violation of the AMA resolution. Further, it is the first overt action in defiance of the resolution by GM." According to Dunn, when then-GM President James Roche was questioned at the Chicago Auto Show, he responded, "I see no harm in it. It doesn't represent any particular change in our position."

At a February 25th press breakfast during that same Chicago Auto Show, Pete Estes spoke about the Camaro and about Chevrolet sales in general. "In its first five months the Camaro has scored an

All the pieces in a '67 Camaro; three of six dresses in David Crystal's "Camaro collection," created in January 1967 and featured in Vogue.

impressive impact on the market," he told reporters. "It is solidly in second place in sales of all domestic small cars and it has been cutting into the volume of the leader—which had a two-and-a-half-year head start. Total sales since introduction day have passed 70,000. On a model-year basis, Camaro is selling about forty percent of Mustang, and in January this figure was forty-five percent.

"Addition of Camaro has increased Chevrolet's overall penetration of small-car domestic sales from twenty-one to twenty-seven percent since last October 1st. Besides helping Chevrolet, it has contributed to the overall growth of the small sports-type market, which has gone up each month since October 1st and now stands at eleven percent of all domestic sales."

Estes explained that February sales had been hurt somewhat by an almost month-long strike at the Norwood, Ohio Camaro assembly plant. He then offered a buyer profile. Ownership of Camaros, he claimed, was almost evenly divided between single-car and multiple-car households. The median age of all buyers was thirty-one, lowest for any Chevrolet except Corvette, and over sixty percent had been to college or were college graduates. The median income was $10,400, which was higher than those for all Chevrolets except Caprice and Corvette.

Almost one in four Camaro owners were women, a majority of them single, while about a third of all owners were single. The Camaro was the first new-car purchase for twenty-five percent of the buyers, and the first Chevrolet purchase for almost half. A good third of the buyers said that they seriously considered Mustang before choosing Camaro.

"Thus it would appear," Estes said, "that Camaro is succeeding in two objectives: first, it is keeping Chevrolet owners who might otherwise leave us to buy a small sports-type car. Secondly, it is drawing new owners to Chevrolet and away from competition."

Estes reported high owner ratings of Camaro's styling, performance and handling. He also reported the high percentage of options being ordered: eighty percent V-8 engines, nearly forty percent Rally Sports, eighty-two percent optional automatic or four-speed manual transmission, forty-four percent power steering, seventy percent whitewalls and wheel covers, twenty-three percent vinyl roofs (the highest of any Chevrolet), and thirteen percent equipped with air conditioning.

He mentioned the recent addition of the 396 V-8 and Turbo Hydra-matic transmission to the option list and added that a collapsible spare tire to increase luggage space and a floor shifter, without console, for the three-speed manual would become available in

March. The SS's nose stripe also would be offered as a separate option, effective immediately.

March issues of some car magazines contained the first Z-28 tests. *Car and Driver,* for one, was impressed but still fairly critical. Why, the author wondered, did Chevy take the cheap route and add only one traction bar on the rear axle when most Firebirds had dual bars as standard equipment?

"Under heavy acceleration," he complained, "reaction to the engine's torque tips the car counterclockwise (viewed from the rear), unloading the right rear wheel. If the right side of the axle isn't tied down, it goes haywire. One traction arm on the right side will control axle judder, but the car still comes off the line sideways. Also, it will behave differently in a right-hand corner than when turning left. Worst of all, under heavy braking the torque is coming from the opposite direction, and the left side of the axle judders violently."

The article heaped some heavy compliments in most other respects, however, especially on the 302 engine: "The 290 hp figure quoted for the Z-28 engine seems ridiculously conservative . . . . It is without a doubt the most responsive American V-8 we've ever tested. . . . Once it begins to pull, it smoothes out and lunges forward like a 426 Hemi." The author compared the Z-28 favorably to a Shelby Mustang, for "almost $1,000 less," and predicted its great success as a race car. Considering the engine's displacement, performance figures were astounding: 6.7 seconds 0-60, 14.9 seconds at 97.0 mph in the quarter and 124 mph top speed.

"With the Z-28," *Car and Driver* concluded, "Chevy is on the way toward making the gutsy stormer the Camaro should have been in the first place. It's an appealing car, as tough and purposeful as an F-5 jet fighter, but a car you could be happy living with. The brakes need a little work, there's that nonsense with the single traction arm . . . and we'd like a wider choice of tires—but it's a start. Any owner who wants to rectify these drawbacks on his own is going to wind up with one of the 1,000 best Camaros ever built."

Race driver/editor Jerry Titus also tested the Z-28 for his *Sports Car Graphic* magazine and came away very impressed. After talking price—$437.10 for the Z-28 option plus another $305 for the required four-speed and power disc brakes—he criticized the use of single-leaf rear springs and, like *Car and Driver,* the single radius rod. More favorably he said that it "*has* apparently eliminated the tramp obtainable on extremely hard braking." He also mentioned the plenum air intake and "tuned runner" manifold as very important features.

"A couple of quick runs through the quarter-mile produced a reading of 15.5 seconds," Titus enthused, "pretty close to GT-350

Camaro was both pace car and competitor at '67 Mid-Ohio Trans-Am race. David Pearson's Cougar (#15) is on the pole next to Jerry Titus' Mustang (#17). Titus won, but George Follmer drove the Penske Camaro from seventh qualifying spot to third-place finish. Below (left): first appearance of Penske/Sunoco Z-28, Daytona, February 1967; (right): Waikiki show car had teakwood grille and side panels, "actuated" taillamps and surfboard mount.

time. Cornering power and attitude were *very* impressive and, even without racing tires and adequate roll stiffness, gave plain indication that the Camaro is going to be completely competitive from a roadability standpoint. Its understeer is mild, braking ability is excellent (though the stock linings quickly gave up the ghost) and out-of-the-corner power can be applied early; all prime attributes in sedan racing.

"Is Chevrolet back in racing?" he asked in conclusion. "No. Will it be? Probably not in the immediate future. Where the Z-28 *is* significant is in a breakthrough of the stubborn policy to hold back options and hardware that would enable customers to be more competitive."

Car Life reported on a pair of Camaros, both coupes, in its March issue: an SS-350 four-speed and a 250 cubic-inch six with the standard three-speed manual transmission. The optional six, it said, represented "quite a bargain in on-the-road performance" for its $26.35 price, plus "surprising fuel economy" (19-21 mph), and "adequate acceleration." Also, because of the 210 pounds shaved off the front-end weight compared to the 350 V-8, it offered "a balanced feeling in driving and cornering." Performance clocked out at 11.4 seconds 0-60, 18.5 seconds at 75.0 mph in the quarter-mile and 104 mph top speed. The only real complaint was the balky three-speed column shifter.

"The SS-350 really blossoms as a personal/luxury/HP sort of car," said the author in comparison, " . . . but balance, handling and braking (with the standard drum brakes) are not as good as with the Big Six." Other optional engines were discussed briefly, as were the car's computer-aided chassis design, its optional front disc and sintered metallic drum brakes, and "inordinately nimble" handling. On the gripe list were reflections from the SS's steering wheel, "odd refractions" from the cone-shaped plastic instrument covers, and some general fit-and-finish faults.

"'Fun-to-drive' keynotes the Camaro," the article concluded. "*CL* testers can't remember when they've had cars with such a high Fun Factor." The test SS-350, incidentally, did 0-60 in 7.8 seconds, the quarter in 15.8 seconds at 89.0 mph, and 120 mph on the top end.

Chevrolet launched a nationwide Camaro "Pacesetter" sales campaign in April in recognition of the Indy pace car tie-in. Featured on the specially-equipped Camaros were free hood stripe and floor-mounted three-speed shifter, plus discounted Powerglide, power steering and power brake option. Advertising support included large newspaper ads, network TV and radio spots, and dealer promotional material.

The pace car itself was an Ermine White convertible with white top and blue interior, deluxe steering wheel and interior trim, SS-396 (325 hp) and Rally Sport packages, Turbo Hydra-matic transmission, Positraction, power steering, power front disc brakes, nylon red-stripe tires, console and instrumentation, pushbutton radio, heavy-duty battery and heavy-duty radiator. No replicas as such were offered for public sale—except the hundred or so actually used for parades and as courtesy vehicles, which were later sold as used cars—but people were urged to go out to their dealers and test-drive similarly-equipped Camaros.

It would be only the third time a Chevrolet would pace the 500. The first had been a 1948 Fleetmaster convertible and the second a 1955 Bel Air. Three-time Indy winner Mauri Rose, a Chevy research and development engineer who had supervised preparation of the 1955 pace car, was picked to drive the Camaro that would pace the May 30th event.

Supplying an Indianapolis 500 pace car involves a lot more than most people realize. Besides the actual car that leads thirty-three nervous drivers around the track at 100-plus mph, there are a couple of fully-prepared backup cars just in case something goes wrong. One hundred or more replicas are provided for use in opening-day and race-day parades and as courtesy loaners for drivers, track officials, race queens, press and various VIPs, as are fifteen three-quarter-ton and half-ton pickups for trackside fire control and safety control duty.

The following were also part of the pace-car deal for the 1967 fifty-first Indy 500: two-page, four-color ads in the festival and race programs; six painted billboards on highways leading to the track during the month of May; a full-page ad in the race-day *Indianapolis Star-News;* hundreds of pocket-size notebooks for distribution at race headquarters and in the press room; a color TV as a prize for the pole-sitting car's chief mechanic; about a thousand favors at the pole mechanic's banquet; some six hundred favors for "handicappers" at the 500 festival parade; and countless other small items such as coasters for various parties and luncheons. Although a tremendously complicated and expensive proposition, it was great exposure for a car like the Camaro.

The pace car's first public function was the elaborate opening-day parade and ceremony on Saturday, April 29th. Following a breakfast program with the Mayor, forty-three pace car replicas led a lengthy caravan from Indianapolis' Murat Temple to the Speedway, then lined up three abreast for two parade laps of the track. While announcer Tom Carnegie gave the official welcome to those present, a

Meet the masked marvel.

Meet Camaro. Masked because it carries Rally Sport equipment with hideaway headlights. A marvel because it's an SS 350: telltale domed hood, rally stripe and Camaro's biggest V8.

Over 3,200 pounds of driving machine nestled between four fat red-stripe tires, an SS 350 carries the 295-horsepower 350-cubic-

inch V8. So you know it's some other kind of Camaro.

For a suspension, it has special high-rate springs—coil in front, single-leaf in back—and stiffer shocks at all four corners. And with its exceptionally wide 59" tread, we assure you an SS 350 handles the way a sporting machine should.

And for your added safety,

every Camaro—be it SS 350 or not—comes with such protective conveniences as the GM-developed energy-absorbing steering column, dual master cylinder brake system with warning light, folding front seat back latches and shoulder belt anchors. Try one on at your Chevrolet dealer's. It's a ball-and-a-half.

Command Performance

Camaro By Chevrolet
CHEVROLET

---

pace car driven by 1966 USAC National Champion Mario Andretti, with Chevrolet general manager Pete Estes as a passenger, broke through a huge paper checkered flag imprinted with "Second Fifty" to commemorate the beginning of the second fifty years of the event.

Andretti parked the car in front of the pit wall VIP area and he and Estes proceeded to the podium. A time capsule to be opened on May 1st, 2017 was loaded with Indianapolis memorabilia, including a picture of the '67 Camaro pace car, and sealed. Boy scouts and marching bands performed, the Queen and her Court were introduced, Andretti said a few words, there was some additional pomp and ceremony, and then Estes stepped to the microphone, next to Speedway president Tony Hulman.

"Chevrolet is very pleased to have the Camaro selected as the car to pace the 1967 Indianapolis 500," he said. "We think it is appropriate that the sporty Camaro is the car of your choice this year, because it is the newest design to be offered by Chevrolet, and it was designed to appeal to the same kind of people who come here by the thousands to watch this great event. These people love great sports events and they love action, and we know they are going to see the greatest of all sports spectacles here at the Speedway. We are proud to have a part in it. And now, Mr. Hulman, may I present you the keys to the Official Pace Car, the Chevrolet Camaro."

A balloonist ascended. Estes, Hulman, chief starter Harlan Fengler and 500 Festival president Kenneth Hauck then climbed into the pace car for a formal inspection lap of the track; and with that, the festivities were over.

Now what about a GM or Chevrolet Division return to racing? "We don't think racing is economical or necessary," GM Board Chairman Fred Donner flatly told a stockholder when the question came up at the corporation's general meeting. "I've got to go along with the boss," said Pete Estes when questioned a few days later. Then what's with the Indy pace car involvement? "Indy exposure is good for any product," Estes replied.

Back in Detroit on May 2nd, Chevrolet unveiled a trio of Camaro "dream cars." A candy-apple red customized convertible called "Cherokee" sported aluminum wheels, a rear-deck spoiler and twin exhaust pipes. A pearl blue SS-396 convertible called "Cabriolet" was fitted with heavy-duty suspension and engine mounts, and other high-performance components, plus simulated air scoops on the hood. And most unusually, a pearl yellow Camaro coupe called "Californian," with special paint stripes and exhausts exiting from behind the front wheels, was mounted on a matching trailer pulled by a matching Chevrolet pickup customized with Camaro styling cues.

As in the case of the parent car, the noticeably tame names were probably due to criticism from Washington and a resultant increased concern with safety.

In his May issue monthly column, *Car and Driver* editor David E. Davis Jr. featured a Z-28 which he had driven cross-country from GM's Mesa, Arizona Proving Ground to Detroit. Calling it his "crazy black and white race car with the spoiler across the tail," Davis said it ran "like a train" as he kept it "between ninety and a hundred for hours on end, whistling down into the valleys and storming up through the hills on the other side." It was "very noisy and uncomfortable," he said, but it "stuck like glue on the pavement."

Davis' only major complaint, and it was major, was the Camaro's rather primitive, non-rake-adjustable bucket seat. "By the time I got to Joplin," he groaned, "my tail was quite literally numb, and I often drove with one hand, hoisting myself clear of the seat with my left elbow on the armrest and my right hand braced on the center console." Otherwise, Davis had nothing but praise. "On the last day," he wrote, "the Z-28 still ran with brisk authority, and I'd come to love it so much in the mountains that I was almost willing to forgive the seat."

Scoring well in the spring selling season by now, the Camaro was beginning to make some serious dents in the mighty Mustang's market dominance. Surpassing the 100,000 mark in its first seven months, it had thoroughly outstripped all its competition except Mustang and was bringing a surge of attention to Chevrolet from the much-courted youth market that the division never would have had otherwise. And perhaps part of the reason for this success was a multi-faceted ad campaign that stressed different youth messages in different parts of the country, from "mod" in Southern California, Indianapolis, Philadelphia and Miami, to "super-sporting" in Atlanta, Washington and Baltimore, and "plum wild" in St. Louis and Kansas City.

How was the car being received by its first-year buyers? *Popular Mechanics* ran a Camaro "Owners Report" that pinpointed some sore points but generally turned out positive. Highest on the complaint list was the rear suspension—"Rear end hops and winds up like a yo-yo under normal acceleration," griped one respondent—followed by the lack of rear-seat room, the severe rear-fender "turn-under" that collected dirt, mud and stone chips, and the tiny trunk. Highest on the positive side were the Camaro's styling, handling, performance and, surprisingly, economy—in that order.

To return to the racing effort: Penske driver Mark Donohue had written a letter to Vince Piggins following a mid-April Trans-Am at Green Valley, Texas outlining problems the team had encountered and requesting development assistance in solving them. Most serious had been rear-axle wind-up and hop under braking and recurrent losses of front system pressure, one of which had caused him to crash during qualifying. In spite of these troubles, Mark had finished fourth in the race, leaving Chevrolet tied with Mercury for second in points with fifteen each to Ford's sixteen.

Donohue had several requests: a thorough troubleshooting of the

Above (left): product promotion manager Vince Piggins was the man most responsible for seeing that Trans-Am Camaros were competitive.

brake system, some work on lightening the car to get closer to the Ford products, which reportedly had acid-dipped bodies; improvements to the engine's intake manifold for better mixture distribution; and factory homologation of a special lightweight seat and 8.5 inch-wide wheels. He also reported a rumor that the Ford teams were going to 300 cubic-inch engines, and he recommended dual carburetors for the Camaro if they did.

In response, Piggins arranged a three-day brake-test program and

Opposite page (below): Donohue ready to drive Penske/Sunoco car (with controversial vinyl roof). This page: at Sebring; pit stop action.

recommended to Burwell that lightweight body panels be fabricated as soon as possible to bring the car closer to its legal minimum weight of 2640 pounds. Paperwork was already being exchanged with the FIA to legalize the special seat and wider wheels.

In mid-May, four additional competition rear-axle ratios—3.23, 3.42, 3.90 and 4.33:1—were released and given part numbers to better enable Camaro competitors to fine-tune their gearing to the different road-racing tracks. And shortly thereafter, the racing seat and two new wheels, 7x15 and 8x15, but not the requested 8.5 inch ones, were released and ready to enter the parts system. On June 1st, Chevrolet Engineering formally requested four lightweight Camaro bodies with thinner-gauge metal and less interior bracing in non-critical areas to be assembled at the Norwood Fisher Body plant.

A couple of weeks later, a comprehensive program had been formulated and proposed for full-bore development of everything from brake, suspension, frame, engine and drivetrain components to hood and deck pins, fiberglass body panels and plexiglass windows—all for inclusion as standard or optional equipment on the 1968 Z-28 so that it could be used on the race cars. It was even recommended that the 1969 Z-28 get independent rear suspension as well as the Corvette's four-wheel-disc brakes. Like most such proposals, this one asked for everything that could possibly be wanted in the hope that the company would agree to a happy compromise; typically, some of these recommendations were carried out and many were not. But it certainly made an interesting "wish list" for Camaro racers.

As the season progressed the Chevy teams continued to complain about their cars' deficiencies, and the Camaro's weight disadvantage versus the competition topped their gripe list. Some said that even after as much chiseling and stripping of excess metal as possible, the Camaros were still five hundred pounds heavier than the Mustangs and Dodge Darts (Piggins estimates that the actual difference was a bit over two hundred pounds), and requested factory homologation of fiberglass body panels to compensate.

Chevrolet didn't think fiberglass panels would get past the FIA rulemakers, but they were working hard on coming up with some lightweight steel bodies. By using light-gauge steel, Fisher Body was able to trim ninety-five pounds from the body and front-end sheetmetal; and it was found that acid-dipping could remove more than another two hundred pounds. This total reduction of some three hundred pounds, then, would be more than enough to get a racing Camaro down to legal weight.

The only problem was that such shenanigans were illegal. Bodies, like everything else, were supposed to remain as-produced except for

certain specified allowable modifications. Still, if Chevy racers wanted to acid-dip their cars, as other serious competitors already were doing, there was nothing Chevrolet could do to stop them. This led to some funny incidents, with everyone cheating one way or another and simultaneously trying to catch everyone else in the act. At one point, the sibling-rival Ford and Mercury teams even protested each other.

One good story involves the Penske car's vinyl roof. "Penske was acid-dipping his body," Piggins chuckles, "and the sheet metal got so thin that it got a lot of wrinkles in it. So to cover up the wrinkles, he put a vinyl top on it and tried to get away with that on the excuse that it made the car go faster according to our wind tunnel testing. And when he said that we actually got a reduction in drag with the vinyl roof, that started a big rush of everybody putting vinyl tops on their Camaros."

The brake problems were not solved until several races into the season. Among other things, says Piggins, "we found out the Corvette brake bias valve had been hooked up backwards. The result was that the rear was getting most of the load and causing an unstable condition."

The halfway mark in the season was a race at Bryar Motorsport Park in Loudon, New Hampshire, where Donohue again crashed during practice, this time due to a broken rear axle. The car was repaired overnight, but broke another axle during the race and didn't finish. Peter Revson won in a Cougar, followed by Bert Everett in an under-two-liter Porsche. Dick Thompson's Mustang was third overall and second in the big-bore class. Standings with six races to go: Cougar thirty-nine, Mustang thirty-five, Camaro twenty-seven.

By the next event though, a six-hour enduro at Marlboro, Maryland, the Penske car was finally sorted out and fully competitive, and Donohue co-drove with Canadian Craig Fisher to a convincing win. Second was the Mustang of Milt Minter and Allan Moffat, while the Jerry Titus/Jim Adams Mustang finished third. That moved Ford back into the points lead with forty-one to Mercury's thirty-nine and Chevy's thirty-six.

By season's end, Ford had won the championship over its sister division by just two points, largely on the strength of four wins by Titus. Mercury also had scored four wins—two by Revson, one each by Dan Gurney and David Pearson—to Donohue's three for Chevy and Bob Tullius' one for Dodge. Camaro had failed to win the Trans-Am title in its first year, but the Penske team's trio of victories, including the last two in a row, served notice that it would be a serious force to contend with in 1968.

In late September the results of a Z-28 handling development program at the Michigan Proving Ground were reported. Though the test car was on the heavy side at 3334 pounds (curb weight plus driver), it managed to generate a very impressive 0.987 g's on the skidpad with the optimum spring and sway bar combination plus 950-15W Goodyear racing tires on 8x15 wheels. Work was also conducted to determine the best front valance panel and rear spoiler configurations to minimize lift at high speeds. This was followed by Proving Ground coastdown tests and some wind tunnel runs to establish a data base of aerodynamic information for future use.

Of course, Camaro hadn't been on the market for long before hot-rod shops and performance-oriented dealers started dropping 427 engines into it. The first major magazine report on one of these appeared in the July *Motor Trend*. "No matter how many 'hot' cars you've driven," wrote MT's John Ethridge, "the first time you really uncork a Dana Camaro [from Dana Chevrolet of Southgate, California] you're bound to be awe-stricken if not outright panicked at the sheer magnitude of the forces unleashed."

Using the biggest slicks he could stuff under the fenders, Ethridge recorded a quarter-mile run of 12.75 seconds at "a shade over 110 mph," but felt that still more rubber and a smoother-shifting gear linkage than the Muncie his test car had would have put it at or below 12.0 seconds. And this was the "standard" 425 hp four-barrel engine, not the available three-carb 435 hp version.

Dana also offered special Z-28 packages and a dazzling selection of Camaro performance goodies for any taste and budget. Roadracer and Chevy dealer Don Yenko, famous for the Corvair-based Yenko Stinger sports car of a few years earlier, marketed 410 and 450 horsepower 427 Super Camaros as well as race-prepared Z-28's. Chicago's Nickey Chevrolet, in conjunction with Bill Thomas Race Cars of Anaheim, California was also solidly into the 427 Camaro business by mid-'67.

Car and Driver, more interested in road driving than dragging, reported in September on the handling characteristics of a monster-motor Nickey/Thomas 427 Camaro. "We rushed at curves, downshifting and up-revving, and came out tail swung wide in dirt-track style," said the author. "Despite the good forward traction of those wide [rear] tires, the lightly laden tail showed a marked propensity for switching around. . . . An initial understeering tendency resulting from the weight distribution was pretty powerful and had to be countered with plenty of throttle and wheel action for fast cornering, but the lack of body roll lent confidence to the driver under such conditions."

The author found the car's metallic-lined drum brakes more than

'67 Z-28, almost a factory racer and basis for Trans-Am Camaros. It came in any color as long as it was creamy white with black roof and stripes.

adequate for fast two-lane driving, but only "so-so" in instrumented straight-line testing because of a tendency to lock up the rear wheels. Freeway driving at 65 mph was "dull" and the suspension a bit stiff. Operating in suburban traffic proved a pain: "The gears always seemed to need changing, the brakes needed using, the [stiff] steering had to be twisted." Also, surprisingly, the test car had no temperature or pressure gauges. Best quarter-mile run was 13.9 seconds at 108, although the author asserted that the same car, modified for strip work, had done an astounding 11.35 second, 127 mph run in previous testing.

In August, Chevy unveiled another interesting "idea" car called "Waikiki." Based on an SS-350 convertible, it was "tailored for specific use by the sun and surf set . . . to demonstrate the car's versatility as a sports-type vehicle." And it indeed sported interesting features: a removable surfboard carrier, for example, and special taillamps that glowed green when the driver's foot was on the gas pedal, amber when he took it off, and red when he applied the brakes. It also had twin "bullet" mirrors, rectangular headlamps flanking a teakwood bar grille, teakwood bodyside panels, wire wheels, and yellow and okra two-tone paint and interior trim. Included in the display was a small trailer on which sat a "hydro-kart, a sort of motorized surfboard painted to match the car."

That same month, radio station KABC of Los Angeles awarded a 1967 Camaro to Jo Ann Pflug of Hollywood, who had won a talent contest sponsored by the station. The competition was staged for the purpose of picking two young women to broadcast freeway traffic reports from a helicopter, but Ms. Pflug, as you may recall, stayed on the ground to become a leading lady in such films as *M*A*S*H, Catlow* and *Where Does It Hurt?*

Finally, it was reported in August that the Camaro's "lipstick-striped" SS front end, often the butt of jokes even within Chevrolet, was predicted by some researchers to be a trend of the future. The reason, according to *Super Service Station* magazine: cars with "bright color noses" will more easily be spotted by pedestrians.

By model year's end, the '67 Camaro had sold to the tune of 201,134—not the 250-300,000 that Chevy had hoped for, but not bad in a year that was basically disappointing for Chevrolet sales as a whole. Of the 220,906 '67 Camaros produced, 64,842 got the SS package; 25,141 were convertibles (10,675 SS's); 5141 had the 396 engine and only 602 were Z-28's.

Given a two-and-a-half year head start, the class-leading Mustang was still well ahead with almost 443,000 '67's sold. But Chevy was well on its way in the fast-growing ponycar market, and working hard to close the gap.

CHAPTER THREE
Taking the Offensive

Nothing ever stands still in the auto business. While engineers and designers were busy developing and styling the 1969 Camaro and the totally revamped model scheduled for 1970, others were just as busily refining the current car. Thus the 1968 model appeared on September 15th, 1967, little changed externally but significantly improved underneath and inside in everything from spring and shock rates to cockpit ventilation.

The grille, park lamps, taillamps and wheel covers were reshaped. Exterior moldings were revised to better accent the car's "venturi" shape, and the side marker lights required by law were grafted into the fenders front and rear. A new SS nose stripe wrapped to the body "break" line and then bent ninety degrees into a slim side stripe extending nearly to the door's trailing edge.

Functionally, the door vent windows disappeared while GM's dual-level Astro-ventilation improved fresh-air flow inside. Rear shocks were relocated to better control the axle, and suspension travel was increased slightly to help smooth the ride. Softer, more luxurious seat trim plushed up the interior look and feel, and more easily read rectangular gauges replaced the former round ones—but they were still optional and remained in the same console location. More instrument panel padding, shielded door handles and other minor changes improved interior safety.

In addition to the mandated safety features, engines throughout the industry sprouted air pumps, or "air injection reactors," and other paraphernalia to meet 1968's stricter emissions standards. For the first time stickers on the radiator supports provided detailed tune-up instructions to help technicians and home mechanics adjust mixture and timing to smog-level specifications.

Thanks to the hard-working performance engine and chassis

Again in 1969, Camaro paced the Indianapolis 500. 1960 Indy winner Jim Rathmann drove white SS-396 375 hp convertible.

groups, the "factory road racer" Z-28 returned better and stronger in every way—and with a choice of colors for '68—though higher-than-anticipated demand and development hold-ups on the revised 302 engine and M-22 ("rock-crusher") close-ratio heavy-duty transmission caused delivery delays until well into December. Twin four-barrel carburetors, four-wheel disc brakes and a larger 4.5 inch front valance panel replacing the 2.0 inch panel for reduced aerodynamic lift were homologated for Trans-Am series racing. The long list of improved heavy-duty parts included front hubs, rear axles, front and rear brake components, and the brake master cylinder.

The street Z-28 package remained a bargain at $400.25 over the base Camaro coupe price of $2694. The required power front disc brakes ($100.10) and four-speed transmission ($184.35 for the M-20 or close-ratio M-21, $310.70 for the special M-22) raised the ante to nearly $3400, but at that price the car still represented lots of excitement per dollar. Other Z-28 options included the aerodynamic front valance and rear spoiler package ($32.68) and positraction rear axle ($42.15). The latter was recommended with the standard 3.73 and optional 3.07, 3.31 and 3.55:1 ratios and mandatory with 4.10, 4.56 and 4.88 gearing.

By now the ponycar phenomenon had captured the country's imagination. Combined with the parallel and interrelated musclecar movement, it was seemingly turning the whole industry into an automotive youth boutique. Camaro promotional photos for '68, for example, show such things as a droopy-eyed basset hound eyeing a new "houndstooth" checked seat upholstery design and a leggy model stretching some multicolored tape striping around Camaro's nose.

Parade, the nationally-circulated Sunday supplement magazine, ran a story called "How Youth Has Changed the Look of the '68 Models" in its October 1st issue. "Youth is climbing into the driver's seat," said author Patricia Chapman, "not only on the nation's highways (the majority of U.S. drivers are under thirty-four) but . . . in the capital of Autoland itself. The youthquake in Detroit has brought a new generation of cars—and a new generation of automakers."

Chapman attributed much of this excitement to youthful designers, a majority of whom "have yet to reach their thirtieth birthdays." Seventy-four percent of Ford's designers, she pointed out, were under thirty-five. The average was mid-twenties at GM, twenty-seven at Chrysler and thirty-two at American Motors. Chapman asserted that Detroit's four styling vice presidents—GM's Bill Mitchell, Ford's Gene Bordinat, Chrysler's Elwood Engle and AM's

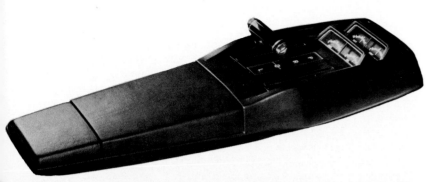

Dick Teague—"have shifted an industry attuned to old, boxy, chrome-laden autos to the sleek, sophisticated autos of today."

All four were profiled and quoted in the article about the fast-growing youth market. "Today you've got to be young, there are no squares any more," said Mitchell, who was credited with starting the youth-car look with the wire-wheeled, bucket-seated Corvair Monza in 1961. "Youth appeal or not," he added, "cars should change progressively. Each car should have a strong identity."

And all four predicted where auto design would go in the years to follow. They saw more luxury cars and more chrome coming down the road, but also a wider selection of options, more bright, psychedelic colors, wilder interior decor ("with today's checks perhaps giving way to flowers by 1970"), and more personal and custom cars, some styled expressly for women. They also foresaw safer autos, some specialized for superhighways and others for urban use, and cars powered by electricity and gas turbine engines.

By late November product performance manager Vince Piggins had put together his proposed assistance and parts development program. This included only token involvement in NHRA drag and NASCAR stock-car racing (due to '68 season rules unfavorable to Chevy products) but increased emphasis on the SCCA Trans-Am road racing series. Daytona car builder Smokey Yunick would continue Camaro development work and campaign his own very trick Camaro, which had been banned from the fall 1967 Riverside, California event as being far from legal.

The Penske team would continue to field one car for engineer/driver Mark Donohue and would add a second for Canadian driver Craig Fisher, with backing from Fisher's sponsor, Terry Godsall of Montreal. The Sunoco financing would continue, as would the parts and development support from Chevrolet. The latter would include, for starters, two prepared cars and ten Traco-built 302 racing engines.

In December, Penske conducted extensive tests of his 1968-version cars at the Marlboro race course in Maryland, primarily to check out suspension changes and evaluate a new-design distributor and a special four-barrel carburetor. By this time, the Penske Camaro's front subframe was rigidly fastened to the body, the safety roll cage was welded to the subframe and to the rear body above the spring shackles, and the front control arm bushings were of solid material—all to achieve sufficient body/chassis stiffness for optimum handling.

Both the racing distributor, with higher initial advance, and the new carburetor, with mechanically operated secondaries and a center-mounted accelerator pump discharge nozzle, proved superior

to standard Z-28 units and were recommended for production release. The latter was intended as a back-up in case the two-four-barrel set-up did not prove satisfactory for all uses. The handling tests also went well, but it was recommended that a new traction bar or radius rod be developed to prevent brake hop with the improved 1968 brakes.

Four Camaros and five Mustangs, two of them factory-prepared, started the Daytona 24-Hour race on February 4th, 1968, running in the Trans-Am class. The Number 6 Penske car driven by Donohue and Bob Johnson qualified fastest and was quicker at all times than even the factory Mustangs with their new tunnel-port 302 engines. All but one of the Trans-Am entries lost time for repairs in the pits, however, and that one finished first in class and a remarkable fourth overall. Unfortunately, of the nine entries, it was the Mustang of Jerry Titus and Ronnie Bucknum.

The Penske car had to replace cracked cylinder heads at 13.5 hours, the private entries of Bill Boye and Joey Chitwood suffered

suspension problems and a fourth Camaro entered by Hugh Heishman retired early in the race with unspecified troubles. But the fully-equipped Penske racer with all 1968 updates including four-wheel discs and twin four-barrel carbs was not only competitive but dominant before its head troubles. The stage was set for Chevy to win the twelve-race 1968 series.

Indeed, the Penske Camaros finished one-two in class and an astounding third and fourth overall in the March twelve-hour enduro at Sebring, Florida. *Time* magazine, for one, saw this as a symbol of Detroit's growing interest in automotive muscle, "a burgeoning off-track trend toward faster road cars—and Ralph Nader be damned." Citing mushrooming buyer interest in high-performance cars and engines, not to mention "racing stripes, special identifying fender emblems and 'spoilers,' " the April 5th article estimated that "muscle buffs last year spent some $500 million on optional high-performance equipment—despite the fact that the cars greatly exceed speeds that are safe and/or legal on most U.S. highways."

Interior and exterior shots of sportier looking 1968 Camaro. Page opposite: console-stirrup shift for Powerglide transmission; front and rear views of RS coupe. This page (above): Sport Coupe; (below): SS-350; recessed door handle was one of several newly introduced safety features.

AIR DISTRIBUTED TO EACH CYLINDER

FILTERED AIR INTO AIR PUMP

A

B

E

C

B

GASES BURNED HERE

D

EXHAUST

UNBURNED HYDROCARBONS AND CARBON MONOXIDE

THIS ENGINE IS EQUIPPED TO REDUCE EXHAUST EMISSIONS

THE FOLLOWING ADJUSTMENTS ARE NECESSARY TO MAINTAIN THE EFFECTIVENESS OF THE SYST

(With engine at operating temperature, choke open, air cleaner installed, air conditioning off)

1. Set mixture screw(s) for max. idle rpm and adjust speed screw to obtain 750 RPM IN NEUTRAL
2. Set ignition timing at 4° BTC with vacuum advance line plugged.
3. Adjust mixture screw in to obtain a 20 rpm drop (lean roll).
4. Adjust mixture screw out ¼ turn.
5. Repeat steps 3 and 4 for second mixture screw (if so equipped).
6. Readjust speed screw if necessary to specified idle rpm.

See Service Manual for Additional Tune-Up Instructions

Page opposite (above): '68 Z-28 was much improved and offered choice of colors; (below); 307 cu.in. V-8 with Air Injection Reactor System; engine calibration sticker was new for '68. This page: 302 cu. in. Z-28 engine; new houndstooth upholstery, with hound; aftermarket nose striping, with model.

Undaunted, Chevrolet announced availability of the two-four-barrel cross-ram Z-28 induction system just a couple of weeks later. Available as service parts through Chevrolet dealers, the two-part conversion kits included the carburetors, cable-type linkage, a large oval air cleaner with ducting to connect it to the cowl plenum chamber, and a cast aluminum intake manifold "designed to take advantage of the pulse ram induction effect of the modern valve-in-head engine."

"The object," said a press release, was "to construct inlet passages of a precise length to set up a resonant frequency which will cause a reinforced wave of fuel mixture to reach the normal fuel-air pile-up behind the inlet valve at the instant of opening." Unlike vertical or partially-horizontal ram tubes, the Chevrolet cross-ram manifold was "discretely designed to take advantage of the horizontal ram concept, providing maximum tuning within the space allotted, and still fit neatly within the regular engine compartment, requiring only minor revisions to the hood underside." Of course, the cross ram set-up was not recommended for street use since there was no exhaust cross-over for heating the carburetor pads, and no provision for chokes, and the thing wasn't designed to run much under 4000 rpm anyway.

Road & Track tested a street Z-28 with the 800 cfm single carb and dealer-installed tuned headers for its June 1968 issue. Were the authors impressed? "Who says GM isn't in racing?" they asked. "If the Z-28 isn't a bona fide racing car—in street clothing for this test—

then we've never seen one. . . . Getting off the line in acceleration tests the car slews smoothly to the right but, even with the clutch dropped at 4500 rpm, it gets off to a relatively leisurely start until the engine can get up over the 4000 hump. Then, hold on! From there it revs so freely that it seems it could go on forever. . . . Chevrolet rates this engine at 280 bhp at 5800 rpm, which may be true as far as it goes, but we think the curve keeps climbing to something more like 350 bhp at 6200."

The article complained about the Z-28's clutch, which was "reluctant to re-engage after our rather unmerciful shifts" above 7000 rpm, and its "stiff and notchy" Muncie shift linkage, "aggravated by Chevrolet's dumb sliding-plate shift lever seal." There were no complaints about handling: "[it's] a stable, near-neutral car that has no trouble setting excellent lap times around any reasonably smooth course," but the testers didn't like the car's power steering, calling it "so lacking in feel that one has to learn to drive without the help of feedback from the tires . . . and that's not much fun." Zero-to-sixty acceleration was clocked at 6.9 seconds, the quarter-mile at 14.9 seconds and 100 mph, and top speed at 132 mph.

The following month *Car and Driver* reported a Z-28 versus Tunnel-Port Mustang comparison test, with both cars factory-modified within reason. "What we wanted for this test were cars that any enthusiast could duplicate with factory parts and yet have performance and handling far beyond the sporty cars," explained technical editor Pat Bedard. In other words, "Trans-Am racers for

Roger Penske (left) and Mark Donohue teamed for ten Trans-Am wins and first Chevy Championship in '68; Donohue in action, Mid-Ohio course.

the street." Racing twin-four-barrel setups, tuned headers and four-wheel disc brakes were permissible, but mufflers were required at all times.

The Camaro turned up show-car pretty and decked out with power steering and brakes, custom interior and even a console. At 3480 pounds, it was 260 pounds above its base curb weight, and was equipped with optional Koni shocks, heavy-duty valve springs, transistor ignition, heavy-duty L-88 clutch and flywheel and a 4.10:1 rear axle. It maintained its standard 11.0:1 compression ratio and E70-15 tires on 15x6-inch wheels. The Mustang, in addition to its 12.5:1 compression ratio, dry deck and tunnel port 302 engine, boasted special suspension all around and mysterious F60 15 tires—a size that didn't officially exist at the time—on 15x7 inch mag wheels, but was handicapped slightly by a 3.91:1 rear axle. It weighed in at 3282 pounds, 111 pounds over its listed base curb.

The Z-28 was slightly quicker at the drag strip with a best run of 13.77 seconds at 107.39 mph to the Mustang's 13.96 at 106.13, and its far-superior four-wheel discs sucked it down from 80 mph in 209 feet versus the Ford's 248 feet. Despite spongy brakes (Ford's four-wheel discs were still under development) and because of its stiffer suspension, trick tires and wider wheels, the Mustang won the lap-time contest at Connecticut's 1.5-mile Lime Rock road racing course at 1:08.8 versus the Z-28's 1:09.2.

Racer Sam Posey, who tested both cars at Lime Rock, criticized the Camaro's rear-axle hop under braking, understeer in bumpy cor-ners and "absolutely terrible" shift linkage, but was impressed by the engine's torque and the car's overall handling and feel. He was surprised at the low lap time, saying "that would have put us somewhere in the middle of the Trans-Am grid here last year, which is pretty intriguing since it's really a street car." He also wondered what it would have done on the Mustang's trick, experimental tires. Other performance figures were as close as they were impressive: 5.3 seconds zero-to-sixty for the Z-28 versus 5.4 for the Mustang and 132 mph top speed as opposed to the Mustang's 131.

Another Z-28 test was reported in the September *Car Life*. "For the person who wants the best-performing non-race car built in this country," the article stated, "the Z-28 appears the only way to go. Chevrolet rates the Z-28's 302-cid V-8 at a laughable 290 bhp. Four hundred comes much nearer the truth. This is a fistful of energy any way you dissect it." Rated high were the car's "fierce acceleration, exuberant cornering and superb brakes," but the author added that these qualities were offset by "little quirks—its lumpy idle, lousy gas mileage, poor low-speed torque, noisy engine and stiff ride."

Car Life also griped about the four-speed shift linkage but labeled the transmission itself "a delight to use, beautifully suited to any track or road condition." Also praised were the test car's disc/drum brakes ("matched the two Vettes we tested this year") and 17.1 power steering ("not only light and quick but also positive"). But the author criticized the car's handling on non-smooth surfaces, commenting: "in the rough, where there are bumps, ridges, gravel, loose

Left: Bob Johnson in #16 Penske/Sunoco Camaro leads Jerry Titus' Mustang. Titus finished second, Johnson fourth; Donohue wins Mid-Ohio Trans-Am.

sand, or anything else, the suspension's stiffness creates a good deal of sideways hopping."

There was no criticism, though, about the improved '68 Z-28's performance as a race car. After the Sebring victory, Donohue knocked down several more wins in a row in the Penske car and ended the season with a total of ten in thirteen events, easily pocketing the series title for Chevrolet. Only two race wins went to Mustangs, and one to Craig Fisher in the other Penske car, which had been converted to a "Canadian Firebird" but still ran the Chevy 302 engine. "We got all the early problems behind us in '68," says performance manager Piggins. "We got the proper springs, spring loads, got the car balanced right. Donohue was probably most responsible for that. We did a lot of work with him at the Proving Ground to get the proper handling characteristics and cornering attitudes. We took it to a few of the tracks for testing as well."

Meanwhile, the designers back at GM Styling had never quit working on the Camaro, trying new concepts on paper and in clay to improve the '68, restyle for '69 and create an all-new Camaro for the '70 model year. Among the ideas tried and rejected for '68 were a Nomad-type two-door wagon (Kammback) version, a duck-tailed luxury coupe with no rear quarter window and a partial vinyl roof, and an aerodynamic-looking fastback.

The sexy and unique Kammback made it into clay but no further because management felt it would be too expensive to produce for its fairly limited market appeal. The fastback, obviously an answer to Mustang's 2+2, looked every inch a starting point for the next-generation Z-28 road racer with its longer, narrower grille opening, functional front fender vents and built-in rear spoiler, but it met with opposition from upper management. "This corporation has had some pretty bad experiences with fastback models in the past," explains Irv Rybicki, who by July 1967 was the executive in charge of all GM exterior design. "There were a lot of people downtown who had no desire to do a fastback of any kind, even including a sports model. Anything fastback appeals to a certain group out there and that's it, and you can't ever push it beyond that number." Too bad.

Another dealership cashing in on the demand for ultra-high performance machinery was Baldwin Chevrolet of Baldwin, Long Island, New York, which announced in 1968 that it was the second-largest such producer in the U.S., right after the Ford-owned Shelby Mustang operation. Baldwin offered what it termed the "Fantastic Five": SS-427 conversions of Camaros, Chevelles, Corvettes, Chevy II's and full-size Chevies. Of the "straight-stock" SS-427 Camaro, priced at only $3795, Baldwin said that it is "dyno-tuned and ready to

This page: "Nomad" wagon in clay and (bottom): model with vinyl roof, wraparound window and taillamps. Page opposite: wild-looking Trans-Am race car concept; proposed '68 has half-vinyl roof, ducktail spoiler and knock-off alloy wheels; fastback with extended nose, fender vents.

blow the doors off any Detroit stocker. And, when fitted with our recommended Super-Bite suspension option, it will run away and hide from production Sting Rays." That was Phase I. Phase II, of course, was even stronger, and a Baldwin Phase III SS-427 Camaro was guaranteed to turn "at least" 120 mph in 11.5 seconds with an "approved" driver on an AHRA or NHRA-sanctioned drag strip.

When '68 model production figures were totalled, the results were only a slight improvement over '67. Of the 235,147 1968 Camaros built, 184,200 were equipped with V-8 engines and 7199 of those were Z-28's with the special 302 V-8.

As is typical in the industry, design work on the '69 Camaro had begun almost as soon as the '67 design was finished. In mid-October 1966, already reacting to criticism that the first Camaro, though pretty, was less "hairy chested" than it should have been, the designers were sketching wide tired, broad shouldered, muscular looking concepts with large, mostly horizontal-theme taillamps. Both sporty fastbacks and more "formal" notchbacks were tried, with fender "blisters" modelled after those on the legendary Mercedes 300 SL sports cars. Beginning at the lower front corners of both wheel openings, these slim bulges swept up, then rearward into horizontal character lines and provided clearance for larger wheels and tires even as the wheel cutouts themselves were flattened on top. Early models had low, Corvette-like grille openings with overhanging bumpers, but by the spring of '67 the grille designs had become merely enlarged versions of the original full-width theme.

Since the '69 car was a facelift, not a complete restyle, these ideas were assimilated into a fresh look on essentially the original body.

Headlamps were set near the ends of a new, V-shaped eggcrate grille, and large, round park lamps below the bumper gave a "driving light" effect. Triple simulated louvers were moulded into the rear quarters just ahead of the wheel openings, and the taillamps took on a longer, slimmer shape with three sections instead of the former two. These details plus the lower wheel arches, emphasized by what Chevy called "trailing windsplits that give an illusion of motion," achieved the more aggressive appearance that was desired.

Inside was a revised instrument panel with rectangular-theme instrumentation replacing the old circular dials in a "Corvette-type individualized cockpit." The bucket seats were improved with larger cushions and "more comfortable contours." Hidden headlamp doors on the RS-option front end featured triple horizontal openings with clear lenses so the lights would shine through if the doors failed to open and flanked a blacked-out grille opening. SS models came with a special raised-center hood, revised nose stripes, front disc brakes and white-lettered "wide-oval" tires on seven-inch-wide wheels. The Z-28 was little-changed in theme but greatly improved in detail, including (as an option) the latest Corvette-type four-wheel disc brakes, thanks to the extensive racing development program.

Several exterior striping combinations were available, and interesting new options included a "Space Saver" inflatable spare tire; stainless steel and rubber fender guards to protect the lower body from road splash, dirt and stones; and headlamp washer nozzles (standard on the RS). Other options were a 250 hp, 9.0:1, regular-gas 350 engine and a resilient body-color front bumper that could take minor impacts without damage. The three-speed Turbo Hydra-matic

69 F

Row above: three proposed "hairy" rear end treatments for '69. Center row: January 1967 notchback, hatchback and fastback side treatments, all w...

69 NOTCH BACK

Row below: winter 1967 proposal for low-mouthed, pointy-nosed '69 version shown next to '67 Mustang; Corvette-like front designs shown on draw...

...nder "blisters," "frenched" headlamps and underslung grille openings.

...e way to more conventional nose on clay model in February 1967.

transmission became available on all models, though a low-cost "Torque-Drive" automatic was retained as an option with six-cylinder engines. A new Hurst shifter replaced the old Muncie linkage on the optional four-speed manual gearbox. Among the many engineering improvements were ignition/steering-column/ transmission locks (required by law) and beefed-up block for the 307/ 327/350 V-8's with four-bolt main bearing caps for 300, 350 and 370 hp versions.

Chevy was still heavily into "cute" promotional photos, most featuring buxom, miniskirted models, and 1969 produced a bumper crop. A Z-28 was pictured with paper eyeballs staring fixedly at the sexy young woman leaning on its fender. A fetching little lady sat crosslegged on an SS-350 to demonstrate the Space-saver spare, which, it was said, could fit inside the hatbox she carried in an adjoining photo. A more warmly-dressed woman was shown backing through heavy snow, aided by a device in the trunk that spread some sort of traction spray on the rear tire treads. There was also a photo of star running-back O.J. Simpson, nattily dressed in tie and double-breasted coat, with his own SS-396. A more serious promotional gimmick was a complex auto-show display that alternately mated a coupe body with two different front-end/powertrain sections on turntables to demonstrate the inner differences between a base six-cylinder coupe and an SS-350.

One commentary on Chevrolet's schizophrenic attitude toward racing was provided in *Sports Car Graphic's* October 1968 issue, which profiled the '69 model ponycars. "A ho-hum Camaro started down the road in '66," said the magazine, "and reached a fork where the sign pointing left said 'race cars'; the one to the right, 'sporty cars.' Restrained by GM corporate policy from fielding a works team in the Trans-Am series, Chevrolet took both roads anyway. . . . Chevrolet, as is widely known, doesn't participate in automobile competition and will be delighted to sell you a Z-28 race car, as well as a less hirsute boulevard *voiture.*"

With both chassis and engine well developed and one SCCA Trans-Am championship under their belts, the road-racing forces concentrated on more subtle speed-seeking improvements for the '69 season. One fairly new (for autos) science worth examining was aerodynamics—altering the body shape for less wind drag and, at the same time, more pavement-gripping downforce front and rear. The Camaro designers had toyed with a built-in rear spoiler late in the '69 facelift program, but Piggins' performance group had more radical ideas, mocking up a wild-looking Z-28 with huge spoilers and side fairings integrating them into the fenders. Neither concept reached production, but a '68 type add-on rear spoiler and a small front air

dam were ultimately approved as Z-28 standard equipment, and were therefore legal under the '69 Trans-Am racing rules.

Although some wind tunnel work was done, most aerodynamic research in those days was strictly trial and error. Then-styling vice president Bill Mitchell recalls working with Smokey Yunick to improve the aerodynamics of certain GM products that were expected to find their ways onto race tracks. "We used to go down to Daytona," he says, "and Smokey would show me the miles per hour he could get from different windshield configurations, the scoops underneath, the rear deck and spoiler shapes, the windows . . . you could add up how many miles per hour a car could pick up. We changed a lot of front ends on Chevrolets from what he said. The divisions may have been using wind tunnels, but we didn't. It's amazing the amount of real aerodynamics that came from proven tests at Daytona at that time."

Very curiously, one so-called "dream car" that made the auto show rounds early in 1969 was based on a '68 SS-396 Camaro. Dubbed "Caribe," it was a bright red "dream pickup" with a headerless windshield, open-topped cockpit, targa-style roll bar and a five-foot vinyl-lined, teakwood-floored pickup bed replacing the back seat and trunk. It also featured a modified grille opening with small, high-intensity headlamps, G70 wide oval tires, with "brushed aluminum sidewall inserts" on fifteen-inch aluminum wheels, high-frequency flashing rear stop-lamps, and a hot beverage dispenser and cup storage box in the console.

The January 1969 *Hot Rod* stated that "Chevy's Z-28 runs a tight

race, on a dollar-for-dollar basis, with Plymouth's 'Cuda 340 for first place in performance machinery. By performance, we're talking about low 13's with open headers and sticky rear tires. Or high 13's with street tires and closed headers." Author Steve Kelly praised the '69 Z's new Hurst shifter, its steering and engine response and the performance of its clutch in drag-strip duty, but criticized its non-supportive seatbacks, lack of rearward seat adjustment for better legroom and its console-located instruments which "aren't even convenient for passenger viewing, except maybe back-seat passengers." Best quarter-mile run, after much tuning, fiddling and addition of a 4.88:1 rear axle, 9.00-9.50x14 M&H tires, E/T traction bars and a competition Hurst linkage, was 13.11 seconds at 106.76 mph; but Kelly said the potential was there for much more with further work. "The Z-28 . . . is probably the biggest sleeper ever to hit a new-car showroom," he concluded.

On January 28th, 1969 it was announced that a Camaro would again pace the Indianapolis 500 race and would be given to the winner. To be driven by 1960 Indy winner Jim Rathmann, it was a white SS-396, 375 hp convertible with Turbo Hydra-matic transmission, power front disc brakes and steering, ducted hood, positraction, "Hugger Orange" stripes and trim, fifteen-inch rally wheels and rear spoiler. Inside, it offered a sport steering wheel, console, special instrumentation, and custom black and orange houndstooth upholstery. On the occasion, Estes called Camaro "the type of automobile that appeals to the millions of people throughout the world who enjoy the action and excitement of the famous Indianapolis

Above: aggressive front designs that would lead to production version; below: the search for the right rear treatment in mid-1967.

speed classic." This time, replicas of the pace car would be offered for sale to the public.

Soon after, leading stock-car sanctioning body NASCAR announced that for the second consecutive year it, too, had chosen Camaro as its official pace car for the 1969 season. Why would GM allow Chevrolet pace cars in light of its anti-racing stance? "No car manufacturer is going to turn down the chance for this terrific exposure to hundreds of thousands at the speedway itself and to many millions of people watching television," offered an Indianapolis spokesman in *Ward's Automotive Reports.*

Also in January, General Motors decided to promote Pete Estes to Car and Truck vice president, and John Z. DeLorean, who had also succeeded Estes three-and-a-half years earlier as Pontiac Division general manager, was picked to replace him. DeLorean was playing golf in Palm Springs, California on February 1st when he got the word by phone from Detroit. "I'll be back as soon as I finish the round," he said. "No," replied group vice president Roger Kyes, "you'll come back right now." And he did.

A brilliant product man and car enthusiast who had trained at both Chrysler and Packard before moving to Pontiac, DeLorean had climbed from director of advanced engineering to chief engineer and then to general manager when Estes had been promoted to head Chevrolet in July 1965. At forty, he was the youngest man ever to run a GM division, and he looked and thought more like his youthful customers than a General Motors executive. His hair and sideburns were long, at least by GM standards, his dress flashy and his outlook decidedly liberal. As a result, he often clashed with his conservative corporate bosses, and his preference for socializing with celebrities and jet-setters instead of them didn't help the relationship.

Still, he had achieved a solid reputation, first under Bunkie Knudsen and then Estes, and as general manager had followed their leads very effectively in moving Pontiac from nowhere into a heady third place in industry sales. He seemed just the man to revitalize and reorganize the massive Chevrolet Division, which had lost much of its lead to Ford despite Estes' best efforts. "This is the most exciting challenge I've ever had," DeLorean told *Detroit News* columnist Bob Irvin. Asked if he could help Camaro take over Mustang's leadership in the sporty car market, he replied, "I guarantee one thing—we're going to try."

The February *Motor Trend* reported that Chevy was planning to put its ZL-1 aluminum 427 engine in a small number of 1969 Camaros, something that must have set performance-oriented hearts palpitating throughout the land. "Just imagine," said the magazine,

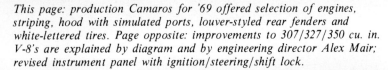

This page: production Camaros for '69 offered selection of engines, striping, hood with simulated ports, louver-styled rear fenders and white-lettered tires. Page opposite: improvements to 307/327/350 cu. in. V-8's are explained by diagram and by engineering director Alex Mair; revised instrument panel with ignition/steering/shift lock.

"a Z-28-weight car with 125 more inches. Can't you just see all those people at Chrysler and Ford reaching for their bottles of Excedrin?"

In March Camaro stylists were toying with a ZL-1 concept that, had it reached production, would have been the meanest looking factory-built car on the road. All in black with deep front chin spoiler and blacked-out headlamp covers framing a special bar grille with "ZL-1" badge, it was set off by special metallic gold striping, a Z-28-type rear spoiler, huge wheels and tires and enormous dual exhausts.

About the engine, *Cars* magazine said: "It can develop well over 600 horses with minor tuning on pump gas and one four-barrel carb, can rev safely at 7600 rpm for long periods, and weighs only about 520 pounds with all accessories—less than a standard 327 engine. Even at an in-the-crate price of up to $3000 it is sure to have a tremendous impact on the whole racing world, from dragsters and funny cars to the exotic Can-Am sports racers." *Cars* predicted that only 50 ZL-1 Camaros would be built—to qualify them for drag-racing Super Stock—and that they would have an advantage in traction and weight distribution over the Boss 429 Mustangs, whose engines weighed nearly a hundred pounds more.

While the ZL-1 was intended strictly for drag-racing competition, there was justified concern within Chevrolet Engineering that some might find their ways into the wrong hands and be used on the street. Aside from the obvious potential warranty problems, there would also be driveability troubles with the engine's open-plenum manifold and lack of either a choke or inlet manifold exhaust heat, not to mention the fact that its power output suffered badly with exhaust

IMPROVED 307-327-350 CU. IN. V-8 CYLINDER BLOCK

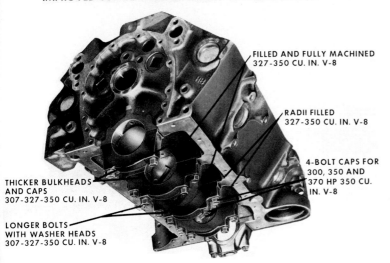

FILLED AND FULLY MACHINED
327-350 CU. IN. V-8

RADII FILLED
327-350 CU. IN. V-8

4-BOLT CAPS FOR
300, 350 AND
370 HP 350 CU.
IN. V-8

THICKER BULKHEADS
AND CAPS
307-327-350 CU. IN. V-8

LONGER BOLTS
WITH WASHER HEADS
307-327-350 CU. IN. V-8

backpressure from a street muffler system. Vince Piggins' suggestion was to build the fifty full-race ZL-1's required to qualify in NHRA Super Stock "C," then de-tune the engine for eligibility in the slightly slower "D" class—and also for the street—and build fifty more.

At least one show-quality development car, dressed like the super-sexy Design Staff concept in gold on black, was built for street use by a few fortunate designers and engineers. Suspension development was completed in early May, and addition of a rear stabilizer bar and glass-belted F70x15 tires was recommended. The car was deemed too expensive already, however, and it was figured that serious racers would develop their own tire/chassis combinations anyway. Then in mid-June a cost-cutting de-proliferation committee decided that the ZL-1 was an "unsaleable option" because of its cost and recommended cancellation.

As it turned out (and according to sketchy and often conflicting documentation), sixty-nine ZL-1 Camaros were built and, like the Boss 429's they were designed to blow away, were fairly conservative in appearance. Using the basic Z-28 body and chassis without the stripes and trim, they cost about $8,000 and weighed approximately 3300 pounds. The all-aluminum (block, heads and intake manifold) 427 engine had an 850 cfm Holley Quad carburetor, 2.30x1.88 inch valves, a .579/.620 inch lift camshaft, solid lifters, 396-type exhaust manifolds connected to dual street exhausts, 116.8 cc open chambers and the Z-28's plenum fresh air intake system. Goodyear GT E70x15 tires were mounted on six-inch-wide wheels, and either a heavy-duty four-speed or automatic transmission and a 4.10:1 12-bolt positrac-

This page: promotional photos for '69 model year included more leggy models, star running-back O.J. Simpson with SS-396 convertible and two options: hatbox-sized inflatable spare and tire traction spray device. Opposite (above): design staff's concept of an integrated rear spoiler, and three shots of effective spoilers as conceived by performance group.

tion rear end put all that power to the ground. What powerhouses they were, and what rare collector's items for their lucky owners today!

In mid-March, the new Chevy general manager found himself accepting the Trans-Am manufacturer's trophy from SCCA director of professional racing Jim Kaser in recognition of the Camaro's domination of that series the previous year. And in May came another very different honor, the *Car and Driver* Reader's Choice Poll award as the "best sporty car." Chevy's Corvette was voted "best all-around car," so both Corvette chief engineer Zora Arkus-Duntov and Camaro chief engineer Lloyd Reuss were on hand at the award ceremony in New York to accept their respective trophies.

A new rash of road tests began with a Z-28 report in the April *Cars*. Unable to get a factory test car, the magazine's staff arranged to borrow one from the Baldwin Chevrolet/Motion Performance group, and loved it despite a few shortcomings. "The Z-28 Camaro," they said, "is the type of ponycar that must be driven to be believed and appreciated as it comes on much stronger in person than it does on paper." The car's stock 3.70:1 gearing, "stiff and sluggish" four-speed linkage, uncontrolled rear axle and a clutch that "didn't want to know about high-rpm power shifting" made drag-type runs difficult, but they found it an excellent street and highway thrasher. After adding 4.56:1 gears, dual-quad carburetors and manifold, tube headers and M/P's Super-Bite suspension, however, they recorded a 5.5 second 0-60 time, and quarter-mile runs in the 13.3 second range at 106 mph. While they found the dual quads "too expensive and too much of a top-end deal to be fully appreciated under normal conditions," they called the Z-28 "the quickest and fastest under-300 hp sportster we have ever driven!"

Car Life came down hard on the SS-396's poorly located rear axle in its May issue, saying: "The rear suspension is plain vanilla, weak linkage between axle and car, and it drags the 396 Camaro down to the level of just another Camaro. . . . At the mere suggestion of work, the axle leaps and hops, shudders and bucks. . . . Starting, stopping or turning, whatever the rest of the car wants to do, the rear suspension won't let it do it." Handling was badly affected by the heavy big-block engine up front, leading to "massive initial understeer, severe final oversteer and a general feeling of wishy-washy before and during the transition." In addition, too-light steering combined with the light rear end required constant driver correction on wet or uneven pavement. *Car Life* did praise the body-colored plastic front bumper, the cold-air hood, the seats and the placement of controls, but in general the article was downbeat. Performance figures were 6.8

This page (above): mini-pickup "Caribe" show car was based on '68; (below): official portrait of 1969 Indianapolis Pace Car; Indy starter Harlan Fengler. Page opposite: on February 1, 1969 Pete Estes gives reins of Chevy Div. to John DeLorean; ZL-1 concept became running prototype, but was not released for production; in 1969 Corvette and Camaro receive Car and Driver's *"Readers' Choice" awards.*

seconds 0-60, 14.8 seconds at 99 mph in the quarter mile and 126 mph top speed.

On the other hand, an August *Car Life* Z-28 report was far more positive. With its optional dual carbs that were "too much for the street, four-wheel disc brakes and a 4.10:1 rear axle, the test car ran 0-60 in 7.4 seconds and a quarter-mile in 15.1 seconds at 95 mph, and recorded a top speed of 133 mph, without modification. "The engine," said the magazine, "didn't begin to work until 3000, and didn't develop any power until 5,000. Then the Great Magic Switch has been flipped, and the power comes on with that brassy blaring call to battle that only comes in bottles labeled small-block Chevrolet." Other comments: "The four-wheel discs made a good braking system better. . . . The package includes front and rear spoilers, which work. . . . The Z-28 steering is light and quick and has road feel . . . very high cornering power, while not requiring expert reactions to keep things under control. . . . The high-back bucket seats are new this year and very comfortable. . . . It's a race car that doesn't have to be raced . . . a delight to drive."

Rival *Road Test* reported on the same car, without dual quads, in the same month, and reached many of the same conclusions. "From the time you turn the key," said the author, "you feel that it's a car that's meant to be raced. The engine idles at 2000 rpm, the twin pipes have a high-pitched snarl, the steering is light and precise, and the cornering flat and fast." *Road Test* praised the Z's close-ratio four-speed, its handling, its four-wheel disc brakes, its new bucket seats and the visibility from inside its cockpit, but criticized the optional gauge placement and the lack of vent windows. Drag-strip performance was "not as quick as we had thought" at 15.4 seconds and 94 mph, probably because the car was only 450 miles old and was not specially tuned. In conclusion, the article said, "the Z-28 is definitely a 'man's car,' and not for little old ladies, of whatever gender. The clutch action is heavy, as befitting a racing car, and fast shifts take a fair amount of muscle. The car responds very quickly to anything the driver does, so it's not a car for casual, arm over the seatback type of driving."

Also in August *Car and Driver* reported on a project car based on a Z-28 Camaro with a special new LT-1 performance engine, which was essentially a Z-28 engine stroked to 350 cubic inches. Rated at 370 hp, it was being developed by Chevrolet to become the Z-28 engine for 1970. With help from racer Mark Donohue and the Penske organization, *Car and Driver*'s "Blue Maxi" Camaro achieved 13.7 seconds at 104 mph quarter-mile and 5.4 seconds 0-60 performance with its 3.73:1 rear axle, plus near-incredible .97g stop-

ping grip from its power four-wheel discs and Goodyear F60x15 tires on 8.5x15 American Racing aluminum wheels. As for handling, said the article, "The car is enormously responsive, easy to direct and is almost flawless in transient situations."

When the model year rolled to a close that fall, Camaro production had improved slightly to 243,085 units, 17,998 of them Z-28's and 3675 Indy Pace Car replicas, but model-year sales totaled 50,000 less at only 193,986. This difference was largely because the all-new '70 model would debut some five months late in February 1970, so '69 model production was extended through late 1969. But it was at least partly due to growing safety and environmental concern among the public and the resulting federal legislation, plus a slightly sagging U.S. economy.

Above: Start of Trans-Am Michigan International Speedway: Parnelli Jones (#15) and George Follmer (#16) lead Donohue (#6), Horst Kwech (#2) and Firebirds of Craig Fisher and Jerry Titus. Jones was winner.

This page (above): start of Mid-Ohio race with Donohue on pole inside Parnelli Jones. Below (opposite page): Jones and Donohue battle for lead; Ron Bucknum finally wins at Mid-Ohio, showing battle scars.

In the '69 Trans-Am series, Ford won four of the first five races before Donohue and the Penske Chevrolet machine got rolling. Then Donohue took six out of the next seven and, assisted by two wins from Ron Bucknum in a sister Sunoco Camaro, bagged the series title for the second straight year. Significantly, there had been serious entries from Pontiac (Jerry Titus and Milt Minter in Firebirds) and American Motors (Bob Tullius and Ron Grable in Javelins) in addition to the two Shelby and two Bud Moore Mustangs driven by the likes of Peter Revson, Dan Gurney, Parnelli Jones and George Follmer. Mercury Division was out, but both Plymouth and Dodge were planning to join. It looked like all-out factory warfare was in store for the 1970 racing season.

Not to mention in the showrooms and on the streets.

CHAPTER FOUR

Redesign

"In those days we felt that four years was about as long as we dared go with anything . . . three years really," says then-Chevrolet Division general manager and GM vice president Pete Estes. "So we started working on a new Camaro immediately after the '67 was announced.

"We weren't leading, you see. That was the problem. We were playing catch-up with Ford all the time. At least it seemed that way to me. We were struggling; we just couldn't get ahead of them to save our souls. I was arguing with Don Frey [Estes' neighbor, friendly rival and Ford Division general manager] all the time about who was going to be number one in the industry. Boy, they gave us a heck of a tussle.

"So we said that this second Camaro has got to be the ultimate, a baby Corvette; it's got to have that kind of image. It was intended to be an honest-to-God sports car, and we didn't hesitate to say that. It had to be better handling than the first car, have plenty of performance and an enduring life. We put our best chassis guys on it, made it lower, cheated the inside room as tight as we could, put a new stub frame under it, changed the front suspension, improved the rear suspension and widened the tread. We had big arguments about whether we should try to save the old stub frame, how much we were going to spend on the car, how new it really had to be. We had a big fuss with management about redesigning the car that fast, changing everything on it.

"We also really worked hard on the styling of that second one. We said it had to be the most beautiful automobile we have ever designed, and Bill Mitchell [then-GM Design vice president] really did a job on it. He had it in a special room, and nobody got in there except us. We wanted it to last us like a Ferrari—that was the idea.

Collection of Camaro concepts developed during mid-June '66 were long, low, sleek and show the inspiration of Corvette.

There's no reason to change cars so often if you do the job right.

"I rarely went two days without being in the studio. Most of the good-looking cars at General Motors were done without too much Fourteenth Floor [corporate management] involvement, and we got this one done almost before they knew about it, without anyone saying a word. We always tried to do that. Didn't always make it, but we always tried."

As is usually the case, particularly with an exciting car that's fun to work on, the designers in Henry Haga's Chevrolet Number Two Studio were plotting their next-generation Camaro even before the first one was launched. A series of full-scale tape drawings from mid-June 1966, though fairly far-out, already shows some of the design thinking that would go into the finished product. Obviously influenced by the forthcoming '68 Corvette, these concepts were low and sleek, with long, tapered noses, rounded contours, prominent wheels and tires filling large fender cut-outs.

Based on these drawings a handsome clay model with a split grille and Corvette-like humped fenders was completed in August while additional concepts were explored on paper. By early September the model's grille opening was back to a version of the original Camaro's wide, blacked-out mouth. Its fenders were flatter, and it had grown some lower-body sculpturing around the wheel openings and an unfortunate vinyl-covered roof. Three weeks later, about the time the '67's started hitting the streets, its contours had become more angular, the rocker sculpturing was gone and so was the vinyl top. In addition, its roofline ended in a fairly severe angle, its rear window was frenched into the pillars, and on one side of the rear deck was a high-mounted brake light similar to those on later Oldsmobile Toronados.

A sexy, bobtailed, two-seat convertible was designed on paper, and in early October 1966 its aerodynamic ducktail was applied to a nice looking, slim-pillared four-seater with both its windshield and its rear window wrapped far around into the side view. At the same time, Bill Porter's Pontiac Firebird studio, working independently, came up with essentially the roof and window shape that the finished car would get—and the wrap-around rear window variation that would not reach production until 1975.

"We had a competition going, as we do in any car program where two or more divisions share body parts," explains then-assistant exterior design executive Irv Rybicki. "As you know, the upper structure was shared between the Firebird and the Camaro, while the lower-body sheet metal was specific to the two divisions. We started two distinctly different design programs. At one point we were lean-

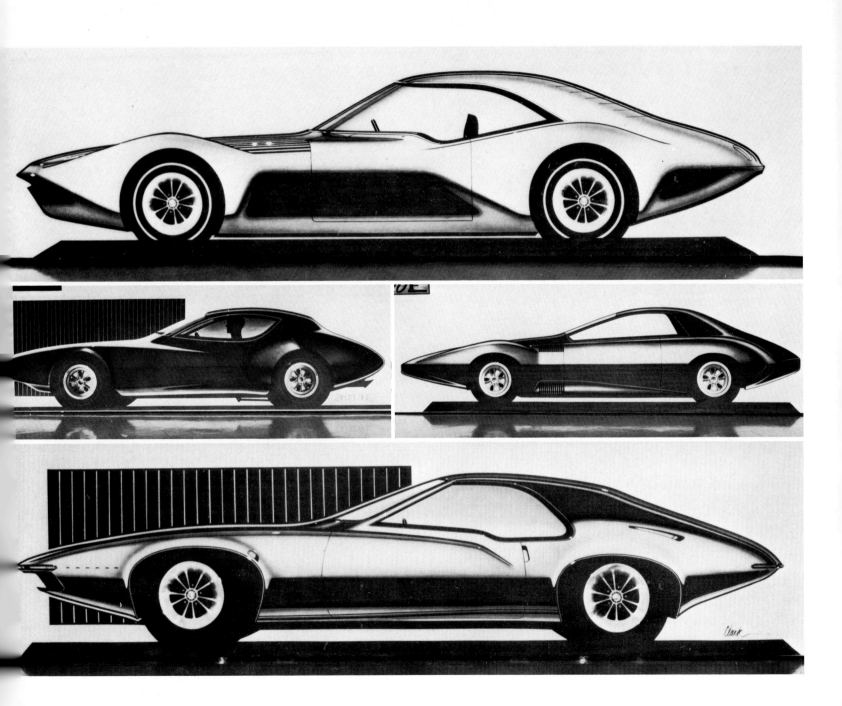

ing toward the Pontiac upper, and we made that the common upper and sent the groups on their way to develop the lowers to go along with that upper."

"The studios were a lot more segregated then," studio chief Haga explains. "There were fewer studios but more security between them. We really didn't know what was happening in the Pontiac studio, but our bosses did because they were coordinating things. At one time when we were working on the '70-½ Camaro, the car was suddenly moved out of our studio and put in the Pontiac room to execute a certain part of the upper. We didn't know what had happened. Then we found out that they were also working on the car, and they had a little different upper treatment that looked pretty good. Suddenly the decision was made to go that way."

"The ground rules for both groups," continues Rybicki, "were to go very fluid and very wild, yet clean and simple. I'm not a guy for bric-a-brac and lace. That's not what an automobile is, never was, never will be in my view. We used to change automobiles every three to six years in those days, but that is not what we were aiming at. We wanted a car that was pure, like something that came out of Italy, and so clean it would live for ten years. That was the goal, and every designer got behind it and worked that way.

"Some felt the first-generation car was not individual enough, didn't telegraph a youthful-enough quality in its forms. I thought it was a pretty smooth-looking coupe, but I didn't see the two-plus-two aspects we were after. The cowl wasn't low enough, and a lot of things couldn't happen because it had been tied in with the new Chevy II we were going to do a year later.

"So on the second car, before we ever put clay on a model, we

This page (above): William L. Mitchell was vice president in charge of the GM Design Staff when the second-series Camaro was designed; Dc Holls was Chevrolet group chief designer; mid-August 1966 clay model with humped fenders and split grille; late August, mid-September ideas were more refined, had wraparound windshield and rear window. Page posite: another view of mid-August clay model, shown with '67 Camar

spent about two-and-a-half months in our vehicle packaging room just getting the seats down, moving the frame out and working with the cross-section to get the proper anatomy. I believed then, and I believe today, that if you can package a car right, get the proportions, size of glass, the thickness-of-body to length-of-hood and length-of-deck, the proper cross-section for the length and height of the vehicle, then you're going to get a good-looking piece regardless of what body configurations you use on the sheet metal. That was our basic premise on the '70-½ car."

"The first one, to me, had no real identity, no blood and guts. It was a real committee car," adds the outspoken Mitchell. "There were three top executives—Gordon, who was president; Goodman, who was head of Fisher Body; and Goad, who was in charge of the Tech Center. One chopped the front, one chopped the back, and they just cooled it down to nothing. They didn't see it as a hot sports car. They weren't sports oriented, any of them, didn't think that way, and each one took a piece out of it.

"It was such a contrast to the second one, which we did really fast, with no interference. We were in the mood, and for some reason nobody bothered us. We had started to separate the studios at that time, so the Camaro wasn't done alongside a Nova. We got the Camaro and the Corvette together, and the guys working on them were different types. All the pictures on their walls were race cars. They were sneaky bastards."

Rybicki puts it a bit more softly. "I think the heavy corporate focus on that first car was there because our friends in Dearborn were doing a whale of a job with the Mustang. We didn't have anything, so just about everyone who was anyone in this corporation focused on that project. But once it was out there, once we had a program to challenge the Mustang, they all relaxed and backed off. That gave us time to go over here and start planning the new car."

By mid-summer of 1967 some of the drawings were sleeker and sexier than ever. Several, like one lovely open-top targa concept, were heavily influenced by the Corvette. Others, significantly, had the long doors and single side-window style that would eventually characterize the production car. Another was sort of a smoothed-out version of the '69 design—not bad, but not original. But the model that seemed to be getting the most attention had grown rather dumpy-looking, more like a two-door coupe than a real sports car.

At one point Mitchell returned from an overseas trip and blew his shiny top: "I came back from Europe one day, and they had a front on that car that could have been a Nova! I said, 'Christ, you've got a Nova, you've got a nothing! A sports car can't have the same kind of front on it as a regular passenger car!' I walked down the hall, and one of those pictures in the hall leading to my office showed a car with a front on it that really grabbed me. I said, 'Just take that off the wall and make it like that.' And that's when we started getting the snaky fronts on that car."

The program moved along fairly smoothly and rapidly after that. Frontal themes became dominated by large, low, mouth-like grille openings that were as far as possible below the headlamp plane. The first renderings to display this feature dated back to late July, and a very long, low, swoopy model based on them was completed in mid-October. Shortly after the beginning of 1968 a lovely fiberglass model nearly identical to the finished product that would go on sale more than two years later sat on Hank Haga's studio floor.

Dave Holls, Chevrolet group chief designer and Haga's immediate boss at the time, remembers the second-generation F-car program as "heaven, the most fun project I've ever been involved in. Everybody was with it, loved it and got excited about it. The feeling was 'OK, we've answered the Mustang but we haven't exceeded it. Now it's time to take the lead.' It was sort of 'lock the doors and don't let anybody in here—we're going to do this one ourselves.'"

Haga describes the overall theme as contrasted to the '67-'69 car, saying, "The first Camaro had one major design flaw: proportion. The cowl was too high and the dash-to-front-axle too short, because these areas were to be shared by the new 1968 Nova. Also the execution of the rear quarter window did not help its sportiness in the side view. It looked more like a two-door hardtop than an exotic sports car.

"The second generation was very much more a designer's car. It had the proportion, it had the dash-to-axle and it had the low cowl because it was specific and did not have to share any of these important elements with any other models. It was more of a 'shape' car, not as much involved with looking like the widest architecture front and rear as it was with forms and tapered shapes that tucked in behind the rear wheels and in front of the front wheels. It became more wheel-and-tire accented and more masculine looking."

Adds Holls: "The most unique thing about that car was the development of the roof and windshield, the two-window-type roof without a quarter window. While that may not sound like much, it just hadn't been done since the '36 Ford or something. That gave it an intimate feeling and some tremendous advantages. One was that we got rid of the cost of that quarter window and put the savings into other things we needed. We had to have a long door so we wouldn't have a big, blind rear quarter, and that dictated a wrap-around windshield. That windshield and the one-piece side window were key items in the architecture of the car."

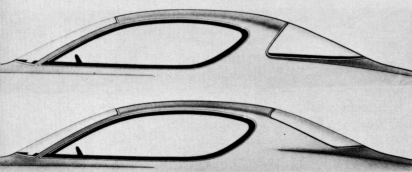

"The long door meant easy access to the rear seats and elimination of the quarter window," explains Haga. "The angle of the number three pillar gave the upper a close-coupled look that was more reminiscent of a two-passenger sporty vehicle than a two-plus-two. Again, as with the original Camaro, the design theme was simple: one peak line along the sides interrupted by accented wheel arches. The big difference was, at last, proper proportions."

Most Camaro lovers would agree that the '70-½'s frontal styling was another key element in its overall appeal. "Initially the car carried a simple loop front end," says Haga, "which was evolved from the previous Camaro. But Bill Mitchell was not content with such an easy solution. He wanted a front end that had a much fresher and more distinct character. After many weeks of searching for a design, the general direction of a vertical 'radiator' flanked by sheet metal 'catwalks' between the fenders and hood was selected."

Two related but different faces were designed, one with a full-width bumper and outboard parking lamps in the valence below it, the second with an open, unobstructed grille flanked by tiny "bumperettes" and round park lamps in the catwalk between it and the headlamps. Though favored by nearly everyone, this latter treatment, influenced as it was by the British Jaguar sedan, had three strikes against it from the beginning: it would be expensive to manufacture, had essentially no bumper protection and required that the front license plate be mounted off-center, something the Corvette designers had never been allowed to do despite cooling problems with a center-mounted plate.

Says Dave Holls: "We'd tried lots of ordinary fronts, but when we got to that one, it gave the car kind of an expensive look all of a sudden. Estes looked at it, and he said: 'My God, it looks like a thousand dollars more car with that nose!' I never thought we'd go to press with the more expensive version, with just that little rubber bar in the middle for protection. I thought at the last minute we were going to

1966 styling efforts: page opposite (top): September 2nd clay model with lower-body sculpturing, vinyl top; (center): same model in three weeks with new roof, smooth sides, high-mounted brakelights; (bottom): roof treatments anticipate '70½ (lower) and '75 (upper) models; model with new roof and wrapped rear window compared to '66 Camaro. This page: rear-end treatments dating from September and December of that year.

have a corporate review, and the more conservative element might have said, 'Well, we just can't do a thing like that, it's got no bumper.' Also, we really had a bind on cost, had to have a base car that came in at the right price—pretty inexpensive. But once we got that nose, that was key. Nothing changed after that."

Surprisingly, Haga recalls no hassle over the offset license plate. "We wanted that," he says, "because we wanted to save what became the Rally Sport front. We had two front ends going, and they looked great. And the impasse between the low-cost version and the alternate, expensive proposal was resolved when the one was selected for the base car and the other for the up-option model, which of course was the split-bumper, urethane-nosed RS version." At one point Mitchell had them go back and try an Aston-Martin-like version with the grille below the bumper much wider than the part above it, but it soon became obvious that the symmetrical "mouth" was a better solution.

"It's interesting to note," says Haga, moving to the rear of the car, "that most of the designers and enthusiasts wanted to raise the tail and give it a more aggressive look. They were out-voted, however, by some of the corporation elders who firmly believed that the rear end should terminate in a very slim, horizontal loop." Inside that loop were set two pairs of the traditional Chevrolet round taillamps. While they had wanted to get away from the Corvair look in doing the first-generation car, it was apparently decided that identification with the round-taillamped Corvette wouldn't be a bad thing this time around. "It got a sportier flair with the round taillamps," says Haga.

Again it was George Angersbach's Chevrolet Number Two Interior Studio that was charged with the responsibility for designing a cockpit in keeping with the striking new exterior that Haga's group was hatching. "We felt that '70-½ was our opportunity to do the in-

Opposite (top): Clay model compared with Ferrari; (bottom): series of four late 1966 and early 1967 concepts, showing various similarities to Corvette. Other photos: many of the fall 1966 renderings seemed too unoriginal, stodgy and sedan-like for the tastes of Bill Mitchell.

terior the way we really wanted it," says Angersbach, "because it was an all-new instrument panel, the construction of which was primarily plastic. That's when we set up our studios, interior and exterior, next to one another. Being next-door to Hank, it became sort of a family affair, and we really got rolling on that car."

With the objective of making the new Camaro's interior much sportier, more innovative and more driver-oriented than the previous one, in mid-1967 Angersbach's people started cranking out some really revolutionary concepts, most with instrument clusters isolated from the right-side passenger and wrapping around the driver into the side door panel. As these were translated into life-size mock-ups in seating bucks and became more practical and less expensive from a manufacturing standpoint, the wrap-around instrumentation idea was retained. The final result was one of the most attractive, exciting and usable instrument panels ever built, with large central speedometer and tach, twin pairs of smaller round gauges on either side, switches for lights and wipers outboard to the left and a matching lighter and accessory switch to the right.

There was only one body style for the second-generation Camaro, a semi-fastback coupe with a roof that, in Irv Rybicki's words, "just pours out onto the rear deck very easily." But that certainly was not because the designers didn't propose anything else. "There was a very slick-looking convertible mocked up on the clay model," Haga recalls, "but it was shelved because of the high tooling costs needed for a relatively small number of sales. Later we developed the Kammback body style on the '70-½ car. A full-size fiberglass model was built, but the planning group never understood the rationale for this design and, without backing from them, it was dropped because of the tooling costs involved."

On paper at least, there were also a lovely targa-top convertible

and a two-seat roadster version, the latter a favorite of the sports car loving Mitchell. "That was Bill's idea," says Dave Holls. "The studio was never really hot for it. We wanted a convertible, though, and we wanted a hatchback, and that little Kammback wagon . . . but I guess we were so happy to get what we got that we thought, 'Well, we'll fight for that next year.' "

The Kammback version, a beautiful two-door sport wagon reminiscent of the classic Chevy Nomad wagons of 1955-56, actually was conceived on the original Camaro body in 1967, then was further developed on the new car the following year. And the primary reason neither it nor any other additional body style ever was put into production goes back to the desire of the Chevrolet and Pontiac studios to have as distinctly different products as possible, even when based on the same general platform and body shell.

"The second-series Firebird and Camaro had rear quarters which were totally different," Haga explains, "and the tooling was different because the front door sections were different. Camaro had a sharp peak and Firebird had a radius or 'dome' section on the side at a different height from the ground. This was a negative factor when proposing an additional model such as a Kammback or a convertible because you had no common door to blend in the front and rear quarters, and that doubled your tooling costs. Although attempts were made to commonize body sections, the car divisions felt very strongly about the differentiation needed between these two cars. In this case emotional considerations outweighed financial considerations. Most people don't realize that those doors aren't interchangeable."

Any new car so totally dominated by styling is bound to cause problems for the engineers, and the '70-½ Camaro was no exception. Dave Holls remembers that one day when the styling was essentially

Above: first appearance of low, central grille theme in July and August 1967 renderings. Below: one of many experiments with the grille/light/ bumper theme; Corvette-like taillamps reappear in March 1968 drawing.

Above: long-nosed model with new front concept, sculptured fenders and wraparound glass in October '67 gives way to mid-January '68 fiberglass model almost identical to production car. Below: more frontal themes.

complete, the Camaro and Firebird models were sitting in the hall at Design Staff. Mitchell called him and the group from the Pontiac Studio down and said, " 'OK, now, that's it. Are you guys happy?' We said, 'Yes sir! Yes sir!' And he said, 'OK then, don't let anybody screw it up.' And, believe me, it was a struggle to get that car made."

One of the major engineering problems was designing the underbody stamping to get the car as low as it was. "The stretches and contortions that had to be made on that underbody are unbelievable," says Holls. According to Irv Rybicki, another problem was the low cowl height. "We had problems with packaging the cowl," he recalls. "We wanted it as low as we could get it because we were forcing the roof down much lower than the original car's. When we got into it with the engineers, they gave us a bad time about the cowl. They wanted to raise it an inch or an inch-and-a-half to get more room for packaging the air conditioning, instrumentation and so forth, and I can remember fighting the Chevrolet group for months. It was a stand-off, and time was getting short.

"That is the crucial line in the automobile, the base of the windshield and where it is positioned. It sets up everything—height of windshield, height of car, sight lines out over the hood, where you place the driver. I tried to keep Mitchell out of those things, but we were getting nowhere. So I had to get Bill into the studio one day, and in his inimitable fashion, he gave them a speech they wouldn't forget for a while. They went back, and then we got the cowl where we wanted it.

"But we were not interfered with at all in the interior packaging," Rybicki continues. "We did that here in our vehicle development studio, laid out the seats, the torso, created the cross section. Because we'd started much earlier than anyone else in the corporation on the

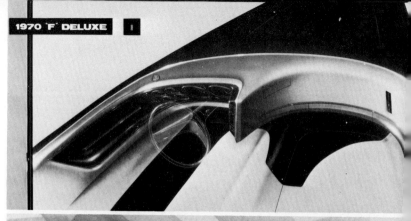

second generation car, I don't think the divisions ever got involved in the interior numbers. We'd done it here when we created the clay, and when they saw the clay, the general managers loved it. They weren't about to move the numbers around inside and disturb that appearance."

The low cowl posed another major problem—clearance between the inner hood and the engine air cleaner. "When you close a hood," explains studio chief Hank Haga, "you have 'overslam.' There are hood bumpers, but the bumpers deflect, and if the hood goes down far enough to bang the air cleaner, you get an imprint in the hood. So you have to have clearance on top of clearance. The engineers felt that the car wouldn't perform unless they had that air cleaner with so much volume into the carburetor, and they kept wanting to push the hood up.

"It was very difficult trying to put our image across. There were a lot of really tough battles, with people getting angry, sleepless nights and lots of time spent in the bar trying to rationalize what we were doing. One day we were trying to do this beautiful, pure car, and an engineer came over and wanted great big chrome bolts through the bumper right on the top surface. He had gone through the proper channels with the paperwork, but some of us were so angry about it that we wrote back, 'no, we don't want any of those chicken droppings on the bumper.' Of course, that went right to the general manager, and I got chewed out about it.

"We had endless fights keeping that hood and cowl down, and lots of impasses, and I guess [then-Chevrolet chief engineer] Alex Mair was Design's champion there. I remember him as really helping out at that time. He was very conscious of what it meant to fine-tune a car's visual character, and he was all for what we were doing. Nearly everyone else wanted to treat this car the same as a big Chevy or Chevy II. It was impossible to get them thinking in terms of a sporty car."

Promoted to director of engineering in 1966, Alex Mair was indeed a champion of the sports-type car at Chevrolet. He had gotten into the first Camaro's development late in the game, after moving over from the Truck Group late in 1965, but he was heavily involved in the second-series Camaro from the very beginning and determined that it was going to be better in every way than the '67-'69—and the competition.

"It was a time when the industry was moving fast," Mair recalls. "We hadn't viewed the first car as a failure, but there were things about it we didn't like. We had done it in a hurry, had gotten it out, and it sort of met the competition. But we viewed the '70-½ car as a

This page: bold early interior concepts had cockpit-style wraparound instrumentation; panel nearing final form in July 1968 retained handsome and practical wraparound effect. Opposite: "Kammback" wagon concepts chief chassis engineer Bob Dorn directed '70 Camaro's development.

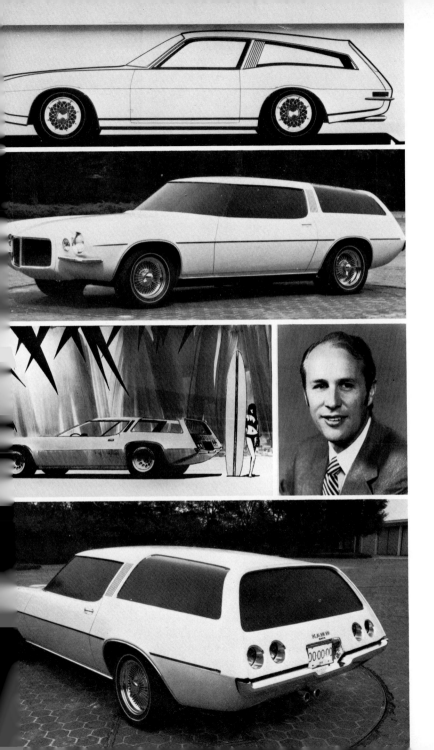

nice opportunity to do it over again. This time we weren't trying to catch up to somebody; we were looking for leadership." To Mair, this meant improved handling, suspension and brakes as well as better styling inside and out, whether or not this created some difficulties for his engineers.

"We looked heavily into the design and styling," he adds, "and Henry Haga had a free hand on it. We had to do new manifolds and carburetors and air cleaners to get under his hood, but we did them. We knew as we moved into 1968 that we weren't going to do any new convertibles, so we didn't have to do the job of working out the shake. The decision had been made, and it had to do with our workload at the time and the crush laws that were coming . . . it was just hard to do convertibles.

"But we did look at whether we needed a notchback and a fastback. None of us can judge for sure what most people will like. We're supposed to be good at that, but it's difficult. The Camaro's styling was exciting, especially for 1970. Henry's group at Design Staff did an outstanding job on it, and it surprised everyone. People who appreciated good-looking cars looked at it and thought it was great. It was neither a fastback nor a notchback but kind of a semi-fastback. It fit either case, appealed to both groups. We felt comfortable, and we didn't need anything else."

One of the key people responsible for re-engineering the Camaro from roof to tire patch was an up-and-coming young engineer named Bob Dorn. A former road racer, Dorn understood what a good handling sports car should be, and it was he who oversaw the new car's chassis design and development under staff engineer Charlie Rubley and passenger car chief engineer Don McPherson.

One of the major chassis changes was moving the steering linkage, gear and all, from behind the front axles to a position in front of them. According to Dorn, this provided better crash protection capability for the driver. "With a collapsible intermediate shaft, you can take up some of the crush without collapsing the steering column," he points out. It also created built-in "lateral compliance understeer" that tended to make the car more predictable during hard cornering. Stabilizing understeer (as opposed to oversteer, which makes the rear end tend to swing wide) was also built into the new front and rear suspensions.

"We put what was basically an intermediate suspension onto a stub frame in a very short time," Dorn relates, "and stuck it under a then-current Camaro. It had a tremendous amount of understeer in it, but it didn't have a lot of steering gain. In other words, it wasn't precise when you turned the wheel, was very 'doggie' on center. So we

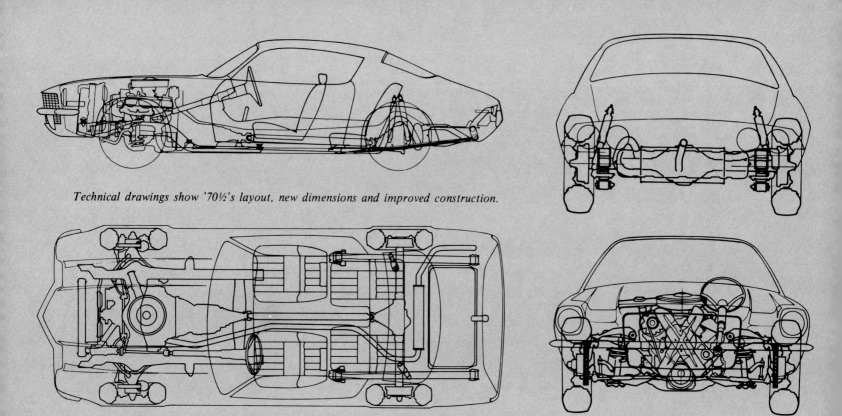

Technical drawings show '70½'s layout, new dimensions and improved construction.

had to work on the steering ratio and the linkage to get the precise response we wanted.

"And when we went to the 'forward steer,' we decided that the time was right to do a whole new front suspension for the corporation using integral cast knuckles, with the caliper mounted directly to the knuckle. It would be the same thing that we would put into the next-generation full-size B-car. We were trying to fit a 396 engine in the Camaro and at the same time use a corporate suspension with the longest possible upper and lower control arms to get the kind of ride that would satisfy Buick, Olds and Pontiac for their B-cars. We had a real time convincing the other divisions that we were doing the right job for their B-cars. If you look at a 396 Camaro, you'll see that the bolts on the upper control arm shaft are within a half-inch of the right-side manifolds. We used the longest arms we could that would still leave room to get that engine in there so we could use the same basic suspension on the big cars.

"One of the other benefits we got from changing to front steer was clearance to remove the oil pans without having to pull the engine or drop the steering linkage. All you had to do was unbolt the front engine mounts, jack the engine up a bit, and you could unbolt the oil pan and take it off.

"Then we looked at the rear suspension, and found that adding understeer there, too, actually made the car more precise, as long as we didn't add too much. We knew we were going to put large engines in the car, so we wanted to be sure to avoid some of the power problems we had had with the previous car. We started with single-leaf springs, but as the car got heavier we had to go to higher-rate monoplates to handle the wind-up conditions, and that made it ride more harshly than we wanted. We ended up having to go to multi-leafs to get the ride frequencies down where we wanted them. And it was during the long-lead-time magazine writers' preview out at Riverside Raceway, just a few months before public introduction, that we convinced

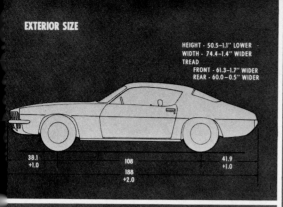

EXTERIOR SIZE

HEIGHT - 50.5–1.1" LOWER
WIDTH - 74.4–1.4" WIDER
TREAD
FRONT - 61.3–1.7" WIDER
REAR - 60.0–0.5" WIDER

38.1 +1.0   108   41.9 +1.0
              188
              +2.0

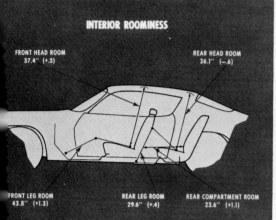

INTERIOR ROOMINESS

FRONT HEAD ROOM 37.4" (+.3)   REAR HEAD ROOM 36.1" (−.6)

FRONT LEG ROOM 43.8" (+1.3)   REAR LEG ROOM 29.6" (+.4)   REAR COMPARTMENT ROOM 23.6" (+1.1)

BODY CONSTRUCTIONAL DETAIL

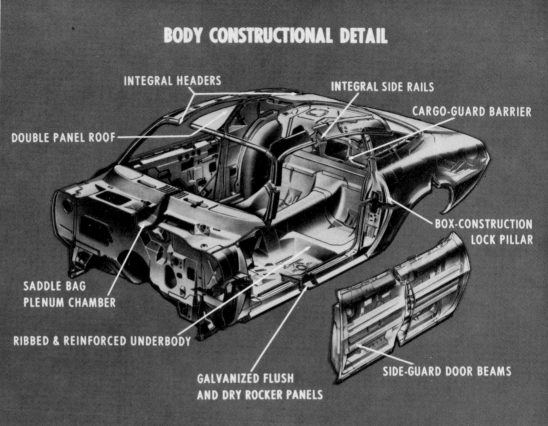

INTEGRAL HEADERS
INTEGRAL SIDE RAILS
CARGO-GUARD BARRIER
DOUBLE PANEL ROOF
BOX-CONSTRUCTION LOCK PILLAR
SADDLE BAG PLENUM CHAMBER
RIBBED & REINFORCED UNDERBODY
SIDE-GUARD DOOR BEAMS
GALVANIZED FLUSH AND DRY ROCKER PANELS

[then-general manager] John DeLorean that we ought to put multi-leaf springs on all Camaros rather than just on the high-performance versions."

The car's new dimensions caused packaging challenges for Dorn's chassis group, particularly in the rear. In effect, the passenger compartment and the body shell around it were both moved three inches rearward relative to the axles. Wheelbase remained the same at 108 inches while the overhangs were stretched an inch both front and rear, yielding a two-inch gain in overall length. The net result was four inches more package space in front and a loss of two inches in back.

"They pulled the front wheels forward," Dorn explains, "which let us pull the engine forward to make room for a really first-class air conditioning system. But they kept the short wheelbase, which sucked the axle up to the rear passenger's butt and made it closer-coupled between the H-point [a specific point inside an interior-

design mannekin] and the rear axle than any car we've ever done. It was a tremendous packaging job trying to put all that stuff in there.

"We were having a hard time locating the axle and the front spring eye. Traditional wisdom said you had to have one-third of the spring between the axle and the spring eye and two-thirds behind, but we couldn't package it that way. We also had to space the spring up off the axle more than anyone had ever done before, and that made us nervous because we'd always tried to keep the spring as close to the axle as possible so we didn't have a lot of rotating moment between them. And the way we got the springs in there at all was to put them outboard of the seat.

"We were working with Computer Analysis Group's Jurgis Mikaila, who used to do all the leaf-spring design calculations. Now it's done by computer, but in those days Jurgis did it on paper. We took drawings to him, and he'd go into his little think-tank and then tell us what kind of stresses we would have, what to do with

Handling development in progress at the GM Proving Ground, Milford, Michigan. Wider tracks, stan

the springs and so forth. We laid all this Camaro data out on paper, gave it to Jurgis, and got back as much information as we could. It all said: 'You guys better be careful.'

"But then we built it into a car, and it turned out to be a whiz-bang, just fantastic! We didn't have the axle control problems we'd anticipated, and we had just the right amount of understeer. You could do anything with it. Go down the road and toss it sideways, it didn't make any difference. The car was super-forgiving. It tracked straight down the road with good on-center feel and without a lot of wind wander. The front suspension was complemented by a rear suspension with enough understeer built into it that it didn't try to steer the car during cornering. Some cars tend to steer the driver, but that Camaro was designed so that the driver could do what he wanted with it without getting into trouble. In fact, I think the car has more ability than all but the best drivers can use."

The overall handling also was improved by means of **treads** that were wider by more than an inch-and-a-half in front and a half-inch in the rear. There was also a standard 15/16-inch front sway bar to control body roll. An optional F41 handling package was developed around the base soft-rate springs but included heavy-duty shock-absorbers and, computer-tuned for each engine-tire combination, a rear sway bar and a larger front bar. Much-improved stopping power was provided by standard manual front disc brakes with new-design integral cast hub/rotors.

One battle the engineers did win over the stylists involved the car's curb stance. The original Camaro had been designed around small tires and sat too high on larger tires, which had prompted management to drop it down, and that had eliminated much of its ride travel. It also had been trimmed with its rear end slightly higher than its front. In doing the second-series suspension, Dorn's chassis group was careful to avoid repeating the ride-height/travel problem and "set it with three-eighths of an inch rake *down* at the back." Later they found that the designers were trying to raise the back end up again and quickly readjusted ride heights to keep the chin-up attitude.

This stance may not have been so good aesthetically, but with plenty of suspension travel—three inches in jounce at four-passenger design load—big-car componentry and better isolation, the re-

-inch front sway bar and optional F-41 package all contributed to substantially improved handling.

engineered Camaro did indeed ride far more softly and smoothly than its predecessors. It was also more comfortable inside, with increased front seat travel, extended front and rear legroom, redesigned seats and five inches additional rear seat entry room because of the long doors, though the rear seat area was still no place for grown people to be.

Another substantial improvement was in sound insulation. Instead of simply piling on heavy, expensive sound-deadening materials, engineers acoustically "tuned" the entire body to eliminate unwanted noise and vibrations from the passenger compartment. Sound barriers and improved sealing of body seams blocked openings where drivetrain and road noises might otherwise have intruded. New "trapped-edge" wind seals around the side windows eliminated almost all wind noise at speed, and a special double-roof design used what was called the "Helmholtzian Principle"—a perforated inner panel and vinyl headliner over a sound-absorbing blanket—to soak up whatever noise did get inside.

Construction of the body itself also was completely new, as were the front stub frame and crossmember. For one thing, the sound ab-

sorbing twin steel roof panels also strengthened the upper structure, and protective safety features such as a steel barrier between the passenger and luggage compartments, side guard door beams and energy-absorbing windshield pillar moldings were added. Provisions for "Astro ventilation," the "saddlebag" plenum chamber between engine and passenger compartments, "flush and dry" galvanized rocker panels and ventless door windows were retained. Up front, the new stub frame was stronger than the old thanks to larger-section side rails and a single large crossmember replacing the two smaller ones formerly used.

Interestingly, it was the engineering problem of trying to provide some semblance of bumper protection for that beautiful Rally Sport front end that almost killed it. "It was the front that management wanted on the car, but it had to pass a mile-and-a-half barrier test," says then-chassis engineer Bob Dorn. "It was our own in-house standard at the time. To do that, it needed a hard-rubber ("endura") ring surrounding it and a narrow protective rubber strip down the center. But they costed that out and decided they couldn't afford it, and that's when they did the other one with a conventional bumper."

Once the less expensive front became standard and the other an option, however, the cost of the optional version was less of a consideration.

Because both designers and engineers were determined to do the job a hundred percent right this time around, the development process took longer than anticipated. It soon became obvious that the car would not be ready for a summer 1969 production start-up and fall introduction, and so the reluctant decision was made to hold off a year and make it a '71 model. A slightly facelifted '69 was quickly prepared in the design studio as a '70 model. Then it was decided to save the facelift money and continue the '69 unchanged as the '70. Publicity photos were even prepared showing a '69 SS-350 coupe clearly labelled "1970." But the final decision was to launch the new car as a '70-½ as soon as it was ready—which turned out to be the unlikely date of February 26th, 1970—and to continue building the '69 model for a few extra months.

Typically, there was some last-minute nervousness among the more conservative Chevrolet managers about the new model's revolutionary design. "This is a phenomenon I've experienced before," says studio chief Hank Haga. "It seems that whenever a really new car is about to be released, hesitation seizes some of the people who have been working on it, either because they fear the responsibility if the car doesn't sell or is not received well by the public, or perhaps more realistically because they really don't know the product. In any event, all anxiety was dispelled one day when race driver Stirling Moss was given a sneak preview several months before announcement day."

"Moss was a pretty good friend of Mitchell's," relates then-design executive Irv Rybicki. "He was out here in Detroit one day, and Bill invited him over for lunch. Bill called me in and said, 'Put those two fiberglass models in the auditorium, I'm going to show them to him.' And I remember Moss' reaction. His eyes were bugging out of his head. 'You're going to sell this as a Chevrolet, a production model?' he asked. When Bill responded in the affirmative, Moss' reply was 'terrific.' We knew we had something then, because he is a fellow who understands machinery. We knew that people who loved cars would gravitate to this thing."

By April 1969 Jim Musser, assistant chief engineer, special products, already was lobbying for increased racing involvement with the slick new Camaro. In addition to continuation of the SCCA Trans-Am series road racing program with the Z-28, Musser proposed using the same basic car in the NASCAR GT small-car class. Beyond even that, he seriously recommended a NASCAR

(Left): Slightly facelifted '69 was readied as '70 model when produc[

Grand National Stock Car effort using a stretched-wheelbase (to 115 inches) ZL-1 427 Camaro. He urged that considerable engine development on both the Z-28 302 V-8 and the aluminum ZL-1 427, as well as aerodynamic work on the new body, begin immediately.

To aid high speed aerodynamics, large front air dams and rear spoilers, as well as "spats" to smooth air flow around the wheel openings, were designed, but there was disagreement about releasing them as part of the new Z-28 package. The more conservative types didn't like their appearance and didn't want them on the car, while the enthusiasts did. Eventually, only a small rear spoiler was released as standard on the Z-28 so it could be used in racing.

But aerodynamic tests soon showed that this conservative spoiler wasn't as effective at high speeds as a taller, full-width one would be, and performance development chief Vince Piggins knew his racing customers would need more downforce at the rear. "Our problem," he relates, "was getting tooling money to build a new spoiler. Also the length of time it would take to get it on the production car. Pontiac already had a large spoiler on the Trans-Am, so we took the Pontiac center section and designed new end caps for it.

"I got ahold of [new general manager] John DeLorean one day

designed Camaro was delayed. (Right): Publicity photos of unchanged '69 labeled "1970" were prepared for fall introduction, but not used.

and told him what we wanted to do, and he agreed. Then he caught Jim MacDonald, who had replaced him as Pontiac's general manager, over at Design Staff and sold him a bill of goods. John told him we wanted to use the Pontiac section and tooling, but that we'd make new end caps so it wouldn't look the same. He said he didn't see anything wrong with that." The problem remained to get this new spoiler into production, and then to get SCCA to allow its use in competition by the time the 1970 season started. But that's a story for the next chapter.

Following his February 1969 move to Chevrolet, performance-oriented John DeLorean involved himself in the new Camaro's final preparation as much as he could. At that point, the car's design was long-since wrapped up and its engineering nearly complete, but he did manage to tune its handling more to his own liking and make a few other last-minute changes.

In mid-August 1969 some 400,000 young people converged on the small town of Woodstock, New York to listen to music and raise a little hell, thereby demonstrating the awesome power of the "youth revolution." "When the young people get together they have 'clout,'" commented *Detroit Free Press* columnist Bob Talbert.

"And 'clout' means influence, which means power." Talbert pointed out that forty-six percent of all Americans were then under twenty-five, that more than twenty-three million were in the eighteen-to-twenty-four age bracket and fully thirty-eight million occupied the twenty-to-thirty-four category.

"These young people are into a massive revolution," he continued. "It is a cultural, life-style revolution. . . . [They are] concerned about social strictures, money, mobility, education, sex, and the peace-war issue." Then he made the point that, like him, the U.S. auto industry "can't get those 400,000 young people out of its mind," and that when asked who had the single biggest influence on the purchase of a car today, youthful Chevrolet general manager John DeLorean had unhesitatingly answered, "the teenager."

"DeLorean," Talbert continued, "a new breed of industry leader, knows and understands that 'young people have new values, new definitions of status, and new life styles. We, as an industry, had better be tuned into this new thinking.'"

Thus was the stage set, and the timing more than ripe, for the February 1970 introduction of Chevrolet's all-new, much-improved and startlingly beautiful second-series Camaro.

CHAPTER FIVE

Act Two

When Chevrolet unveiled its '70-model product recipe in the fall of 1969, two key ingredients were missing: an improved Corvette and the all-new Camaro. "The 1970's will be an unparalleled decade of individual customer choice," proclaimed general manager John DeLorean on that occasion. Chevrolet will continue to set the industry pace with a variety of cars and options which allow each buyer to custom tailor his or her personal transportation."

Yes, but where were the new sports and sporty cars?

"Current models of these companion excitement cars," deadpanned the press release, "will be continued to the end of 1969 with new models to be introduced later in the model year." This caused some confusion in the marketplace, and some less-than-alert buyers that winter drove away in new '69 Camaros thinking they were '70's. At least one was angry enough to sue his Toledo, Ohio dealer, demanding the return of his trade-in and $2300 in damages.

Although we don't know the outcome of that or any similar suits, we do know that people at Chevrolet were wringing their hands in anticipation of their new Camaro's introduction. "We will give an entirely new direction to this market," enthused DeLorean in the January *Motor Trend*. "It is so sensational that I think we will more than make up for lost ground."

At last, on Friday the 13th (that's confidence!) of February 1970, DeLorean held a news conference to preview his division's exciting sporty-car creation, which definitely took top billing over the little-changed Corvette. He predicted that it would soon take over leadership in the ponycar market, which he called "the most hotly contested in the industry," with a more than thirty percent share of the anticipated 600,000-700,000 sales per year.

"This market segment is important beyond its numbers," he said.

Launched in mid-February '70 after series of delays, '70½ Camaro, complete with new emblem, ready for inspection.

"Studies show it is the top single entry point into the domestic market for first-time buyers—those either purchasing their first car or trading in a used car to buy their first new one."

Pointing out that more than forty percent of Camaro buyers were first-timers, compared to an industry average of twenty-two percent, DeLorean added: "The sale of a Camaro-type car gives an automaker his biggest single chance to get new buyers for his products and to begin to cement owner loyalty. The customer may eventually move up to other models because of a growing family and other changing life patterns. But if he is pleased with his Camaro, he'll probably buy one of our other Chevrolets."

Also among the statistics: the first-generation Camaro had enjoyed the highest percentage (over fifty) of buyers aged twenty-five and under of any car in the industry, and fifty-one percent of its buyers had been single people of both sexes. It was also a favorite of women, who bought one out of every four Camaros sold, and of military service people, who accounted for nearly one of ten.

"Innovations in design and engineering make the new Camaro different from any car now offered," DeLorean continued. "Its new long hood, expensive-looking body and highly-improved handling, ride and sound insulation create a completely new car." Base price was up to $2749, more than the '69 base sticker a year earlier but only $22 over the late-'69's tag after a September 1969 increase.

Features emphasized in the press release included: 2.0 inches longer, 1.1 inches lower, 0.4 inches wider than the '69 Camaro; concealed windshield wipers standard on the RS and SS, otherwise optional; ten percent more glass area; five-inch longer doors, with flush door handles; new foam-filled bucket seats with a less upright seatback angle, "semi-bucket" rear seats and more legroom front and rear; new interior, instrument panel and cluster design; acoustical roof and other sound-isolation innovations; and windshield antenna (not such a good idea, as it turned out). In addition, there were standard front disc brakes; 1.7 inch wider front tread, 0.5 inch wider rear; forward-mounted steering with optional variable-ratio power assist; redesigned, stronger front subframe; improved suspension design and geometry front and rear, with thirty percent softer ride; larger (nineteen gallon) fuel tank; E78x14 bias-belted tires on base cars, F70x14 on SS models, F60x15 on the Z-28.

Engine availability for the standard Camaro ranged from the bottom-line 155-hp 250 cu. in. six through a 200-hp 307 V-8 to a 250-hp 350. Another 350 rated at 300 horsepower was standard and a 350-hp 396 optional with the SS package, while the new killer Z-28 engine was still another 350 rated 10 horsepower above the 396 at 360

RALLY SPORT

hp. (A 375-hp 396 became available later on a limited basis; a rumored 450-hp 454 apparently did not.) A three-speed floor shift remained standard and the Powerglide automatic was optional with the base six and the 307 V-8, a four-speed manual standard with all 350's and the 396, and the three-speed Turbo Hydra-matic available with all but the six. A choice of transmission gear ratios was offered with the SS-396 and Z-28, and the special M-22 heavy-duty box with either wide-range or close-ratio gears could be ordered on the Z-28.

Detroit auto writer Bob Irvin drove a new Camaro for a few days and then commented on it in his March 25th *Detroit News* column. "The wait was worth it," he enthused. "It is a beautiful looking automobile, one that makes the Mustang and Barracuda seem like last year's models." Irvin also praised the car's ride and handling and its new full-foam bucket seats. His only criticism concerned the extra-long doors, which made getting in and out difficult when the car was in a tight parking space.

Early advertising was especially creative. Shortly before introduction there was a stunning two-page newspaper spread—a teaser showing the Rally Sport's jutting front profile and revealing just enough information to whet the ponycar buff's appetite. Spring enthusiast magazine ads pushed the theme "A sports car for the four

Highlights of the Rally Sport for 1970 included redesigned instrument panel, flush door handle, headlamps and aggressive front-end profile.

of you," aimed at Corvette fanciers who needed a rear seat for family, friends or "Great Danes." At the same time, several other magazines were running a very different full-page spot: "We've never announced a car at this time before," it explained. "But then nobody's ever announced a car like this before."

The '70-½ Camaro catalog also appealed to the sports-car enthusiast and traded on the Corvette's reputation and popularity. Judging from the Camaro's "low stance," said the copy, "you'd think it grew out of the road. . . . It hangs right in with Corvette. . . . Sort of like a four-place Vette." The Z-28 in particular, it pointed out, is "for the guy who always wanted a performance car that he could drive to work." Both advertising and the catalog revived the old "Hugger" theme, referring to the new Camaro as "Super Hugger."

March car-magazine stories about the new F-cars (Camaro and Firebird), based on mid-winter previews, were generally very positive. "The Firebird and Camaro," said *Car and Driver*, "are the first of a new generation of American GT cars—low, taut and sleek of flank . . . a blend of agility, comfort and silence beyond anything the world had ever seen in a GT car of this price . . . exceptional automobiles." Referring to the Camaro in particular, the article 93

Sport Coupe and introductory ad; opposite: sport coupe and Z-28.

Camaro Sport Coupe with Rally Sport equipment.

New Camaro.

We've never announced a car at this time before.
But then nobody's ever announced
a car like this before.

enthused: "Its shape is smoother than any Detroit effort we can think of . . . the new instrument panel is a brilliant layout, but it still gives the feeling of a posh tourer rather than a taut GT car. . . . The driving position is extremely good and the interior is far more spacious, particularly in the rear seat area, than you would expect in a fastback." It also predicted that the Z-28 would be more popular than before because the new 350 engine was "far more tractable than the old 302" and would be available with an automatic transmission. But *C and D* did strike one sour note, pointing out that these excellent new GM entries were being launched into a market segment ("sport compacts") that was "dying on the vine," having fallen away from a high of thirteen percent of new car sales in 1967 to a mere nine percent two years later.

Road & Track, ever critical of American cars, called the F-cars "strikingly handsome and tasteful," but added that their styling was "backward looking rather than pioneering" because their "resemblance . . . to certain older Ferraris and Maseratis is unmistakable." *R&T* also called "inexcusable" the fact that the new Camaro/Firebird had a cubic foot less luggage space than its predecessor.

Motor Trend felt that the new Camaros, especially the Z-28's, had lost their former racer-like handling and could "no longer, with any integrity, be referred to as 'huggers.' . . . Wheeling the car through tight turns at high speed does produce a good bit of roll," said author A. B. Shuman, "but the machine is always easy to control." Zero-to-sixty performance of the four-speed Z-28 was 7.0 seconds, while a quarter-mile was run in 14.9 seconds at 97 mph . . . which Shuman called "below expectations in view of the supposedly stronger engine."

But *Sports Car Graphic's* Bob Kovacik disagreed. "The standard Camaro for '70 is a better-handling car than ever before," he wrote, "and the Z-28 hasn't lost any of its zing, except maybe slightly in the braking department. . . . Only a few options are missing, like the 302 engine, four-wheel disc brakes, bubble hood and front-mounted spoiler. . . . The stimulating 302 is now history, and in a way it's just as well. . . . [It was] meant more for the racetrack than for street use." Testing an automatic-equipped Z-28, *SCG* reported an 8.7-second zero-to-sixty time and 15.3 seconds at 87.6 mph in the quarter-mile. Kovacik also praised the Camaro's "unusual quietness" and interior comfort. "The driver can really get into the car," he marvelled, "not just atop the seat, and can stretch out and feel like part of it rather than just a passenger on a guided missile."

"Refinements to the Camaro are more noticeable in its appearance than performance," said *Hot Rod's* March report, "which

isn't to say it won't run as good as its ancestors." Author Steve Kelly also praised the new car's room, saying: "Front seat adjustment travel is now good enough to make driving comfortable for six-footers, something the '67-'69 cars never could brag about." *HR*'s best quarter-mile run was 14.93 seconds at 97 mph with two people aboard.

Car Life was impressed by the new Camaro as a whole, which it called "worth the wait" and "a whole light year away from last year's," and especially admired its styling: "The '70 Camaro is so smooth it looks like the clay model was parked in a wind tunnel under the high blast until all unsightly bulges had been trimmed off. . . . It ought to have a booming record in the showrooms."

One of the most interesting stories about the second-generation Camaro is the saga of how the Z-28 got its taller rear spoiler after a smaller, more conservative decklid lip already had been released. You may recall from Chapter Four that any front air dam within certain restrictions was allowed in SCCA Trans-Am racing, and performance-group head Vince Piggins had anticipated a similar allowance for rear spoilers in 1970. But when the '70 rules were announced late in 1969, they required rear aerodynamic devices to be strictly production items, available to anyone. This meant that an effective rear spoiler would have to be designed, tooled, put into production and—according to the rules—installed on a certain number of production cars before it would be race-approved.

Pontiac general manager Jim McDonald agreed to let Chevrolet use the center section from the existing Firebird Trans-Am spoiler, so all Piggins needed was a new set of outer extensions ("end caps") to make the Chevrolet version look suitably different. Designing them was little problem, but it would take a superhuman effort to get them into production in time and (as it turned out) some deft sleight-of-hand to get them approved by the SCCA. And the importance of doing so was amply illustrated by wind-tunnel tests that showed 168 pounds of downforce at the rear wheels at 116 mph with the tall spoiler compared to 112 pounds of *lift* with the smaller one . . . a critical 280 pound difference in the race cars' stability and cornering traction at speed.

A.O. Smith Corporation, builder of Pontiac's spoilers, was quickly contracted to produce the Chevrolet version as well; but they said that even the first end caps from temporary tooling could not be delivered before the end of March, well after the mid-March Sebring 12-hour race. Management approval came in early February, and the first fifty spoilers were promised for April 1st, with a total of three thousand—the maximum that could be made on temporary tool-

ing—to be delivered by the end of April. Permanent tooling would be available in time for 1971 production.

Nineteen-seventy was to be the Trans-Am series' biggest year. American Motors had wooed two-time series winner Roger Penske and his ace engineer/driver Mark Donohue away from Chevrolet to help build their Javelin's reputation, and there would be a second car for Peter Revson. Undaunted, Chevrolet would have the capable services of Jim Hall and his Chaparral organization (of Can-Am racing series fame) to run a two-car Camaro team. Another strong Camaro effort was expected from the Owens-Corning-backed duo of Tony DeLorenzo and Jerry Thompson, who had won SCCA's national amateur championship the year before in Owens-Corning Corvettes. George Follmer and Parnelli Jones would be back to spearhead the high-buck Ford Mustang forces. Pontiac was out to win with under-the-table support of *Sports Car Graphic* editor (and former Mustang driver) Jerry Titus and Canadian Craig Fisher in Firebird Trans-Ams, the cars that bore the series' name. And even stock-car-oriented Chrysler Corporation would come out to play with a pair of Plymouth Barracudas for Dan Gurney and Swede Savage and Dodge Challengers for Sam Posey and Tony Adamowicz.

It was understandable, then, that some of the Pontiac people were a little miffed that Chevrolet had essentially "stolen" their trick Trans-Am rear spoiler. Apparently unaware that his general manager had OK'd the deal, one Pontiac purchasing executive even wrote A.O. Smith a terse letter, saying: "We wish to advise that under no circumstances are any Pontiac tools purchased for the production of this spoiler to be used or shared in any way with any other division for the production of competitive spoiler assemblies unless approved by Pontiac in writing." Presumably, he was soon informed that MacDonald had given verbal approval to Chevy general manager DeLorean, and that was that.

Piggins had ideas about getting the first twenty spoilers installed on production Z-28's in time to get them legalized before the March 21st Sebring event, but he was frustrated by production hold-ups and the paperwork necessary to get such special service from an assembly plant. Then SCCA announced that it would not allow the new Camaro to run at Sebring anyway because fewer than the required 8200 '70-½ Z-28's would be built by then. This requirement, if strictly enforced, also could have scuttled the new rear spoiler for the whole season, since only 3000 sets of the end caps could be built on the temporary tools, 5200 less than necessary for SCCA "homologation." There was nothing left to do but try to bamboozle the SCCA officials into believing that the required number of new Z-28's could quickly

1970 engine options included 300 hp 350 V-8 and 360 hp 350 cu.in. Z-28 (which was rated 370 hp in ZL-1 Corvette, as pictured here).

be produced with the larger spoiler when fewer than half could actually be built prior to the late-summer arrival of the permanent tools.

Piggins told SCCA officials that company policy prevented his complying with their request to send computer sheets verifying production and the names of dealers receiving their cars, but he did offer to supply build schedules, show them the production line and cooperate in any other way. Then he tried to get the first thirty spoilers installed at the Norwood Camaro/Firebird plant during the first week of April so he could bring the SCCA technical people through in hopes of obtaining approval well before the first Trans-Am race at Laguna Seca, California on April 19th. Again his plans were delayed, because only a few sample pieces were available by then and they didn't fit very well. Even as a photo and an announcement about the special spoiler were released to the press on April 2nd, A.O. Smith, Chevrolet and Fisher Body engineers were working to improve the pieces' fit and Piggins was still trying to get the first few to the assembly line for installation.

The photo showed a Z-28 sporting the big spoiler and included an explanatory caption. "A fiberglass-reinforced plastic air spoiler is available as optional equipment on the 1970 Z-28 Camaro," it said. "Factory installed, the rear deck spoiler improves the car's airflow characteristics. Although the Z-28 has been available with an optional spoiler, this is a new design."

On April 8th, the spoiler was inspected by Chevrolet, Fisher Body and Norwood assembly plant personnel and was approved for production by the plant manager. A.O. Smith was instructed to begin shipment immediately. As soon as the first batch arrived, installation would begin at the Z-28 build-rate of seven cars per hour. One problem that would slow things up a bit, however, was that the early spoilers made on temporary tooling were of a low-temperature material that would not survive the heat of paint-drying ovens. Thus, they would have to be air-dried after painting.

At last, on April 20th, 1970, the race-designed rear spoilers entered production at Norwood. Piggins brought SCCA technical chief John Timanus in on April 23rd (just after the Laguna Seca race) and, as he put it, "assured him of the legitimacy of this option." There was only a handful installed on Camaros by then and about fifty more in the plant, but he and the production people managed to put on a convincing show. "We had these fifty spoilers hanging on the racks," he recalls with a grin. "The paint was still wet on them, and I walked him through and showed him those. They had just started installing them on Camaros, but there were a lot of Pontiacs around with the similar spoiler. He asked why Pontiac had so many more spoilers than Chevrolet, and I said, 'Well, they're brand new, but we're turning them out hand over fist.' We really sold him a bill of goods on that."

The spoiler was tentatively approved for racing beginning at a May 9th event near Dallas, Texas, but Piggins' battle wasn't over yet. It seems American Motors was having similar troubles getting its Javelin rear spoiler into production, and Penske was raising a smoke screen around his own rule-bending by complaining that Chevrolet was cheating. "Penske was telling them it wasn't in production," he says, "and here they had that Donohue spoiler, the one with the autograph on the back, on three or four cars. They were allowed to run it, but SCCA wouldn't let us run ours for the first race and was hedging on it for the second one, even after I had waltzed John through the plant and showed him what we were doing."

So Piggins' assistant, John Pierce, grabbed a half-dozen spoilers, hand-carried them down to Dallas, installed them on cars at a dealership and drove the cars out to the track. "We had them parked in the infield," Piggins relates, "to show that the spoilers were stock. And then the race was rained out." But the point had been made; the spoilers were approved for the next event at Mid-Ohio.

Meanwhile, the new Camaro was getting off to a much smoother start in the showroom sales race. It nearly caught the lofty Mustang in March, the first full month after its introduction, and by April had become the industry's top-selling ponycar. A third shift was added at the Norwood plant (boosting total Camaro production to more than 1150 per day), and plans were made to keep the full three shifts going right through the traditional late summer model-changeover period since the car would be essentially unchanged for '71. "Dealers credit the success of the new Camaro to its international styling, improved ride and handling and favorable price position," crowed a May 22nd press release. Ninety percent of the '70-½ Camaros sold through May 10th had V-8 engines, one-third were equipped with air conditioning and one-fourth with the Rally Sport option, according to the release.

In the May 1970 *Sports Car Graphic* was an unusual test of a 1969 Z-28 road-racing car owned by amateur driver Gerry Gregory and built by Dick Guldstrand. It may not have been the equivalent of a Penske-prepared Camaro or a Bud Moore factory Mustang—it hadn't won a race in 1969—but it *was* certainly faster than just about anything else ever tested by the magazine. "Right off the street (with muffler cores removed)," said author Paul Van Valkenburgh, "it turned 116 mph in 12.8 seconds" despite being a circuit car set up for

turns rather than a drag racer designed for traction off the line. Top speed was "only . . . 143 mph at 7,500 with the 4:11 gear . . . [but] with the proper gearing it should reach 160 mph at sea level on a nice day." Lateral acceleration on a skid pad was a phenomenal 0.97g, while braking deceleration (after the racing pads were hot) was measured at an equally amazing 0.99g! Subjectively, the handling felt superb with predictable throttle response, minimum roll and precise steering, perhaps . . . with excess understeer . . . [but] flat and always controllable at a level which would drive any stock sedan off the cliff." Zero-to-sixty miles per hour took 5.0 seconds; zero-to-one hundred a mere 10.4.

Also in May came the first full road tests of the '70-½ Camaro. *Car and Driver* called the Z-28 "an automobile of uncommon merit . . . every bit as much at home on the narrow, twisting streets of Monte Carlo or in the courtyard of a villa overlooking the Mediterranean as it is on Interstate 80. It's a Camaro like none before . . . a stunning machine from almost any vantage point. . . . Somehow, though, the Z-28 is not as thrilling as it once was. It's more tolerant of driving techniques now, more mature in its behavior . . . a car of brilliant performance for its displacement and with prep-

school manners."

C and D felt that the car displayed "exceptional road handling— probably the best Detroit has ever produced. . . . But in more demanding situations . . . the Camaro is disappointing. It understeers heavily." The brakes were praised as "up to any touring demands," while the seats were damned as "just the inverse of a bucket . . . easier to fall out of than in to." Other criticisms were leveled at the long doors (difficult entry/exit "in a narrow parking slot") and the auxiliary gauges ("very small and . . . likely to be blocked by the steering wheel"). Performance figures were: 5.8 seconds 0-60, 14.2 seconds at 100.3 mph in the quarter-mile, and 118 mph top speed.

Car Life, testing an automatic-equipped Z-28, came to some similar and some very different conclusions. "The 1970 Z-28 Camaro is not a perfect car. It is merely great," said the magazine. It called the new LT-1 350 engine (rated at 360 hp in the Z-28 and 370 hp in the Corvette) "the strongest mid-range V-8 on the market," but complained that it was hard to start when cold and hard to shut off when hot. Handling also drew mixed reviews: "Cornering grip borders on the fanatical. . . . In the upper speed ranges the car is very neutral." But cornering hard at low speeds produced "more un-

dersteer than we expected."

Brakes drew praise as being "equal to the LT-1's power" and interior quietness also received high marks ("5,000 lb. of quiet packed into a 3,500-lb. car"). In defense of vision to the outside the reviewer commented that "blind spots are not as bad as we would have thought." Improvements in seating also attracted attention; the rear seats were "much, much better than before," while front seating rated "eight out of ten" thanks to general comfort, "good back angle and more than enough legroom." The only gripe about front seating was that there was "no lateral support during cornering." The long door ("limits the opening width"), plastic rimmed steering wheel ("not in keeping with the car"), smaller trunk ("the new car's only leap backward") and placement of the heater controls and ashtray ("hard to reach and see") were criticized. Performance was 6.5 seconds zero-to-sixty, 14.5 seconds at 98.8 mph in the quarter-mile. Conclusion: "The Z-28 is as close to a mild-mannered racing car as the industry has come."

Taking a slightly different tack, *Road & Track* tested a milder-mannered Rally Sport with the 300-hp 350 engine, automatic transmission, and both SS and handling packages. Right off, the

Chevrolet general manager John DeLorean with second wife, model y Harmon; long, low-nosed race-car concepts were drawn in May lovely Kammback model was dusted off and proposed again for '71.

magazine called the new Camaro "the first serious effort since the 1963 Corvette to create a real American GT." "Greatly improved suspension," "aesthetically successful," and "clearly more comfortable than the old" were just some of the positive comments in the opening paragraph. Driving it about a week before public introduction, *R&T* "greatly enjoyed the reactions of people on the streets to it. Some practically crashed into trees gawking at its European snout and graceful lines, but we got the feeling several times that drivers of older Camaros were ignoring it. Did they feel abandoned, or did they simply not realize it was a Camaro?"

The magazine appreciated the car's increased seat travel, optional tilt steering wheel and remote-control outside mirror, new "bi-level" air conditioning, quick power steering, and generally "pleasant, responsive, solid" driving feel. Ride was described as "still on the stiff and jiggly side" but "better than any other ponycar we've driven," and handling (on smooth pavement, at least) displayed "less understeer than before." "Now it's possible," asserted the author, "to get it into a neutral cornering attitude by a mere tweak of the steering wheel and then keep it there with the throttle." Criticized were the tiny trunk, the lack of an oil-pressure gauge or trip odometer, placement of the heater/air conditioning controls (obscured by the steering wheel spoke), front seats (poor lateral support and no backrest angle adjustment) and rear seating accommodations (low cushions and minimal legroom, "which means knees-in-the-air"). The brakes performed well in panic stops and felt good in everyday use but faded drastically in repeated stops. Reported performance figures were 8.8 seconds zero-to-sixty and 16.6 seconds and 86 mph in the quarter-mile.

All things considered, *R&T* called the '70-½ Camaro "nice to drive in the day-in-day-out routine and an exceedingly good long-distance touring car." In fact, "we'll have to say it's the best American car we've ever driven, and more importantly it's one of the most satisfying cars for all-around use we've ever driven."

Although delighted with such a favorable evaluation, especially from a magazine known for its strong import-car bias, Chevrolet Engineering took exception to *R&T's* description of the Camaro's brake fade resistance as "pretty terrible." Convinced that the car's brakes had been insufficiently broken in ("burnished") before the test, engineer J.P. Konwinski brought a Z-28 with well-burnished front pads to the magazine's office and invited engineering editor Ron Wakefield to try it. Wakefield agreed, and discovered to his amazement that it had excellent fade resistance. He later tested still another Z-28, first with "green" brakes and then with the pads well

Selection of proposal drawings and scale model clay versio[ns]

burnished, and got similar results. So *R&T* upgraded its rating in the November issue, and Wakefield vowed always to burnish brakes in the future before testing them.

The next Z-28 article appeared in the June *Road Test*, which had a lot of favorable comment and very little negative to say. "The looks are long and racy without the common Detroit flaw of overstatement. . . . The sound is probably as close as you'll ever get to a full-race Trans-Am car and still be street-legal. . . . We found the steering very light and racy to use, and never did run into a situation where we did not feel in complete control. . . . The brakes pull the ton and three-quarters of pony car down to a smooth stop . . . over and over, in dry weather or in the rain. . . . The four speed manual . . . was smooth, if a little heavy-feeling, and easy to use."

In the negative column were the small trunk, "wretched" shoulder harness (a separate belt in 1970), placement of the ash tray ("pulls open right into the driver's kneecap") and heater controls (to see them, the driver must "scrounge down and twist around to the left, or turn the steering wheel hard right or left"), lack of headroom (with a hat, or especially a crash helmet) and difficult access to the low driver's seat (aided, however, by the tilt-wheel option). Best dragstrip time was 14.41 seconds and 100.2 mph, and fuel economy averaged about 13.0 miles per gallon. "It's true," the article concluded, "that five thou is a lot of bread, but if a pony car is what you want, and you want it hot and saucy, we can't think of anything on the market that we'd give a higher recommendation to than the 1970 Z-28 Camaro. It's as close to being a true Grand Touring or sports car, by anyone's definition, as anything Detroit has ever produced."

Also in June, *Sports Car Graphic* compared a Z-28 Camaro to an LT-1 Corvette it had tested earlier, and the Camaro came out the two-seater's equal in nearly every way. Both recorded top speeds of 120 mph (with 4.10:1 gearing), braking deceleration of 0.86*g*, and skidpad acceleration of 0.76*g*. The Corvette's performance figures were not given, but the Z-28 did zero-to-sixty in 6.5 seconds and a quarter-mile in 14.6 seconds at 98.3 mph. Interestingly, the Camaro displayed only 2.8 degrees of roll on the skidpad compared to the Corvette's 4.0 degrees. "Apparently stiffer anti-roll bars on the Z-28 make up for the more sophisticated Stingray suspension," the magazine surmised.

SCG praised the Camaro's Astro-ventilation ("actually works without vent windows, and at velocity you can get great gobs of air with the windows up, resulting in really quiet cruising and no wind whistle"); and the only real criticisms involved rear axle hop at the limit of traction under heavy braking ("been doing it for years"). The

reviewer found the front seats "better than last year's" but groused about "no lateral support, a board back and vinyl-covered brick for a head stopper." He also mentioned handling performance that "may be degenerating toward better ride—at least compared to its sister Firebird Trans-Am." The bottom line, though, was extremely positive: "Seldom have we seen an all-new model with so few drawbacks. It's quiet, quick, beautiful, and all the parts look and act as though they belong together."

Road Test ran two back-to-back Camaro articles in August, the first an SS-396 test and the second a comprehensive owners' survey. "The SS-396," the magazine summarized in its test article,"handles well on the highways and byways, stops firmly, corners anywhere, has more than sufficient power to meet any conceivable situation, and most important, it is fun to drive. The clean and simple styling has definite European tones, in fact the roofline is so low that the tall driver clonks his head entering and exiting just like he would in an Italian GT." Quarter-mile performance was reported as 15.3 seconds at 92.7 mph.

Living space up front was fine, it said, but rear seat comfort and accommodation were called "minimal" and the trunk "ridiculously small." Complaints were also lodged against the "lack of stowage

...ne during summer of 1969 explored design concepts for '72 model.

space in the cockpit" and "blind spots to the rear caused by the fastback styling." But *Road Test* concluded that "the car is a responsive machine, makes wonderful noises, causes small boys to whistle, and causes gas station attendants to wash all the windows and ask questions about the performance. Yes, folks, we think the 1970 Camaro with SS options is the neatest thing we have ever driven from Detroit's mass production lines. Chevrolet can truthfully state that they have, at last, built a real American Grand Touring car."

Because it dealt with owners' feelings rather than test results and editorial opinions, the owners' survey proved especially interesting. "Despite the current trend away from high-performance cars, the Camaro people seem to identify with performance, racing, and the sports car mystique," said the article. "The predominant theme running through the survey lists mentioned the sporty looks and the fine handling qualities of the car as reasons for buying. Of course, many mentioned marque loyalty as well." And, like owners of other popular ponycars, Camaro people tended to band together in groups and clubs, attend and compete in performance events together, and cheer for their favorites from organized parking and viewing areas.

Forty-eight percent of the owners of '67-'69 models surveyed said that they would buy another Camaro, and over half of the 37 percent

who would not listed an SS Chevelle as their probable next choice. This lent credence to Chevrolet's theory that Camaro buyers would stick with the marque when they outgrew their ponycars and indicated that performance cars were still attractive to a good portion of the market. Among the "likes" listed were the Camaro's power, handling, size, ease of maintenance, economy of operation, power disc brakes, safety, general reliability and—believe it or not—front bucket seats. In the "dislike" column were harsh ride, small trunk, console location of the auxiliary gauges, hard shifting of the four-speed transmission, stone damage to paint due to the lower body curvatures, and rattles and shoddy quality control in earlier models. Owners of performance versions also complained of rear axle hop under acceleration and early rear lockup under hard braking. The only frequently-mentioned first-year replacement item was the muffler.

But the most universal gripe was Chevy's dealer service, which thirty-six percent listed as "poor to shocking" and another twenty-nine rated "fair or average." Only twenty-two percent said their dealer service was "excellent" and thirteen percent said it was "good." "The owners quoted exorbitant prices for parts and labor ... and extreme delays, often days, in retrieving their cars from the most routine check-up." Thirty-eight percent, in fact, said they did their own service, and some claimed that dealers didn't even stock parts for their cars, though they were available elsewhere at more reasonable prices. Disturbingly, many reported that their experiences with dealers were bad enough to keep them from buying another Chevrolet—or in some cases, any GM car.

Nevertheless, *Road Test's* survey indicated that: "On the whole, Camaro owners are fond of their cars and are true members of the sporty-car set ... willing to put up with dealer service in order to get warranty satisfaction but ... convinced that general service is better and cheaper on the outside. The typical Camaro driver is a real enthusiast who likes to drive hard enough to appreciate good handling in a car, and he is pleased with the racing success and competitive image of the Camaro. A good many Camaro owners participate in an occasional rally or slalom and have a measure of success in grass roots competition."

Back in the design studio, the Camaro stylists had been hard at work dreaming up ideas for future model variations as well as the next-generation F-car. Aerodynamic racing versions with long, low noses were sketched and studied but never seriously considered for production. Early in 1969 the lovely Kammback was dusted off and re-proposed as a '71 addition. Several new concept drawings were created as possible '72 models, and by mid-'69 some were reproduced

in clay to provide full-scale, three dimensional perspectives for evaluation.

John DeLorean, who had just taken over as Chevrolet's general manager, was promoting a grandiose scheme to combine the X- (Nova) and F- (Camaro/Firebird) bodies into a single basic car with different sheet metal. Called the K-body, this same body/frame (unibody) platform also eventually would have been shortened to accommodate the second-generation subcompact Vega and stretched to replace the mid-size Monte Carlo/Grand Prix specialty cars. There was even a two-seater version, which some people (not DeLorean) believed could have replaced the Corvette. The idea might have simplified manufacturing and production, eliminated thousands of parts through commonality of chassis components, produced smaller and much lighter cars model-for-model, and saved millions of dollars. In fact, it's the same thing that foreign makers have done for years and the domestic companies began to catch onto in the late 1970's.

The first K-car models were completed in November 1969, and by the following January the Camaro versions, at least, had evolved into a very handsome fastback and, yes, another Kammback sport-wagon variation, both proposed for the '73 model year. By May, two months after the '70-½'s introduction, another sleek fastback model

was done, complete with battering ram bumpers to meet the government's upcoming damageability standards. By July both fastback and Kammback were redone into sleeker and still-prettier shapes with a low, two-segment grille and wrapover rear glass. "We looked at both front-wheel drive and conventional drive and assessed the economics of the two," says DeLorean. "The car that was designed could take either one so we could slowly phase into front-wheel drive as we got rid of the conventional. If they had done that, they could have saved a bloody fortune."

What happened to DeLorean's K-car idea? "The corporation killed it," he laments. "Primarily it was [then-GM president] Ed Cole who killed it. He had a way of destroying you without ever really saying no. He would always send things back for further study. Finally it would get to the point where we had studied the hell out of something, and by then everyone was bored with the idea and it would just disappear. That's what happened to the K.... He just further-studied it until it died."

Jim Hall's Chaparral Camaro debuted at the Leguna Seca sports car course in Monterey, California, site of the first 1970 SCCA Trans-Am event on April 18th; in the next day's contest it proved noncompetitive with the factory Ford Mustangs. Vince Piggins was there, and when he returned to Detroit he wrote a letter expressing his

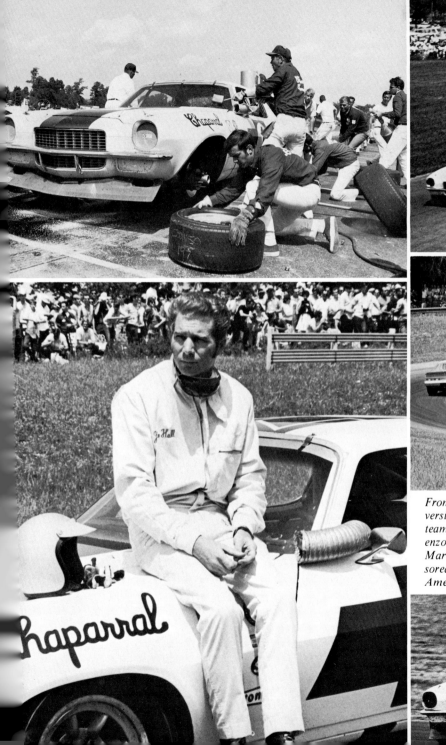

From the 1970 Trans-Am series: Page opposite (above): Jim Hall's controversial racing Camaro debuted at the Laguna Seca race course; Chaparral team performs engine change prior to Mid-Ohio race; (below): Tony DeLorenzo's Owens-Corning Camaro (#3), Ed Leslie's Chaparral Camaro (#2) and Mark Donohue's Penske/Sunoco Javelin (#6) in action; Owens-Corning-sponsored Tony DeLorenzo. This page: action at Mid-Ohio; Jim Hall, one of America's best-ever race driver/builders with his Chaparral at Mid-Ohio.

concern to then-passenger-car chief engineer Don McPherson, with copies to DeLorean, then-engineering director Alex Mair and other members of the hierarchy. "The results of heavy expenditures on race-oriented engine development over the past two years of Trans-Am activity," he pointed out, "have provided Ford with a stock-block small V-8 of superior horsepower potential and apparent reliability.

"Ford is presently claiming 465-475 hp using single 4-bbl. carburetion on their 302 Boss engine. The best we have been able to produce with the Z-28 is 440-445 hp. Their power advantage is clearly evident on acceleration and top-end performance." Piggins went on to explain that the Chevy small-block engine was handicapped by its smaller valves and ports ("Ford has port and valve sizes the equal of our 454 Mark engine"), and he strongly recommended a program to produce a competitive new cylinder head for the high-performance Z-28 engine.

"My concern with Ford's obvious performance superiority beyond the immediate Trans-Am activity is the terrific impact this engine is bound to create in aftermarket sales," he continued, "where, since 1955, Chevrolet small V-8 engines have been dominant. Currently this total-performance market is 65% Chevrolet-oriented and *Speed and Custom Dealer* magazine reports sales will reach $700 million annually by mid-1970. Success of the Ford small-block V-8 will see Chevrolet power replaced for most end-product performance usages such as in Formula "A" (road-racing) cars, USAC Championship cars and most special applications where rules require stock-block, pushrod engines. Loss of this prestigious market is bound to have an effect on our overall sales picture in 1971."

But the country and the auto industry were deep into a recession by mid-1970. Money was tight, people were being laid off, and low-priority engineering programs were being cut back, delayed and even cancelled. The killer small-block head was never done, and Chevrolet's Trans-Am road-racing program suffered throughout what would be its last season. Despite the efforts and considerable talents of Jim Hall and his Chaparral organization and independents such as the Owens Corning-backed Tony DeLorenzo and Jerry Thompson, the larger, heavier, underpowered new Camaros won only one event—Vic Elford in Hall's number two car at Watkins Glen, New York. Another, at Brainerd, Minnesota, was taken by the versatile Milt Minter in a '69 Camaro owned and entered by wealthy sportsman Roy Woods, but Ford drivers Parnelli Jones and George Follmer won six races and the championship, while Mark Donohue took the other three in Penske's AMC Javelin. Chevrolet finished

Views of '70½ Z-28: three piece tail spoiler in mid-year ad; this page: Z-28 with standard rear spoiler; Car and Driver *tests early car.*

third in the manufacturer's championship with forty points to AMC's fifty-nine and Ford's seventy-two. Luckily, Ford also dropped its racing efforts after that year, the potent Boss 302 engine was left to die, and Piggins' dire predictions about the future of Chevrolet's performance-leading image never came true.

An exciting full-color ad that was run in race programs that season (and the next) used a rear shot of a dark green Z-28 with the taller optional spoiler, spinning its wheels lustily on a dirt road. "The new Camaro Z-28," said the copy, "is as good looking underneath as it is on top. With a Turbo-Fire 350 cubic inch V-8. And with a Hurst shifter that comes along for the ride when you order the four-speed. Then there's the suspension that lets you feel the road without feeling the bumps. And the quick ratio steering. And the special wheels with the F60x15 tires. And on, and on, and on."

When the model-year closed that September, Chevrolet had produced slightly less than 125,000 '70-½ Camaros, nearly fifty percent less than the number of '69's built the year before. Only 8733 were Z-28's, versus the previous year's 20,302. Model year sales totalled 148,301 including the extra '69 cars produced prior to the new Camaro's late introduction, compared to Mustang's 170,000. After a strong early-year start, Camaro sales had fizzled due to the recession, criticism of youth-oriented cars by self-appointed safety advocates, high insurance rates, and other special and political factors.

Pete Estes, newly appointed group executive in charge of GM's overseas operations, had been Chevrolet's general manager during most of the new car's development, although he had served for a year as car and truck group executive during the time that the car was actually launched. He feels that the timing was wrong. "We should have called it a '71," he says. "We learned something from that. You can be early, but you can't be late. We fought like mad in the division to call it a '71, but we lost, and probably rightly so. February was too early to reasonably call it a '71. . . . I think there are some states where you can't register them that early anyway. The earliest you can do that, based on our experience and some others', is about April. And you can't be later than the first week in November, so there's a no-man's land in there as far as I'm concerned. You can announce extra models in a current line, but you can't put out a brand new car in that period."

Just as the '71's were announced, GM was hit by a massive UAW strike that shut down production completely for a record seventy days, allowing Ford Division to outsell Chevrolet for the calendar year with 1,621,846 vehicles delivered, as opposed to Chevy's 1,504,522. And that was just the beginning of new general manager John DeLorean's troubles. Federal emissions and safety regulations would be much tougher for '71 models, and GM had decided to cut drastically the compression ratios of all its engines so they could burn low-octane unleaded fuel and to begin rating them with more realistic SAE net horsepower figures. The result would be enormous drops in rated horsepower across the board, partly real and partly due to the new rating system. It looked like the final curtain for performance cars, at least at General Motors, and the beginning of lean times for the new Camaro in just its second season on the market.

CHAPTER SIX

On the Precipice

Nineteen seventy-one marked the beginning of a very unusual decade in the life of American industry in general, not to mention the automobile industry. Even a youthful, exciting car like the Camaro felt the influence of the times. It was a decade of development and refinement, of little exterior change save a couple of facelifts front and rear, and even less interior evolution.

The rival Mustang grew overlarge for '71, sunk to small and spiritless for '74, and was totally revamped again for '79, while GM's beautiful F-cars remained essentially the same, but got better every year. They weathered two crippling strikes and a serious sales slump that nearly caused their cancellation. Then they recovered and prospered through two separate fuel crises, and withstood an era of regulatory overkill to emerge sole survivors of their original ponycar class.

So little changed was the 1971 Camaro—introduced under the cloud of a United Auto Workers strike that stretched from September 14th to November 22nd, 1970—that Chevrolet even re-used some of the '70-½ photos in the '71 catalog. The most important changes were under the hoods: low-compression engines designed to run on low-octane unleaded fuel. Two sets of horsepower numbers were published to help ease the transition from traditionally inflated gross figures to more realistic net ratings for the coming age of lowered expectations. The 250 cubic-inch six was rated at 145 hp gross and 110 hp net; the 307 V-8 at 200 gross/140 net; the 2 bbl. 350 at 245/165; the 4 bbl. SS-350 at 270/210; the SS-396 (really 402 cubic inches) at 300/260; and the Z-28 350 at 330/275.

Inside were new and much more comfortable high-back front bucket seats with an optional, two-position seatback adjuster for the driver, plus a new cushioned-center steering wheel and soft black

Proposed 400 cu.in. Z-28 engine was not okayed, but reviewers gave '71 Z-28 and other Camaros an enthusiastic welcome.

control knobs to meet the latest safety standards. There was also a new spoiler option, available on any Camaro, which included a front air dam and the tall, wrap-around spoiler the racers had struggled to get into production the year before.

As early as March 1970, anticipating the coming horsepower loss for '71, performance group head Vince Piggins had written a memo to then-passenger car chief engineer Don McPherson recommending development of a new 400 cubic-inch Z-28 engine. "I would anticipate a reduction in market penetration on our performance oriented models," it said, "particularly if Ford, Chrysler, and American Motors retain their premium fuel engines for another year. The Z-28, which made it on performance, would not be successful as just a styling vehicle. The market serviced by this option is a knowledgeable one, and is influenced little, if any, by performance advertising and racing stripes alone."

Piggins suggested fitting a small-block 400 cubic-inch engine with the special Z-28 cylinder heads, hi-rise aluminum intake manifold, 800 cfm Holley 4 bbl. carburetor and either the existing L-46 hydraulic-lifter camshaft or a new one designed for maximum torque. With a 3.73:1 rear axle ratio and manual transmission, or a 3.42:1 with automatic, he calculated that acceleration would remain "as good or better than" that of the '70 350 cubic-inch Z-28 "by concentrating on maximum mid-range torque characteristics rather than gross power at very high rpm." And he predicted that this approach would produce lower emissions and noise levels.

Piggins also recommended a similar treatment for the LS-7 454 cubic-inch engine for use in both Chevelle and Camaro, pointing out that the lower rated horsepower numbers would give customers a break on fast-rising insurance premiums for so-called "muscle cars" without a corresponding loss in street performance. He had a strong motive for wanting to save the LS-7 454 and the four-bolt main bearing 400. They and their associated "heavy duty" service parts, he said, would put Chevrolet in "the best competitive position possible since 1963" in drag and other forms of racing due to "proposed rules changes in most associations for 1971."

A prototype 400 engine built to the above specifications was installed in a test car and evaluated by McPherson and then-Camaro chief engineer Bob Dorn, and both pronounced it "impressive and highly acceptable." At the end of June 1970 Piggins formally proposed it as a special-order Z-28 option beginning in mid-1971, to become standard in the '72 Z-28. Under the section marked "Reason for request," he stated: "To retain performance superiority to Mach I Mustang and Dodge Challenger on regular fuel. With hydraulic

This page: the '71 look—SS-350 and interior. Opposite: elaborate car show attraction was a favorite over many years.

cam and 8.8:1 C.R., horsepower rating can be 295 advertised. Reasonable insurance rates will prevail and help sales." And, he added, "This base '400' block is in heavy demand for specialized performance small block engines from 302 cubic inches to 440 cubic inches. Future rules for Indianapolis and Stock Car Racing will use this basic block to achieve favorable bore/stroke ratios at 355 and 366 cubic inches."

But GM management was concerned about the street durability of a high performance small-block engine opened to 400 cubic inches, well beyond the intentions of those who designed the original 265 cubic-inch version back in the early 1950's. Development money was tight in 1970 and the Camaro, after a strong start, was not selling all that well at mid-year. The whole youth-oriented ponycar class seemed in danger of being stifled by high insurance rates and pressure from the emissions and safety forces gaining strength in Washington. Also, by the September '71 model introduction, GM was suffering acutely, its production stopped cold by the UAW strike.

Two days before the October 30th, 1970 Planning Committee meeting, Piggins made his final pitch in a memo to Chevy general manager John DeLorean. He pointed out that dealer/racer Don Yenko had requested a special order of 250 400-cubic-inch Z-28's and that the field durability question could be answered at minimal risk by filling Yenko's order as a "trial balloon" to see how 250 such cars would perform—and last—on the street.

"Ford Mustang for 1971," he argued, "has five models in three series with nine engine options; three of which are high performance, high compression engines. The 1971 Camaro needs a shot in the arm that the 400 cubic-inch engine could provide to retain some street performance image and also give us a real dragstrip sleeper that could put us back in the winner's circle for the Manufacturer's Trophy in 1971 . . . . This engine is presently in wide usage in the Super Modified circuits opened up to the limit of 440 cubic inches. Durability is excellent . . . . The new 1971 NASCAR 366 engine displacement limit for Grand National cars will put this 400 cubic-inch engine destroked to 366 in demand in the 1971 Chevelle for this class. . . . Unless you lend your support to this one, I'm afraid we may lose it."

But the 400 cubic-inch Z-28 was not approved. There were small-block 400's available in full-size Chevys for many years, and big-block 400's (the same 402 cubic-inch "Mark" engines that were called "396's" in Camaros) in Chevelles, Monte Carlos and big Chevys. And the venerable small-block in 366 cubic-inch form did indeed become the class of NASCAR racing throughout the 1970's and

into the '80's. But Piggins' proposed lightweight, high torque, low compression 400 never made it into a production Z-28, something which didn't help a continuing slump for the high-performance Camaro that eventually would lead to its cancellation as a model—and may have marked the beginning of what almost became the end for GM's F-cars as a whole.

Nevertheless, even with reduced engine power and responsiveness for '71 that lost it points with the drag and street-racing set, Camaro remained the favorite in its class among sports-car oriented enthusiasts. It handily won *Car and Driver's* 1971 Reader's Choice Poll among ponycars, receiving twice as many votes as the Mustang. It was also named one of the Ten Best Automobiles of the year—winner of the Best $4,000-6,000 Sedan category, and the only domestic car on the list—by *Road & Track* magazine. The other nine *R&T* winners were Toyota's Corona, BMW's 2002, Mercedes Benz' 280SE and 300SEL 6.3, Fiat's 850, Datsun's 240-Z, Alfa Romeo's 1750, Porsche's 911 and Ferrari's 365GTB/4—some pretty prestigious company.

"The Chevrolet Camaro," stated the magazine that rarely has praised any American product, "proves that Detroit can build a good, aesthetically pleasing road car for a reasonable price. Its classification as a sedan is somewhat equivocal; we could have easily called it a Sports/GT, but whatever the category, it is an outstanding car. Chevrolet engineers seriously tried to incorporate in it some lessons learned from European GT's and in doing so gave it adequate suspension, standard front disc brakes, a good driving position and wide wheels and tires. Meanwhile, the stylists were giving it an astonishingly beautiful body, albeit an overlarge and not particularly space-efficient one. But for less than $5,000 one can buy a Camaro 350SS and it's one great hunk of car for that money."

Car and Driver tested a Z-28 for its May 1971 issue and called it "very definitely a driver's car, quiet and comfortable except for the upright seat, with extremely quick power steering, accurate short-throw shifter and powerful brakes . . . . As a racer, however, it would appear to be all over for the Z-28, at least as far as the Trans-Am (series) is concerned. There will be no factory cars this year, under the table or otherwise, and an independent, no matter how good he is, won't have a chance against the Penske Javelin."

About the Camaro in general, *C and D* pointed out that it was then "neck and neck" in the market with its Ford rival and "it appears that the Camaro is finally going to outsell the Mustang." That, the magazine asserted, would make it "first in line for second fiddle, because the sporty car market itself is withering like last year's

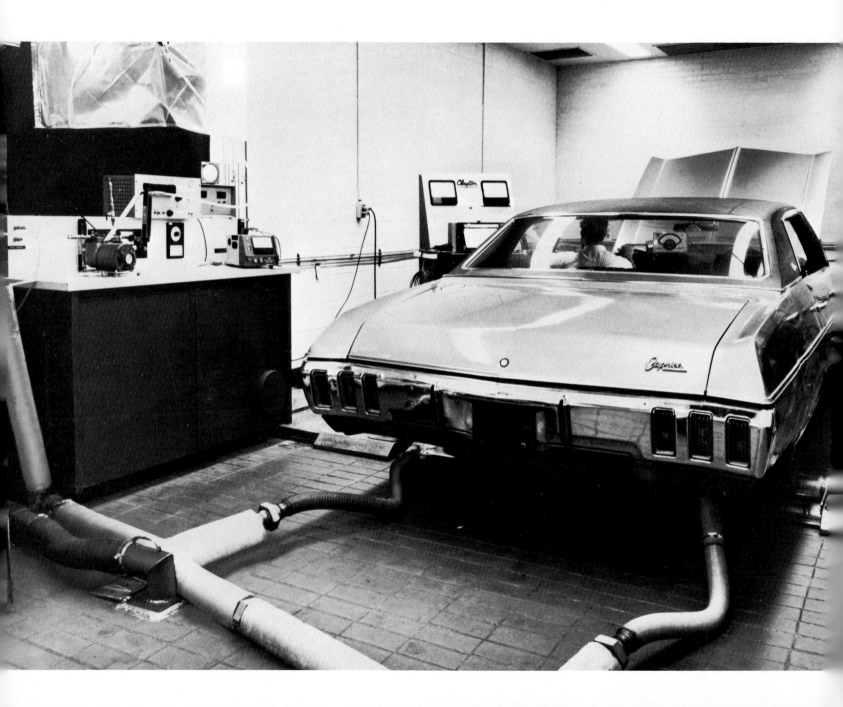

roses." The new bucket seats were criticized because their backs were non-adjustable and too vertical for comfort, "so that the seat feels like a half folded-up lawn chair. A two-position backrest, like the Vega's, or a recliner mechanism like most bucket-seat imports, is a logical addition and it is a measure of Chevrolet's nearsightedness that one is not available in an otherwise well-planned car." (Chevy says a two-position back rest was an available option.)

The article also lamented GM's early move to unleaded fuel and low compression ratios—9.0:1 in the Z-28 versus 1970's 11.0:1, both of which lowered the engine's power output and worsened its part-throttle driveability, "particularly before it was fully warmed up." Performance figures for the test car, equipped with a close-ratio four-speed and a 3.73:1 rear axle, were 6.7 seconds 0-60 mph, 15.1 seconds at 95 mph in the quarter-mile and a respectable 130 mph top speed.

There were kind words, as usual, for Camaro's design and its driving character: "GM stylists must be a benevolent sort. Instead of marauding over the project, drawing lines and molding shapes that obscure the car's function, they have released a car that is almost understated by Detroit standards. The virtue of that will be more obvious as time passes; when today's Camaros still look attractive on tomorrow's freeways . . . . Its styling is functional, honest rather than tricky, and to the driver the Camaro feels compact and agile—qualities which we feel are prerequisites for any sporty car and which are unfortunately absent in the Mustang."

Of necessity, safety concerns played a far greater part in the design of the Camaro during the Seventies. Not content to legislate just passenger safety, the muscle-flexing National Highway Traffic Safety Administration (NHTSA) felt compelled to protect the cars as well. The first federal bumper standards, effective with '73 models, had industry designers and engineers scrambling to meet them with reasonably attractive solutions by mid-1970. The most aesthetically pleasing approach involved "soft end caps" supported by spring mounted reinforcement bars that would allow them to bounce back undamaged after minor impacts.

A full-size drawing of a proposed '73 Camaro using this approach—and otherwise little changed except for the addition of louvers on the front fenders and behind the side windows—hung on the studio wall by mid-July; by October 1st there were two "soft-nosed" clay models vying for attention. Both had head- and park lamps "frenched" into the body and grilles split horizontally by full-width, body-colored bumpers that gave the look of no bumpers at all. One sported a blacked-out, open-mouthed grille, a thin-section bumper and aggressive looking triple hood ducts, but it was the other

Coping with new regulations: emissions research at Chevrolet Engineering and chassis development on computer controlled ride simulator.

slightly cleaner, more rounded look with a fatter bumper and a fine-mesh grille pattern that prevailed. In back, above a matching hidden bumper, were full-width, two-colored, wraparound taillamps divided into four horizontal sections by thin chrome strips.

By year's end there were some radical new Camaro designs on the wall as well, but most attention centered on the handsome, soft-ended model—now minus its fender vents—that was being examined and photographed in a mid-December snowstorm in the viewing area behind the GM design building. It was too late to tool for '73-model production (beginning in the summer of '72), and the soft end caps were judged too expensive an investment for a car with badly sagging sales in what seemed a fast-fading market—a car that might not survive more than another year or two. But it was an interesting and attractive approach to NHTSA's so-called "safety" bumpers, and worthy of further investigation.

None of the corporate and divisional executives who viewed that car on that December day could have realized that what they were looking at was essentially the '78 Camaro, to be unveiled some seven years later. The designers returned to their studio, some to dream up further futuristic sporty-car concepts on paper while others struggled with the more mundane task of beefing up the existing bumpers as a stopgap measure for the '73 model . . . if there was to be a '73 model.

Sales were indeed sinking fast when the '71 model year ground to a close, with 116,627 Camaros delivered compared to 148,000 the year before and 194,000 in model year '69. Of these, approximately ten percent had the six-cylinder engine, forty-nine percent the 307 V-8,

forty percent were 350-powered and just one percent were equipped with the 396 (402) big-block V-8. Only 4863 were Z-28's.

Then-general sales manager Bob Lund recalls trying to counteract the slump: "I remember the struggle we were having to move them," he says. "We did all kinds of unique things to merchandise them, and we challenged our field organization to come up with their own ideas as well. One of our regional managers, for example, developed some unique vinyl tops . . . some very gaudy looking vinyl tops that he was putting on in the field." Proving once again that as designers, sales people make excellent sales people.

Camaro had not outsold the redesigned Mustang in 1971 as some had predicted it might. But the other prediction—that it wouldn't stand a chance without factory support in the Trans-Am racing series—had come dismally true: Penske's AMC-backed Javelin took the title, and the Chevrolet independents had scored not a single victory.

When the '72 Camaros were introduced in the fall of 1971—again with little change save a "bolder looking, large grid pattern standard grille," a relocated hood latch, "refinements" to the chassis and the six-cylinder engine, a quicker 24:1 manual steering ratio, improved emissions controls and a special system for California's tougher standards, a new four-speed transmission shifter, a "wet-look" vinyl roof option, a wider white stripe on the whitewall tires, and addition of the four-spoke "sport" steering wheel as standard equipment—there were already rumors both inside and outside General Motors that the year would be Camaro's last. One sign that the car might be in trouble was a lowering of dealer profit margins on it from twenty-one to just seventeen percent, which allowed a token $133 reduction in its base price.

"Quality is the keynote of the Chevrolet Motor Division's 1972 product program," pledged John DeLorean at an August 31st press conference. "From the luxury Caprice to the economy Vega, we have limited the changes in our 1972 models to refinements and product improvements, while we concentrated on building each car better than ever before." This was a sincere statement from a general manager genuinely concerned with Chevrolet's quality reputation, which had been slipping seriously. Still, the "no-change" year also had had a very practical but unspoken reason behind it: the corporation had been hurt so badly by the late-1970 strike that nearly all product programs scheduled for '72 had been postponed a full year.

The Camaro catalog for 1972 led with a bold message on its cover: "If you're looking for the closest thing to a Vette yet, you've come to the right catalog." Inside it implied that Camaro was a four-seat

Page opposite: Bob Lund, then-Chevrolet general sales manager, talking with interviewer in 1971. This page, above: July 1970 drawing for proposed '73 facelift; "soft" design proposals for '73, resembling eventual '78 car; (below): some wild concepts on paper for '73 on display in December 1970.

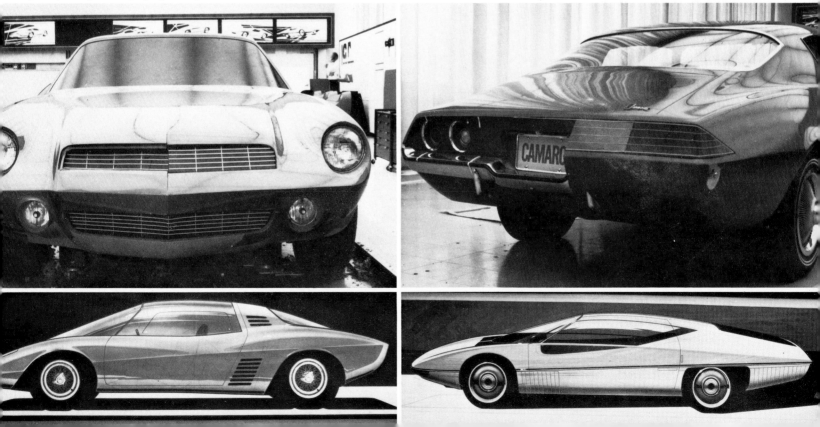

sports car that could do anything Corvette could at a much lower price. Advertising in non-automotive publications stressed the *Road & Track* "World's Ten Best Cars" recognition but moved Camaro under the Chevrolet divisional umbrella theme: "Building a better way to see the U.S.A." Appropriate for Impalas and Chevelles, perhaps, but most unexciting for a once-strong "image" car.

By now, America was irrevocably entrenched in an era of anti-car consumerism. Soured by the Vietnam war, youth unrest, Nixonism and the inevitable recession that followed the wartime boom, and spurred by the bleatings of self-appointed saviors, the people were newly aware of highway carnage and environmental pillage. They needed someone or something to blame, and the automobile was a convenient scapegoat. Suddenly the country's love affair with its cars, after a long and blissful honeymoon, had decayed into a troubled marriage of convenience. Many in government and the media were calling for separation and eventual divorce.

The September 18th issue of *Business Week* magazine featured a commentary called "Americans Put the Car in its Place." "They may not love it as they once did," it began, "but they need it as a 'household utility.'" Virginia Knauer, Office of Consumer Affairs director, Donald Petersen, then-Ford Motor Company vice president for car planning and research, and others were quoted. "There was a time when everyone wanted the biggest, fastest, flashiest car around as a status symbol," said Mrs. Knauer. "Now more people worry about durability, cheapness of fuel consumption, and pollution." Said Petersen: "Excesses in size, flamboyance, and needless styling changes, which were gobbled up in the late 1950's, are behind us. The swing is back to a different balance between exterior appearance and interior room," and he estimated that by 1980

half of all cars could be compact-size or smaller.

"The car in America has been dying a slow death as a symbol of economic and social status," said the article's author. But "love object or not," he correctly pointed out that "the automobile pervades American life. One out of every six jobs depends on it in some way. Our whole mode of living revolves around it . . . . To do away with the car would be to stop America in its tracks." Then he concluded with the disturbing opinion of one interviewee: "The day will come," she predicted, "when buying a car will be like buying a washing machine—you'll just order it from a catalog and wait until it is delivered." A thought to chill the spines of automakers and enthusiasts alike.

An innovative approach to promoting the Camaro—combining specific model and equipment packages for specific needs, desires and budgets—was begun with the '72 model. An informal handout outlining these packages was distributed to magazine editors at the summer long-lead press preview, with the suggestion that they tailor their test cars accordingly. One publication that took Chevrolet up on the idea was *Road & Track,* which tested three such "packaged" cars for its April 1972 issue.

A so-called "Budget GT," equipped with the 2 bbl. 350 V-8 engine (now rated at 165 hp), four-speed transmission, 3.08:1 axle ratio with positraction, F-41 sports suspension, power brakes and steering, F70x14 bias belted tires and 14x7 Rally wheels, special instrumentation, AM/FM radio and the Rally Sport appearance package, priced out at $3850. Its mid-range powertrain was "a most satisfactory combination," said the article, "quiet and at least acceptably smooth for a 1972 emissions controlled engine." There was some tendency to stall when the engine was cold, but the four-speed linkage was "a

*Opposite: Berlinetta clay model with soft end caps proposed for '73.
Above: proposed beefed-up bumpers for '73; the '72 Camaros.*

pleasure to operate, in contrast to the overly stiff Camaro linkage of earlier years." The variable-ratio power steering was "quick, albeit lacking in feel," and the optional handling suspension stiffened the ride but provided "a useful increase in cornering power."

A "Luxury GT," at $4365, had the same 2 bbl. engine with automatic transmission and a 2.73:1 axle and was loaded with everything on the budget car plus tinted glass, rear window defroster, air conditioning, clock, tilt steering wheel and custom interior—but not the performance-oriented sport suspension, positraction or gauge package. Its standard suspension proved softer and had "lower cornering power and more initial understeer," but it "jiggled less on rough surfaces." The powertrain gave "effortless, noiseless and turbine-smooth performance," yet moved the car from rest "as quickly as the driver could wish." The air conditioning rated "an unequivocated endorsement."

And a "Performance GT," a Z-28 with automatic transmission, 4.10:1 rear axle, center console, front and rear spoilers, power steering, tilt wheel, AM radio, Rally Sport and custom interior, was the most expensive car tested at $4558. The $766 Z-28 option itself included the 255 hp 350 engine, dual exhausts, a special handling package, F60x15 tires on 15x7 styled wheels, positraction, a larger radiator, flexible cooling fan and the usual stripes and emblems. It "fairly leaps from rest and gains speed at a good rate," said the magazine, "shifting at redline with a nice touch of wheelspin. The suspension and large tires provide high cornering power and the Z-28 can be driven fast with precision." But *R&T* complained that "there wasn't enough blinding speed to make up for the fuel consumption and engine temperament .... The idle speed is set fast and the transmission usually goes into gear with a bump. Even at the high

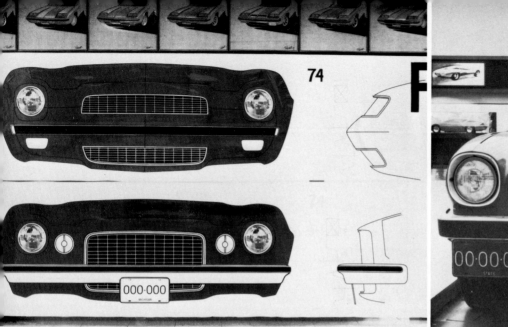

speed the idle is rough," and the engine was noisy and "liable to run-on when warm."

Zero-to-sixty times were 10.5 seconds for the luxury version, 9.8 seconds for the "budget" car and 7.5 seconds for the Z-28; quarter-mile runs were 17.6, 17.2 and 15.5 seconds at 79, 82.5 and 90 mph; and top speeds were 107, 110 and 124 mph, respectively. All three had "good" brakes, though fade resistance was judged "marginal for the Z-28's acceleration capability." They also had two-position adjustable seatbacks, which the testers criticized as "too-upright" and very limited in adjustability—"a good idea, insufficiently executed." The authors didn't pick a favorite, saying that a hydraulic-lifter, 4 bbl. 350 with F-41 suspension and either transmission would be more to their liking, but they did conclude that "the budget car doesn't lack luxury, the performance car doesn't lack comfort and the luxury car doesn't lack performance."

On April 7th, 1972 the UAW struck GM's Norwood, Ohio Camaro/Firebird assembly plant, shutting down production; and it was just about then that GM came closest to dropping the F-cars. There were too many cars, too many model and option variations, too many engines and drivetrains. For years the corporation had grown and prospered under the philosophy of interdivisional competition and diversity—"a car for every purse and purpose," as styling chief Bill Mitchell used to put it—but it was getting too complicated and expensive to test, develop and certify every product

variation for each year's tougher emissions, safety and damageability standards. There was a very real need to de-proliferate, to drop unneeded car lines and models, commonize engines, drivetrains, chassis and internal body parts and share research and development costs among the divisions.

"There was a pressure to reduce our complexity," recalls Alex Mair, who was Chevrolet chief engineer at the time, "and the F-car was selected as one of those to be discontinued. Its sales were not very high, so there was a plan going on to drop it. There was a meeting on the Fourteenth Floor in which the recommendation was made to consider cancelling it. There were proponents each way, and I was one who wanted to keep the car because it still had great value. It was only in its third model year since we had tooled the new one, and I thought it would come back. I wasn't alone, a lot of people did. Both divisions wanted to keep it. There were people at both Chevrolet and Pontiac, people who had worked on it, who strongly wanted it, and that was important."

As then-Camaro chief engineer Bob Dorn remembers it, the Camaro "had been canceled. Mr. Cole [then-GM president Ed Cole] had announced that it was canceled. I don't know what the other reasons were, but the bumper standards were coming upon us for '73, and it looked like we would have to spend a fair amount of money to put a new front end on it. So we said, well, we won't do a new front end . . . we'll gin it up with struts and whatever we have to do. I was

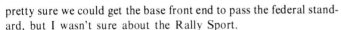

pretty sure we could get the base front end to pass the federal standard, but I wasn't sure about the Rally Sport.

"We got to work on it, and we worked on reducing the tool bill. I don't recall the figure, but it was in the multi-million dollars when we started. When we finished, just by saying we won't do this and we won't do that, we had it down to a very low number because we didn't have to tool new header panels, new bumpers and things like that which really cost a lot of money. We had a lot of reinforcements, a lot of struts and bumper guards, and we spaced the bumpers another half-inch off the car to pass the tests. The RS looked like a NASCAR stock car, it had so many rods and struts behind those little bumpers."

Obviously it would have been a crying shame to cancel those beautiful F-cars after only their third year on the market. "That's what we thought," says Dorn, "and that's why so many people worked on it. From an engineering standpoint, it was the very best car we had at the time, and it would have been illogical to cancel the best car we had. Whether it was Alex Mair or John DeLorean who saved it, or the work we did, I don't know. But management couldn't say we'd have to spend a lot of money on it, and all of that added together to keep the car going."

Once Dorn's engineers had come up with the low-cost bumpers and the decision had been made not to cancel the Camaro for '73, they were faced with the challenge of designing stronger and better

'74 facelift with spring-mounted aluminum bumpers begins to take shape in late '71 and early '72; (below): sleek scale model of January '72.

looking systems for a facelifted '74 model. With soft end caps ruled out at least for the moment, they turned to a solution that was already being developed for the '74 Vega—lightweight, spring-mounted aluminum bumpers—as the next best solution. The stylists conceived some fairly attractive front and rear appearances around them, tried several variations in clay, and by the spring of 1972 the '74 Camaro's look was essentially complete.

Looking ahead, the designers also began development of the next complete restyle. A radical looking high-tailed fastback scale model was displayed in January, and by August several attractive and very European looking drawings—all "glassy" fastbacks with rounded soft ends front and rear—were on the studio walls, while at least one related concept sat on the floor in full-size clay.

The Norwood UAW strike dragged on through the summer, but the June *Hot Rod* struck an upbeat note by reporting on a Chevrolet Engineering experimental Camaro powered by a turbocharged six-cylinder engine. "This six runs like a 350 cubic-inch V-8 with a four-barrel." While a stock six-cylinder, Powerglide car managed only a 20.28-second quarter mile at 67 mph, the turbo-six Camaro with Turbo Hydra-matic did 16.18 seconds at 86 mph. More significantly, the turbo car ran a 50-70 mph passing test in just 5.12 seconds compared to 12.87 seconds for the non-turbo six. "The turbocharged engine started, idled and ran every bit as smoothly and quietly as the stocker," said author C.J. Baker, and was "a pleasant car to drive, exhibiting none of the ill manners that are usually associated with modified engines." But the turbo engine had been built for evaluation purposes only, to learn about its performance, emissions, reliability and economy, and Chevrolet said there were no plans to produce it for sale at that time.

Despite a complete lack of factory-backed cars and the resulting lower level of competition in what had become essentially a semi-pro series, Chevrolet went winless again in Trans-Am ponycar road racing. George Follmer, now piloting a Javelin, won the '72 title for American Motors with four wins in seven races, while Milt Minter took one in a (Chevy-powered "Canadian") Herb Adams Firebird, and Warren Tope won two in a Mustang. Several strong independent Camaro efforts led by Warren Agor, Paul Nichter, Mo Carter, Carl Shafer and Gene Harrington competed well, but Chevrolet finished only fourth in manufacturer points with twenty-four to Pontiac's twenty-eight, Ford's thirty-four and AMC's forty-eight.

When the model year sales race ended in September, with the Norwood assembly plant back in commission on September 25th after a crippling 171-day strike that had stopped Camaro/Firebird production cold since its April beginning, only 70,809 Camaros—a dismal 2575 of them Z-28's—had been delivered compared to Mustang's 120,000. Some seven percent were six-cylinder-powered, forty percent had 307 V-8's, just over fifty-one percent had 350's of one type or another, and less than two percent were equipped with the 402 cubic-inch big-block engine in the last year it would be offered. Though they had suffered no strikes, the other manufacturers were experiencing similar sales problems with their own sporty coupes, and it certainly seemed that the whole ponycar class was fading fast.

The strike not only had killed the last four months of '72 Camaro production, but also had substantially delayed the '73-model start-up. Further, the walk-out had stranded in various stages of completion some 2100 cars, both Camaros and Firebirds, so that they couldn't be shipped to dealers. Since it would have been prohibitively expensive to update these cars to the '73 bumper, emissions and safety standards, they were all unceremoniously crushed and scrapped. "It almost made you want to vomit when they crushed those cars," laments Bob Lund, who was Chevrolet general sales manager at the time. "We were going to build them out and send them to Canada or Europe or some place because their regulations were different from ours, but then it was decided that we couldn't do that either. That strike was a very serious point in the history of the Camaro, one of the most devastating we've ever had."

Chevrolet may have had ponycar sales and strike troubles in 1972, but the division as a whole had enjoyed a tremendous year as the country recovered from recession and pent-up demand for new cars was unleashed, boosted considerably by removal of the seven percent federal excise tax on new cars in the fall of 1971. Records had been set by the full-size Caprice, specialty Monte Carlo, compact Nova, subcompact Vega and Corvette sports car. DeLorean promised more of the same for '73 at the September 8th press review. "In addition," he said, "Chevrolet dealers are undertaking an all new service program, called Service Supremacy, which should result in a giant step toward better service."

Despite its close brush with cancellation and postponement of the originally scheduled facelift, the '73 Camaro bowed in on September 21st, 1972 with significant changes under its skin. Besides addition of the federally mandated bumpers—with big vertical guards protecting the grille on standard cars—the biggest news was a new model called "Type LT." Previously, the option structure had allowed building any sort of Camaro one wanted, but most options added nothing to the "Blue Book" value when it came time to trade or sell. The idea of the LT (from "Lusso Turismo" in Italian, "Luxury Touring" in English) was to create a whole new model that included most of the popular convenience and dress-up equipment, but which would be viewed differently by the blue book in terms of resale value. It was also a marketing move to re-position the Camaro toward a slightly older and more affluent buyer. The LT came complete with the 2 bbl. 350 V-8 engine (now rated at 145 hp), power steering, dual sport mirrors (remote control on the driver's side), lower body side moldings and accent paint treatment, 14x7 Rally wheels, sport instrumentation, luxury seats and interior trim with woodgrain and silver accents, extra sound insulation, and LT emblems inside and out.

All Camaros got a new soft-rim, four-spoke sport steering wheel as standard equipment, molded foam rear seats, an improved seat belt and harness system and a new clutch pedal and pad design that increased foot room for the driver. Exhaust gas recirculation (EGR) was added to all engines to meet '73-model standards. Other engineering improvements included a new ratchet-type automatic transmission floor shifter with a "range selector knob" that replaced the former stirrup handle, a larger radiator with the air conditioning option, higher durability body mounts and a "refined" Delcotron alternator. Also, the Turbo Hydra-matic transmission finally replaced the old two-speed Powerglide as optional with the base six-cylinder engine. New options included redesigned floor console, new-

Opposite: more practical ideas for next-generation Camaro proposed for '76 in August '72; clay and paper quad headlamp proposals for 1976.

look wheel covers, "GT" styled wheels with a special cast urethane coating to give the appearance of aluminum, and the LT's interior decor and sound insulation group. And for the Z-28 were a new hydraulic-lifter 350 engine rated at 245 hp, an open element air cleaner for what Chevy called "power on demand" sound, and air conditioning available as an option for the first time.

The "engineering package" program introduced the year before was expanded to five distinct Camaro variations for '73, and magazine editors requesting test vehicles were again asked to tailor them accordingly. As described by Camaro chief engineer Bob Dorn, these were: "Budget 2+2 . . . a package of basic equipment required to provide a civilized vehicle of 2+2 design without great expense"; "Insurance Special Sports Car . . . provides maximum performance with low insurance premium and low initial cost"; "Luxury Camaro . . . quietest, softest riding Camaro available"; "Super GT . . . the ultimate in GT Camaros. The air conditioned Z-28 is the basis for the package along with the 'Type LT' equipment"; "Maximum Performance . . . includes all options which contribute to acceleration, handling and cornering." With the big-block 402 V-8 discontinued, five engines remained available: the 250 six; the 307 V-8; 2 bbl. and 4 bbl. 350's; and the higher compression Z-28 350. These were rated at 100, 115, 145, 175 and 245 hp, respectively.

Advertising for transition year 1973 concentrated on the new Type LT, "A Very Special Camaro." It also was on the cover of and heavily featured in the 1973 Camaro catalog.

Over the winter of 1972-73, rumors flew that Chevrolet was building an all-new Camaro on the subcompact Vega platform for

Opposite: '72 Trans-Am action at Mid-Ohio includes Warren Agor (#13) leading George Follmer's Roy Woods Javelin and Alfred Ruys de Perez in Mo Carter Camaro (#89); (below): Tuck Thomas in Lancer Stores Camaro was among better independents in '72 Trans-Am. This page: Chevy engineer Dick Hoffman's Camaro built for '73 series; Agor's Camaro in Mid-Ohio paddock in '72; Carl Shafer and Canadian Mo Carter, two of best independent road racers, scored points for Chevrolet in the 1972 series.

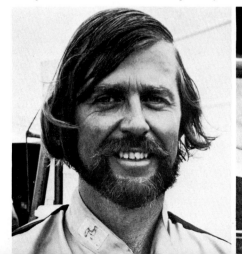

'75—just as Ford's '74 Mustang would be Pinto-based— and that this smaller Camaro would serve as the launching platform for the GM Wankel rotary engine (GMRE) then under development. They began when Chevy general manager DeLorean announced in mid-November that the GMRE would be introduced in a "spectacular 2+2 roadster in the fall of 1974." This led *Detroit News* auto columnist Bob Irvin, for one, to conclude that DeLorean was alluding to a Vega-based Camaro. "GM has been developing a new Camaro for 1975," Irvin wrote in his November 26th column. "The company did a styling exercise of a Camaro based on the Vega body shell. Pininfarina, the Italian design shop, has built such a sporty car." Other publications picked up on Irvin's speculation and reported it as fact, which must have been a source of amusement to those in the know at GM. There was, in fact, no intention to downsize the F-car at that time, with or without the GMRE (which never did reach production). And the car DeLorean referred to was, of course, the '75 Vega-based Monza 2+2.

The February 1973 *Motor Trend* did some speculating of its own about what the facelifted '74 F-cars would look like—not very accurate, but they did get the Camaro's rear appearance about right—and editor Eric Dahlquist added some commentary on a suddenly revived market for the GM ponies. "Against the backdrop of the impending small-sized 1974 Mustang," he wrote, "and the well-known success of the Capri, Toyota Celica, Opel Rally (nee Manta for 1973), the demand for the old, original full-sized sports-personal cars has suddenly blossomed anew. And for once, no one, not even Detroit's legions of marketing whiz-kids, can tell you why. After all, these pony-machines were supposed to be in a headlong dash to the same shallow grave as the Corvair . . . . But they're not.

"Last April, the United Auto Workers struck the Norwood, Ohio assembly plant where both General Motors sporty cars are made. The dealer supply pipeline ran out in April and there was a feeling in some quarters that maybe it was all to the good. Why prolong the inevitable? . . . Even as the last few remaining cars were snatched up, despite fat sticker prices, the value of low mileage '71's began to climb steadily. This doesn't happen to your average Detroit car . . . . What American buyers don't do best is wait long for their automobiles . . . . The first time most of these would-be Camaro/Firebird customers walked out a new-car showroom's front door, flinty-eyed Chevy and Pontiac dealers kissed them goodbye forever. Yet what to their wondering eyes should appear the next month and the month after—the same Camaro/Firebird buyers, waiting, actually *waiting* for their beloved Z-28's and Trans-Ams to rattle up on the transporters once again."

The June *Road Test* featured an upbeat report on the Z-28, which it called "alive and surprisingly healthy" for '73. "The wild engines are gone from the scene," said author Jean Calvin, "the blistering acceleration that made the cars popular among street racers and drag types, and the enormous variety of performance options have passed into history. What remains, in the case of the Z-28, is the zoomy styling, the fine handling, and a far more civilized car . . . . We were pleasantly surprised with the Camaro, and we feel it is more than worthy of wearing the Z-28 emblems in all areas but one, and that is exciting engine performance . . . . The Z-28 handles like a proper sports car, keeps a positive, near-neutral feel going into and coming out of a hard corner . . . . The big brakes with front discs and the power boost also have a very positive feel, and they are well balanced for daily use as well as panic situations . . . . Still missing is a decent reclining mechanism for the seat backs, but maybe next year . . . . The interior finish is well above standard, and the degree of detailing

New Camaro Type LT luxury coupe for '73 offered as standard equipment 145 hp Turbo-Fire 350 cubic-inch V-8 engine and power steering.

in the test car was real quality, putting the Z-28 in the true GT category."

Calvin's only real complaints involved the new de-smogged engine, which was a bit sluggish and slow to warm up, poor visibility of the gauges and heater/AC controls behind the new four-spoke wheel, and inconvenient location of the ashtray. There was no quarter-mile time given, but 0-60 acceleration of the automatic transmission Z-28 was reported as an unimpressive 10.0 seconds, while top speed was estimated at 110 mph.

Car and Driver tested Dorn's "Super GT" package—the combination Z-28 and Type LT—and reported on it in September. "With a pricetag that's actually decreased," the article began, "it's the blue chip investment in a world of inflation." True enough, the '73 was priced at $4067 compared to $4430 for a comparably equipped '71 due to the lifted excise tax (about $290) and inclusion of most of the goodies in the two major option groups. The rest, said the author, "you could consider a rebate from Chevrolet for the 30 horsepower drained during the past two years from under the hood." The engine was called "no more than a pale reminder of the vigor once behind every Z-28 badge. You should not revere it as the semi-racer power-plant it was in the high compression days of 1970. The solid lifter cam has left our midst for '73, as well as the Holley 4 bbl. carburetor and aluminum high-rise intake manifold. That lowers the power peak by 10 hp since last year, and the redline by 500 rpm."

Surprisingly, because the engine's greater low-end torque partially compensated for its lesser high-rpm power, *C and D* found the Z's quarter-mile performance little different from that of the first low compression Z-28's in 1971: 15.2 seconds at 95 mph. Zero-to-sixty acceleration was also respectable at 6.7 seconds, while observed top speed was 123 mph. "Where you lose out," said the author, "is in

'73 Camaro Rally Sport stands in foreground, with Z-28 at rear.

throttle response. The lightning-fast reflexes of the old Z-28 are but a memory. If you rudely mash the throttle these days, you'll very likely get an awkward stumble before the revs climb. Once you pass that transition, however, things are fine." Handling, despite a tire-related tendency to wander somewhat in a straight line, was also judged as excellent: "We found the steering to be quick enough that it's not necessary to change your hand position on the wheel during rapid maneuvers. And the Z-28's steering precision translates every minute correction at the wheel into a definitive action at the road, so you can guide the car exactly where you want it .... There is initial understeer built into the Camaro ... more than we like. But you can easily negate that tendency with the throttle."

On the negative side, *C and D* criticized the engine's intake noise through the "chrome-plated unsilenced air cleaner," the bias-belted 60-series Firestone tires, which were "so stiff that road irregularities caused the interior to creak in protest," and the small, hard-to-see gauges: "Each is but a tiny island in a vast sea of test-tube walnut. And as if that weren't enough, several gauges were cleverly positioned so that you need X-ray vision to take a reading—the Porsche-style four-spoke steering wheel stands rudely in your line of sight." But the magazine concluded that "the Z-28 is still a car with which you can have a passionate affair. Because few cars at any price offer the Camaro's refinement in going, stopping and turning abilities. And that refinement is housed in one of the most hand-somely chiseled forms ever to roll out of Detroit."

The much diminished Trans-Am road-racing series was revamped for '73, with Porsches, Corvettes and other sports cars competing with the ponycars under a new set of international rules similar to those of the successful IMSA (International Motor Sports Association) Camel GT series. There were only six events, of which Camaros won two, one each by Warren Agor and Mo Carter. Two went to Porsche Carreras (Peter Gregg and Milt Minter) and the final two to John Greenwood's killer Corvette. That gave the factory crown to Chevrolet with forty-two points to Porsche's thirty-seven.

The Camaro's marketplace comeback was gathering momentum as the '73 model year closed. Even after the Norwood plant strike had delayed production for several weeks, sales rose to 91,678 units—not great, but not that much worse than the 123,400 posted by Mustang in its last year before shrinking to Pinto size. Encouragingly, 11,575 of those Camaros—almost thirteen percent and about 9000 more than in '72—were Z-28's.

But the American auto industry was about to be dealt a vicious blow by a group of sheiks in the oil-rich Middle East.

CHAPTER SEVEN

Resurrection

The '74 Chevrolets were unveiled on September 20th, 1973 by a division flushed with confidence—some might have called it arrogance—after back-to-back record years. In danger of losing its industry leadership to a fast-rising Ford Division when John DeLorean had taken over in 1969, Chevrolet was now clearly in control. The dynamic but controversial DeLorean had been promoted to GM's Fourteenth Floor corporate management, and new general manager Jim McDonald was promising a third consecutive record "three million-plus sales" year. Little did he know that the course of world history was about to be altered dramatically and irrevocably by a crippling Arab oil embargo.

All '74 cars by law were equipped with one of Washington's lesser ideas, a seatbelt/ignition interlock system that prevented them from being started until front seat passengers had buckled up. There were additional safety, emissions and bumper requirements, along with added equipment, that increased weight and decreased fuel efficiency. For the first time cars destined for the crucial California market had fewer available engines and different tuning calibrations because of that state's tougher emissions standards. Otherwise, engineering improvements across the Chevy line included wear sensors and indicators for disc brake pads and front suspension ball joints, better batteries and redesigned air conditioning systems.

Camaro's spring-mounted aluminum bumpers and the facelift designed around them changed its front and rear appearance but didn't hurt its visual appeal—except for the wrap-around taillamps, which always seemed slightly crooked because they didn't quite fit their fender openings. The Rally Sport model was discontinued, but the Z-28 option remained, complete with a bold, triple-stripe design with huge "Z-28" graphics on hood and decklid. The bumpers,

Two-page '76 advertisement stressed the excitement of IROC contest and Camaro's history of beauty and performance.

designed with two inches of clearance so they could spring back after minor bumps with no damage to the body, had thick rubber impact strips for extra protection, and large steel-reinforced rubber vertical guards were optionally available. Although the system was twice the weight of the '73 bumpers, Chevy estimated that some fifty pounds had been saved by using aluminum face bars instead of steel. Round, RS-style park/signal lamps, like the headlamps, were recessed into "sugar scoop" bezels in the sloping nose outboard of the grille. The luxury LT model sported additional special trim and redesigned badges inside and out, plus standard steel-belted radial tires and new deep-contour bucket seats with ridge-textured fabric inserts.

Other changes and additions included a twenty-one-gallon fuel tank replacing the previous eighteen-gallon one for added range, standard power steering on all V-8 equipped cars, a positive connecting jack that locked into slots in the bumpers, relocation of the horn relay to the inside firewall to protect it from corrosion, a new spherical manual transmission gearshift knob, an optional AM/FM stereo radio and improved-design tailpipe hangers. Engine availability remained as before except that the 307 V-8 was dropped and a new California-spec, single-exhaust 4-bbl. 350 rated at 160 hp was added for cars headed there.

And then, on October 18th, 1973, came the Arab Oil Embargo. It changed the face of the world and the direction of the industry forever. In the short term, it caused gas shortages and long lines of panic-stricken drivers waiting for a few gallons of the suddenly precious stuff. Big cars grew cobwebs on dealer lots while smaller, more fuel-efficient ones, both foreign and domestic, sold out across the country. Plants producing cars and engines that were perceived as gas-guzzlers shut down, putting thousands of workers on the streets and plunging the country into a deep recession. Those few that built more fuel-thrifty American products struggled on overtime trying to meet demand. The domestic makers, sensing a long-term radical shift in consumer preference, labored mightily to squeeze more efficiency out of existing powertrains and to convert production capacity to smaller cars, simultaneously plunging themselves into multi-million-dollar downsizing and new-product programs.

Camaro, not especially fuel efficient but certainly smaller and easier on gas than most domestic products, thrived mightily through it all. The Norwood plant was churning out F-cars on three shifts, and plans were made to re-convert a second facility at Van Nuys, California—which had built F-cars between 1967 and 1971—to ponycar production.

Ironically, even while *Cars* magazine was presenting its "Top Per-

Benny Parsons   Brian Redman   James Hunt   Emerson Fittipaldi   Richard Petty Jody Scheckter A. J. Foyt Mario Andretti Bobby Allison Al Unser David Pearson   Bobby Unser
(not shown)

Gentlemen, start your Camaros.

third annual International Race of
pions is on.
e again, in four fascinating events
widely across the country and the
ar, 12 of the world's winningest
s are competing in 12 identical cars,

identically prepared. A true test of
driving skill.

The cars are Camaros.

That should come as no great surprise.
Camaro's aerodynamic shape makes it a
natural for these events. The profile is low,

the stance is wide, the size is right—and
the feel is terrific. Drivers enjoy driving
Camaros, people enjoy watching them.

Camaro has been a particularly popular
off-road competition car ever since it was
first introduced about 10 years ago.

Chevrolet salutes the 12 distinguished
drivers of the third International
Race of Champions.

Gentlemen, start
your Camaros.

WATCH FOR THE INTERNATIONAL RACE OF CHAMPIONS ON THE ABC TELEVISION NETWORK.

formance Car of the Year" award to the '74 Z-28 because, in the words of editor Fred Mackerodt, "we think it's the best performance package available on the market today," Camaro advertising was stressing more practical virtues. Under the umbrella theme "Chevrolet Makes Sense for America," mid-year magazine ads were trying to make the best of the federal 55 mph speed limit, which had been imposed in January as a "temporary" fuel-saving measure. "Camaro lets you limit your speed without cramping your style," said one. "Look and feel good at 55. . . . As long as you've got to go slower, you may as well do it in style." But another intended for sports and auto magazines showed both a base coupe and a fully decked-out Z-28. "With Camaro, you can be practical. Or go bananas," it said, trying to hit both ends of the sporty car market.

While some in the design studio were working on minor facelift ideas in the spring of 1974, others were charged with conceiving and modelling smaller-sized, sleekly aerodynamic sporty coupes just in case management suddenly decided to radically redesign the Camaro in a big hurry. There was also a sexy, performance-oriented clay model with glassed-in rectangular headlamps, soft front and rear end caps and aggressive looking wheel flares, which eventually evolved into the "Berlinetta" show car. Another project involved a functional racer-look Camaro for Roger Penske's televised International Race of Champions (IROC) series of challenge races that winter, replacing the Porsche Carreras that were used the year before.

Though the total of 135,780 Camaros sold (13,802 of them Z-28's)

CHEVROLET MAKES SENSE FOR AMERICA

EXAMPLE: CAMARO LETS YOU LIMIT YOUR SPEED WITHOUT CRAMPING YOUR STYLE.

Car enthusiasts used to say that a good-looking car "looks like it's moving even when it's standing still." Today's Camaro owners know all about that. They also know how well Camaro moves when it's moving. Because the way it looks is the way it goes.

LOOK AND FEEL GOOD AT 55.
Camaro is a car that's designed to be a joy to drive. The stance is wide and firm. The handling is smooth and stable because of the forward-mounted steering system, the sophisticated suspension and the wide-tread tires and wide-rim wheels. The front disc brakes resist fade, water, heat and dust. Even the sleek new front end incorporates a new improved bumper system.

AS GOOD-LOOKING INSIDE AS OUT.
Make yourself comfortable. Camaro gives you full-foam Strato-bucket seats and door-to-door cut pile carpeting. A soft-rim four-spoke steering wheel and floor-mounted shift add to Camaro's sporty good looks. Flow-through ventilation is standard. Inside the doors, there are steel guard rails.

Overhead, a dou[ble] panel steel roof.

PRICED LESS THAN $3000.
Sound like a lot of car? It is. Sound like a lot of money? It isn't. In fact, at $2889.70[*] the '74 Camaro 6 Sport Cou[pe] is the lowest priced car in its class.

Camaro is available in [6-] and 8-cylinder versions. Plu[s] there's the luxurious Type [LT] and the heavy-duty Z28.

Take the time to check [out] a new Camaro at your Che[vy] dealer's. As long as you've [got] to go slower, you may as w[ell] do it in style.

*Manufacturer's Suggested Retail Price, in[cludes] dealer new vehicle preparation charge. Destination charges, optional equipment, state or local taxes are additional.

Luxurious Type LT and Z-28 for '74, along with Z-28's 350 V-8, 4 bbl engine. Camaro ad of same year stresses timely "fun at 55 mph" theme.

in model year '74 was less than half of the 296,000 figure attained by Ford's conveniently-timed downsized Mustang, it was nearly twice the dismal '72 total and a substantial 44,000-unit improvement over '73. In a year when domestic sales in general had suffered badly, it was a creditable performance that more than vindicated those who had saved the car from extinction two years before.

On March 18th, 1974 the oil embargo had ended as suddenly as it had begun, and gas availability was more or less back to normal—though fuel prices had approximately doubled. Blessed with diehard automotive habits and short memories, the public already was switching back to the larger cars they knew and loved, while Washington was hatching a corporate average fuel economy (CAFE) law to force them into smaller ones like it or not, and Detroit was proceeding with the massive redesign programs to which they were irreversibly committed. The hated seatbelt/ignition interlock was gone, but the "temporary" national speed limit seemed here to stay. So, apparently, was the Camaro.

On September 14, two weeks before the '75 models were announced, the year's first International Race of Champions was run at Michigan International Speedway. A highly promoted, nationally televised series, IROC matched twelve of the world's best drivers in theoretically equal Camaros prepared by Penske Racing under retired supershoe Mark Donohue. In the first IROC the year before, the oval-track aces had fared poorly against the road racers in Porsche Carreras, but they took immediately to the more familiar-

feeling Camaros, with engines and transmissions similar to those in NASCAR stockers. A.J. Foyt, Johnny Rutherford and Bobby Unser represented the Indy drivers; Richard Petty, Bobby Allison, David Pearson and Cale Yarborough were there from NASCAR; and Ronnie Peterson, Emerson Fittipaldi, Graham Hill, Jody Scheckter and George Follmer were picked from the Formula One and GT road-racing ranks. Donohue had cleaned up against a similar selection of champions the year before, but the soundness of switching to specially prepared Camaros was proven when Indy pilot Bobby Unser won this first '74-'75 series event on the Michigan oval. The next two races were set for the Riverside, California road course, and the finale would run on the Daytona tri-oval in February.

Nineteen-seventy-five will go down in history—some say infamy—as the year of the catalytic converter. GM led the industry by opening a plant to manufacture its own and took the giant step of putting them on every one of its '75 products, and the chemical exhaust cleanser has been with us ever since. The principal advantage was that engines could then be calibrated on the "dirtier"—and therefore better running and more fuel efficient—side, and the converter would clean up carbon monoxide (CO) and hydrocarbon (HC) pollutants sufficiently to meet emissions standards. The disadvantages were that the catalyst materials were (and are) rare, expensive and quickly fouled by the lead additives used to raise the octane of gasoline.

This meant that buyers of converter-equipped cars were forever locked into low-octane unleaded fuel, which is more costly and less efficient to produce than leaded fuels. (To make it difficult to intentionally or inadvertently use leaded gas, EPA required manufacturers to put undersized fuel filler necks in all converter-equipped vehicles and fuel retailers to have corresponding small-diameter nozzles on unleaded pumps, and "unleaded fuel only" stickers were required on fuel gauges and filler doors.) Also, low compression engines designed to run on no-lead gas get less work per gallon than do high compression ones. The converters were only effective for 50,000 miles or so, and it was unlikely that car owners would spend the money to replace them unless forced.

The catalysts came as part of an "efficiency system" that also included an electronic "High Energy Ignition System" which was virtually maintenance free and gave a hotter, longer lasting spark; "Outside Air Carburetion" that drew cooler, denser air from outside the engine compartment; "Early Fuel Evaporation" to improve fuel vaporization during warm-up after a cold start; and easier rolling steel belted radial tires. Besides better driveability and some fuel economy improvement over '73-'74 models, there was an added

Above: new grille proposal for '76; proposed complete redesign for '76 in clay. Opposite: soft-bumpered Berlinetta previewed '78 look.

benefit of longer oil, oil filter, chassis lube and other service intervals. Thanks largely to the electronic ignition, the recommended spark plug replacement interval was extended to 22,500 miles from the previous 6000. Economy conscious buyers also could order special highway axle ratios and "Econominder" vacuum gauges to help them save fuel.

Bob Lund, who took over as Chevrolet general manager when McDonald was promoted in November 1974, called the extended service intervals "a giant step forward toward reaching our long-range goal of a 50,000-mile, no-routine maintenance vehicle" and estimated the resulting savings at "about $100 a year or as much as $1000 for the life of the car."

For Camaro in particular it was the year of the wrap-around rear window, which gave a ten percent increase in glass area and created "the illusion of an added triangular quarter window" when viewed from the side. There were also revised Camaro insignias and easier-to-see lettering on the washer/wiper switch. Further changes included a new "Sports Decor" package with sport mirrors and body-color vinyl appliqués on the lower bumpers and door handles; refinements to the six-cylinder engine and air conditioning available with it for the first time; finned aluminum rear brake drums for improved heat dissipation; and (unfortunately) a new single inlet, dual outlet muffler system on all V-8 cars to meet noise level laws in some states.

Early press-preview literature indicated that the Z-28 package was again available with either the standard or the LT model . . . but then it was discontinued at the last minute in the division's zeal to stress fuel economy and "sensible" cars and de-emphasize performance and any semblance of automotive fun. There was a weak explanation that the Z-28 had fallen victim to noise regulations, but it was more likely a casualty of ultra-conservative management thinking following the fuel crisis debacle, lackluster sales and the resulting national recession. Dropping the only Camaro image car would soon prove a major mistake because, as Pontiac's Trans-Am would demonstrate, there was still a market out there lusting for youthful, exciting, performance oriented automobiles even in a new age of lowered expectations. The Camaro's reputation and sales to youthful buyers both would suffer as a result.

Advertising, predictably, focused on the efficiency system and its many benefits—"Improved fuel economy. . . . Surer starting. . . . Faster warmups. . . . Better performance. . . . Fewer and simpler tune-ups. . . . More miles between oil changes and chassis lubes. . . . Cleaner air"—but failed to mention the unleaded gas requirement. The '75 catalog said much of the same, also emphasizing that

"Camaro is and always was a small car. . . . A sensible sporty compact car."

As for the highly visible and promotable IROC series, the world's best drivers might as well have been running in Checker cabs for all Chevrolet seemed to care. A deal had been made to supply the fifteen Camaros, but then Chevy seemed content with whatever exposure it got through normal media coverage. To management, the Camaro was merely a "sporty little compact," not a racer, and they didn't want to talk about performance in 1975. For the record, GP champion Emerson Fittipaldi and NASCAR ace Bobby Allison won the two fall Riverside road races, but Indy driver Bobby Unser took the February Daytona Finale and the '74-'75 IROC title, averaging 167.5 mph on the tri-oval superspeedway.

The spring introduction of a new Rally Sport model restored at least some visual excitement. Available in red, white, silver, yellow or bright blue with flat black grille, hood, roof, rocker panels and rear end panel, the package also included Rally wheels, dual sport mirrors and tri-color accent stripes with "Rally Sport" graphics. Front and rear spoilers, a "Gymkhana Sport Suspension" and special body-color fifteen inch mag-style wheels were available as options.

"The heavily rouged Rally Sport is only a halfhearted hint of the blood-bailing Z-28 of yore," said then-*Car and Driver* editor Stephan Wilkinson in an August 1975 report. "Yet . . . it is still a relatively honest, handsome car, and it's still a competent car. Not exhilarating, not pulse-pounding, not super bad, just 'competent'. . . . Even with the most basic, most easily understandable handling modifications, you or I could turn this stone into Mighty Joe

BIRD'S EYE VIEW OF THE '75 CHEVY — Since all Chevrolets for 1975 are being designed to use only unleaded fuels to improve their fuel economy and meet the very stringent 1975 auto emission standards, extreme precautions have taken by engineers to "fuel-proof" fuel tank intakes against being fed the wrong kind of gasoline that might harm some o emission system components. First (top left) there will be this warning . . . "Unleaded Fuel Only" . . . on the access door the fuel filler to emphasize that anything but unleaded fuel is harmful to the emission system. In addition, the new ty fuel filler neck (bottom left) will have built-in safeguards. The nozzle restrictor will accommodate only the smaller new nozzle which gasoline stations will be using to dispense unleaded fuel under federal regulations. There will also be a new of threaded fuel filler cap (top right) featuring a ratchet tightening device to reduce chances of its being improperly ins and allowing vapors to escape. Only when the cap is closed properly will its ratchet produce a loud clicking noise differences between new and old fuel tank filler openings and fuel filler nozzles are shown in sketches at lower right. The unleaded fuel filler nozzles are smaller in diameter. In the event an attempt is made to introduce the larger nozzle int new filler neck at left, it won't fit. If fuel flow is activated, the restrictor prevents insertion and the deflector cause automatic nozzle shut-off device to stop flow. All Chevrolets will use the new fuel tank that accepts only unleaded f 1975. This new three-point protection system, visual warning (on the instrument panel, filler door area and cap), screw-on fuel filler cap and nozzle restrictor/deflector will help assure that only unleaded fuel is used.

Young." Wilkinson pointed out that the Vega-based Monza 2+2 introduced in the fall of 1974 was a great thing for the Chevy ponycar because dealers had "watched many of the buyers that it attracted into their showrooms depart in Camaros. Bigger engine, slightly bigger interior and trunk, moderately better performance for approximately the same price." With the 155 hp 4-bbl. 350, automatic transmission and a 3.08:1 rear axle, the test car managed a fairly respectable 8.5 seconds 0-60, 16.8 seconds at 82 mph in the quarter mile and a top speed of 116 mph.

The Rally Sport that *Car and Driver* tested didn't have the F-41 Gymkhana suspension or the bigger tires and wheels, but its handling was plenty good "during moderately enthusiastic cornering or sharp transients from lane to lane. . . . When pushed to the limit on the skidpad, however, understeer arrives in embarrassing quantity: The Rally Sport limps around munching its outside front tire which folds under like a rubber eraser." Wilkinson added that the brakes were well-biased—didn't lock-up rear-first and cause sideways sliding in hard stops—but that they "fade rapidly and require surprisingly high pedal pressure." Though the Rally Sport was strictly a "decor exercise—Power by Paint," he felt that it was "reasonably tasteful," with "no signboards or extra emblems or bogus vents/scoops/spoilers." Like others, Wilkinson complained bitterly about the poor gauge visibility: "All four of the peripheral gauges on the panel, outboard of the tach and speedometer, are obscured either by the steering-wheel rim or one of its spokes." But he concluded that "the Camaro is such a strong combination of handling, style and simplicity that it'll probably be around for a long time to come."

In that same issue, Patrick Bedard reported on a very special Camaro prepared by racer/engineer Bill Mitchell (no relation to GM's styling vice president) by direction of Mark Donohue, who was then very much out of retirement and driving boss Penske's Formula One GP car. "A Camaro with track shoes," it was intended to be a road version of the mighty IROC racers that Donohue had engineered the year before. Besides the IROC-style cowcatcher front spoiler, with a driving lamp and a recessed fog lamp, the car had Michelin XWX tires (205/70 front, 215/70 rear) on Minilite racing-type aluminum wheels (7.0 inch front, 9.5 inch rear); stiffened suspension, lowered an inch in front and realigned for more front caster and negative camber; and a carburetor cold-air duct where the left-front park lamp used to be. There were also racing-style windshield clips and rear window straps; racing bucket seats and fat-rimmed steering wheel; even air horns, a European-type headlamp flasher, and a dashboard badge that read: "Camaro by Mark

NEW CAMARO RALLY SPORT.

"Unfair," cried the ordinary cars.

"All's fair in love and cars," retorted Chevrolet, trotting out a knockout new version of Camaro, which was already one of the better looking numbers on the block.

The Camaro Rally Sport is a bright new option package available on either the Sport Coupe or Type LT, in your choice of five colors: red, white, silver, yellow or bright blue metallic.

The hood, roof, grille, rocker panels and rear end panels are painted flat black, with distinctive tri-color stripes and Rally Sport I.D.

Rally wheels and dual sport mirrors are included in the package.

Available options (shown) include front and rear spoilers and special 15-inch body-color wheels with white-lettered tires. (The special wheels are available only with the Gymkhana Sport Suspension.)

If you think it looks

good here, wait until you see it in person.

Wait until you walk around it, sit in it, take it on the road.

But don't wait long. Production is limited, and we'd hate for you to miss out.

Now that makes sense
CHEVROLET MAKES SENSE FOR AMERICA.

Chevrolet

Donohue." Bedard called it "a Camaro that behaves like a Ferrari. . . . When you dial in a steering input, it doesn't wait around." Donohue said, "I want to do a limited number for people who will appreciate them." Depending on the equipment ordered, he planned to sell kits for $3000 or less and a few complete cars for about $9500.

The Camaro designers had been working on the next major facelift, scheduled for the '78 model year, since late 1974. Because the planned additional volume—the Van Nuys plant had resumed F-car production in 1975—justified the soft-ended approach to bumper laws, there was plenty of room for creativity both front and rear. Essentially the front designs kept the traditional Camaro flavor, with low, mouthy grilles, park/signal lamps that looked like driving lights and large single headlamps, most of which were rectangular since the law requiring round lamps was changed for '77. At least one quad-rectangular headlamp approach also was tried and rejected. In back, various full-width, tri-color, wrap-around taillamp treatments were explored. And full-scale drawings of both fastback and "formal" notchback rooflines were produced and evaluated, though neither was seriously considered.

Camaro sales for '75 at 135,102 (versus Mustang's 199,000) nearly duplicated the previous year's performance, despite still-depressed sales of new cars in general as the country struggled to throw off its post-fuel-crisis recession. It's likely that the total would have been better had the performance-oriented Z-28 not been dropped.

For '76 the Camaro bowed in with only minor changes, most necessary to meet the new year's safety and emissions standards or to improve fuel economy. Most significant was replacement of the previous 2-bbl. 350 with a new 2-bbl. 305 cubic-inch (5.0-liter) economy V-8 as standard equipment for all but the base car, which still carried the old 250 (4.1-liter) six. Brake performance was boosted with new front pad and rear lining materials and larger wheel

Page opposite: Rally Sport was revived as paint and trim package in early '75, adding life to a dull period; '75 Mark Donohue/Bill Mitchell modified Camaro with new rear window design. Above: '75 drawings and clay models for next facelift, now scheduled for '78; fastback and notchback ideas.

cylinders for the rears, and a power assist became standard with all V-8 engines. The four-speed manual transmission got a higher 2.85:1 first gear ratio, replacing the previous 2.54:1, and the optional air conditioning was improved with a new "Maximum" mode. In keeping with a "major objective" to "restrict appearance and product refinement changes to those with high perceived value," the only exterior changes were a new lower body molding for the standard car and a brushed aluminum applique between the LT's taillamps. The LT also got redesigned seat trim (again) and a leather-look instrument cluster replacing the previous fake wood. New on the option list were a half vinyl roof treatment covering just the front portion, cruise control and restyled custom wheels.

The catalog urged potential buyers to compare Camaro to economy imports and domestic subcompacts to learn that it represented "more car" at an attractive price with an "economical" six-cylinder standard engine. But—surprise!—Chevrolet had suddenly discovered the IROC racing series, as demonstrated by an impressive two-page color ad spread in January car-enthusiast magazines. "Gentlemen, start your Camaros" it trumpeted under a huge photo of the '75-'76 IROC drivers posing with one of the cars before a spectator-packed speedway grandstand. "Once again," said the copy, "twelve of the world's winningest drivers are competing in twelve identical cars . . . . The cars are Camaros. That should come as no great surprise. Camaro's aerodynamic shape makes it a natural

for these events. The profile is low, the stance is wide, the size is right—and the feel is terrific. Drivers enjoy driving Camaros, people enjoy watching them. Camaro has been a particularly popular off-road competition car ever since it was first introduced about ten years ago." The drivers were: Brian Redman, James Hunt, Emerson Fittipaldi, and Jody Scheckter from international road racing; A.J. Foyt, Mario Andretti, Al Unser and Bobby Unser from USAC Indy cars; and Benny Parsons, Richard Petty, Bobby Allison and David Pearson from NASCAR stock cars.

In retrospect, Chevrolet general manager Bob Lund acknowledges the value of promoting the IROC cars as Camaro image boosters after the post-fuel-crisis doldrums, when American cars and the way they were marketed grew equally boring. "The IROC series provided us with a tremendous impact," he says, "because the public saw those cars on television, and it was an exciting kind of thing. Not only the television but the actual attendance at the races was fantastic, and the people who went out there to watch those rascals run were dyed-in-the-wool fans and supporters of the cars. The drivers loved the cars, we loved the races, and the public loved the races. It did a hell of a job for us." Asked whether he agrees, then, that de-emphasizing Camaro's youthful, fun and performance aspects for two years was a mistake or an overreaction, Lund says: "No, I wouldn't say so. Everything is a product of the times. I think the times kind of demanded, cried for, that de-emphasis, and I think we did the right

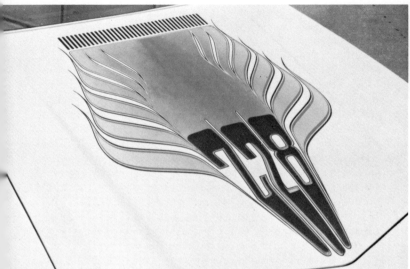

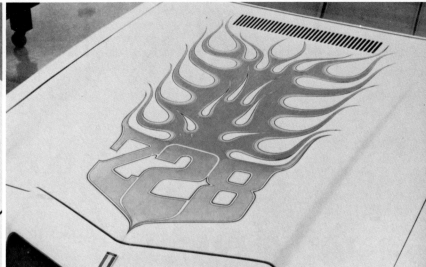

Two views of '76 Type LT Sport Coupe, and the search for a hairy-looking hood decal design to compete with Trans-Am's "Screaming Chicken."

thing at the time. But maybe we shouldn't have stayed out of it so damned long."

Plans were underway at Chevrolet to revive the Z-28, since Pontiac's Trans-Am, the only real performance car left, was enjoying tremendous success (half of all Firebirds sold in 1976 were Trans-Ams) and the performance look, if not the reality, was getting a rebirth in such stripe-and-spoiler cars as Ford's Mustang Cobra II, Chrysler's Plymouth Volare Road Runner and American Motors' Hornet AMX. Development engineer Jack Turner, under new Camaro chief engineer Tom Zimmer, was working out a super handling package while the Camaro designers, now under studio chief Jerry Palmer, were evaluating various visual treatments worthy of going head-to-head with the Trans-Am. At the same time they were working on a slightly smaller third generation Camaro, then scheduled for the '80 model year. Several sleek concept drawings and scale models were produced in early 1976, most of them low-nosed, aerodynamic fastbacks with low beltlines, rounded, sweeping fender shapes and molded-in chin and tail spoilers. The most promising of these became a beautiful clay model with "Camaro Super Spyder" graphics and was viewed and photographed on the GM Design Center viewing court in late May.

It was a good year for Camaro, the best since 1969, with sales of 163,653 versus 179,000 for the smaller Mustang. Clearly the Chevrolet ponycar was on its way up again and its arch rival sliding

137

downward, though Mustang had enjoyed a boost from surprising acceptance of the paper-tiger Cobra II among excitement-starved buyers. There was even a victory by Camaro driver Joe Chamberlain on the 1976 Trans-Am racing circuit, a series now largely dominated by smaller and more agile Porsches and the occasional good Corvette.

The most exciting Camaro news at the '77 model introduction were three new colors for the Rally Sport paint-and-trim package: medium gray, dark blue metallic, and buckskin metallic. As in '76 only three engines were available—4.1 liter (250) six, 5.0 liter (305) V-8, and 5.7 liter (350) V-8—but now the six came standard in all Camaros, not just the base car. Also, the V-8/automatic axle ratio was reduced from 2.73 to 2.56:1 as Chevy engineers strained to squeeze out a few more drops of fuel economy. Horsepower ratings actually went up for 49-state engines: from 105 to 110 for the six, 140 to 145 for the small V-8, 165 to 170 for the 350. But they went down for the same engines certified for California, to a sickly 90, 135 and 160, respectively. Also, all California Camaros were automatic-only; now enthusiasts in that state would really begin to feel the sting of its much tougher emissions standards. Both three-speed and four-speed manual shift linkages were redesigned for smoother shifting action and easier service adjustment, and the reverse slot was relocated from upper left to lower left because it was easier to move it that way after lifting to disengage the four-speed's reverse inhibitor. Finally, the Space-Saver spare tire inflator was changed from the freon-type to a new, refillable carbon dioxide unit, which also gave double the inflation pressure in sub-zero temperatures.

The reborn Z-28 wasn't quite ready for the fall 1976 introduction, but those who attended the Riverside, California IROC races in the fall couldn't help noticing large and very obvious "Z-28 Camaro" lettering on the cars. You didn't have to be a genius to figure out what Chevy had up its sleeve. Another promising sign was that Camaro advertising and the '77 catalog were emphasizing driving pleasure again. "We're looking for people who love to drive" headlined the October print ad, which ran in both enthusiast and general interest magazines. For some people, said the copy, "driving an automobile is about as exhilarating as riding an escalator." But not, it pointed out, for Camaro drivers. "It's definitely a driver's car. It sits low and stands wide and moves like it really means it. Camaro is quick, quiet, tight and tough. All of which translates to a very special 'feel.' The spirit of Camaro. The lift the car can give you, even just driving to work . . . . Driving gloves are optional."

Star of the Chevrolet section at the January 1977 Detroit auto

show was a sexy Camaro show car called "Berlinetta," the first such styling exercise for public display in years. Little changed since it was first photographed as a concept in clay in 1974, it sported "bumperless" soft front and rear ends; upper and lower eggcrate grilles; recessed, glass-covered rectangular headlamps; and flared fenders with an integral front spoiler. Like the many "dream cars" of earlier days, it was heavily pinstriped (in gold) on the outside and highly polished and engine-turned in the cockpit. On its hood were racing-style hold-down pins, twin instrument nacelles and a raised center section with "ZL-1 Can-Am" identification. Under it was a real, live, ZL-1 427 engine like those favored in unlimited SCCA Can-Am sports car road racing. Why did Chevrolet suddenly decide to revive the idea car concept? *Automotive News* on January 3rd ran sneak previews of the coming '78 facelifted Camaro . . . and guess what? Except for the park/signal lamps and round headlamps instead of rectangular, its front end looked a whole lot like the Berlinetta. It was the old trick of previewing next year's styling on this year's show car; and it did draw renewed attention to the Camaro and what still could be done to freshen its now seven-year-old body. It also previewed a new nameplate that would adorn a production Camaro model beginning in '79.

Then on January 14th came the announcement that so many of the country's car enthusiasts had been waiting for. "A new Camaro Z-28 model," said the press release, "combining a jaunty look with special sport driving equipment, will be introduced . . . marking the return of the sportster made famous on road and track since the Camaro's debut ten years ago." Fittingly, there would be a Daytona Speedway press breakfast to debut the car just before the February IROC finale, and another a week later at the Chicago Auto Show.

Early on the morning of February 18th, 1977, in the Goodyear tower on the fourth turn of the world-famous Daytona International Speedway, Chevy general manager Bob Lund welcomed the assembled press, introduced Camaro chief engineer Tom Zimmer and development engineer Jack Turner, made a few opening remarks, and then began his pitch:

> We discontinued the Z-28 in 1974 because our engineers had maintained all along that the car had to be very special. It had to have *substantially* better performance than our standard Camaro or we wouldn't keep it on the market. We reached that point in 1974 when, due to regulatory pressures, we were unable to satisfy those objectives.
>
> But within a year, demand for the Camaro increased

Above: Mo Carter's IMSA Camaro at Mid-Ohio in August 1975. Below, left: two January '76 design concepts for Camaro planned for '80. Bottom left and right: handsome scale model proposals for '80 in March-April 1976 had aerodynamic noses, low beltlines and rounded fenders.

April 1976 clay developed from one of scale models featured molded-in spoilers and Super Spyder graphics; lovely Berlinetta anticipated '78.

greatly, and the market began to return to the more limited specialty vehicle market. The decision to reactivate the Z-28 became obvious months ago, when Camaro enthusiasts simply demanded we bring the car back.

Using certifiable, numerically high axle ratios and performance transmissions, with dual exhaust outlets, we managed to achieve more efficient power output from our 350 cubic-inch V-8 engine. But then, more efficient performance alone does not make the Z-28 what it is.

Our engineers could have pulled the same special suspension parts off the shelf from 1974, because the standard suspension and body for the Camaro are still similar. But they didn't. They wanted to apply Chevrolet's latest state-of-the-art in vehicle dynamics. The result is a better balanced suspension, a much more refined Z-28.

The new Z-28 suspension doesn't know speed. By that I mean our engineers have given us a car that handles equally well in either low or high speed ranges, making it both predictable and responsive at all times, and over all types of road surface. We firmly believe the Z-28 may well prove to be the best handling production vehicle ever built, and that it will set a new standard for production cars of the future.

Refined shock absorbers, rather than the traditional heavy-duty type, help maintain wheel control on hard, rough corners. This, combined with higher spring rates, helps to minimize driver bounce and fatigue usually associated with sporty-type vehicles, particularly on long freeway trips. In short, it's a driver's car. We haven't compared it to all of the foreign cars in detail, but we have no reason to believe there is a better handling vehicle anywhere!

The Camaro Z-28 is intended for the macho

Return of the Z-28 in mid-'77: Tom Zimmer, who became Camaro chief engineer in late '76, stands with car and special parts; new 350 engine.

enthusiast. Today the enthusiast wants a special breed of aspiration car. He wants a car with functional sophistication and with finesse. He wants his car to be aggressive, quick, agile, and dependable. He is very critical, and we welcome his appraisal of the Z-28.

Lund said he expected '77 Camaro production to top 200,000 units, and that 20-25,000 of those would be Z-28's despite the late introduction; he added that production could be adjusted upward if demand was higher. He pointed out that Camaro buyers at the time averaged $21,200 in annual income and 27.2 years of age, that 58.2 percent were single and 66 percent male—a perfect market profile toward which to re-launch the Z-28. Counting the Corvette and the Monza Spider, he promised that Chevrolet would be producing 85,000 to 90,000 "specialty" cars a year and would continue to lead and dominate the specialty-car market. Then he invited the press to drive some new Z-28's on Daytona's infield road course.

Four years later, as this book was being written, he viewed the rebirth this way: "It was just that we felt we had developed something that was extremely popular at one time in the history of the car, and we had dropped it. Pontiac had come in with their Trans-Am and were eating our lunch. We determined that, by God, that had to stop. So we resurrected the Z-28, which was a household word, so to speak, a byword with the kids. If you had a Z, you were right on top of things. So we brought it back in, and it did help us a lot."

Though the new engine was rated identically to the everyday 350 available in any Camaro—170 hp at 3800 rpm, 160 hp in California—its less restrictive exhaust system and other small refinements (which didn't require an expensive EPA emissions recertification), plus the numerically higher axle ratios it drove through, gave it noticeably better performance. Except in California, the standard drivetrain was a heavy-duty Borg Warner four-speed with a 2.64:1 first gear, coupled to an 11-inch high capacity clutch and a 3.73:1 rear axle. A Turbo Hydra-matic (recalibrated for full-throttle shifts at a high 4900 rpm) with a 3.42:1 axle was optional. Exhaust from both cylinder banks was piped through a single large catalytic converter, then split into dual pipes with only small resonators, no mufflers. This gave a lovely, mellow sound and, said Chevy, forty percent less backpressure than the stock system at 4000 rpm. EPA fuel economy ratings, newly required on every car's factory price sticker, were 14 city, 18 highway with the 49-state four-speed and 15 city, 20 highway with the automatic.

As Lund has said, the suspension was not off-the-shelf F-41 but a specially developed system of front and rear stabilizer bars, spring

rates, shock valving, bushings, grommets and rear spring shackles, all tuned to the car's substantial GR70-15 steel belted radials and unique to the Z-28. The steering ratio was reduced from 16:1 to 14:1 for higher effort and more precise road feel. Available with seven exterior colors, the tasteful visual package included body colored wheels, spoilers, mirrors, and bumpers; blacked-out grille, rear end panel, head and taillamp bezels, rocker panels, moldings and license plate opening; a NACA duct-shaped hood decal; wheelhouse and rocker panel accent stripes; and various Z-28 decals and emblems. Inside were a full complement of instruments, a Z-28 steering hub insert and a specific shift knob on a new Inland shifter. Production of

the reborn Z-28 began on February 1st, 1977. Its first public showing was at the late-February Chicago Auto Show, and its retail price was $5,170.60.

"The Z-28—The Camaro's Camaro," said the ad that ran in the March, April and May magazines. "You remember this car. Low and lean. Born to run. It's back. The Z-28." After listing the appearance and performance equipment, it concluded: "Z-28. We won't build many. So, if you want to move 'Z' style, you better get moving."

Hot Rod ran a "Resurrection of Z" story in April under the subhead: " 'The best Chevrolet ever built,'—the Z-28 Camaro—is back, 143

stronger, quicker and faster than when it left in 1974, with 15-second, 90-mph quarter-miles and handling that borders on the incredible!" Author Jim McCraw observed that the new engine "flat ran out of power and rpm at 5000," yet still produced the "quickest and fastest stock-vehicle quarter-mile times we've seen around here in years, the four-speed car hitting 15.35 at 91 mph after a handful of quarter-mile break-ins!" Top speed was 110 mph. While these numbers would have been scoffed at just a few years earlier, they were downright impressive for smog-controlled, economy-engineered 1977. "This engine is definitely *not* the original 302, nor is it the LT-1 350, but it sounds terrific, it's a lot stingier with gasoline than either of the aforementioned powerplants, and it's cleaner and easier on the atmosphere."

McCraw complimented the four-speed shifter and the brakes, then moved into his handling evaluation: "We're here to tell you that the car is a complete ball to drive . . . unbelievably well-balanced, flat, and almost completely neutral. During off-road 105-mph lane changes . . . the feeling was that every single component in the steering and suspension was united and cohesive in responding to steering inputs. Everything happens right now, and only to the extent of inputs. Nothing more and nothing less. Steering feel in the wheel and the seat of the pants is excellent, and overall the feeling of this new Z-28 is one of lightness and extreme agility. . . . The group of engineers and designers that brought the Z-28 out of the ashes stronger than it has been in years is to be congratulated. They have done a terrific job."

Car and Driver countered with an April Z-28/Trans-Am comparison test. After driving the new Z at the Arizona GM Proving Ground, the author tried it on a "bumpy, twisting mountain road," and was duly impressed. "There the Camaro revealed itself as a road machine of the first rank. Its 350 V-8 . . . sang that special, keening song that issues only from good Chevy small-blocks, while the Z-28 blitzed up the canyons and charged over the arroyos. It was as close to being a neutral steerer as any car with a heavy iron engine tucked up front probably can be and could be easily kicked into more gentle oversteer/understeer conditions by easy application of the throttle or brake." On the skidpad it lost to the more stiffly-sprung Trans-Am .74g to .80, but it beat the 400 cubic-inch, 200 hp Pontiac in straight-line acceleration—8.6 seconds 0-60 to the T/A's 9.3, and 16.3 seconds at 83 mph in the quarter (much slower than *Hot Rod's* car) to 16.9 seconds at 82 mph. "Limited by the redline and the 3.73 rear axle," however, its top speed was a mere 105 mph versus the 3.23-axled T/A's 110.

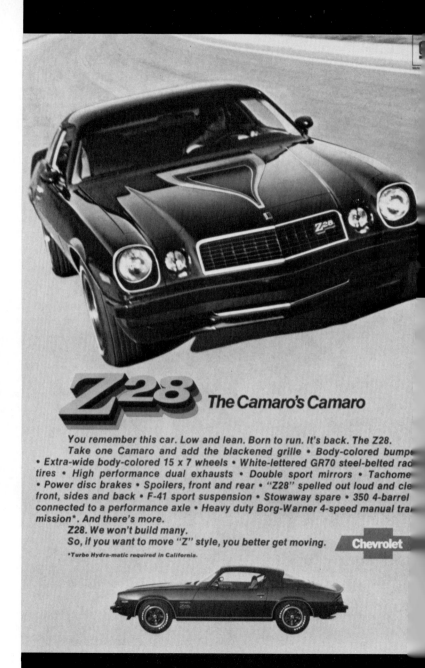

Advertisement heralding the return of the Z-28 in 1977. 1978 Indianapolis 500 "Official Car," a Z-28, on paper and in the flesh in October 1977.

In June, *Motor Trend's* Bob Hall reported 8.0-second 0-60's and 15.4-second, 90 mph quarter-miles from an automatic-equipped Z-28—indicating either that *C and D's* car was unusually slow, or that his and *HR's* were atypically fast. As quick as the car was, though, he said that "its most outstanding characteristic is its handling." He found it "nothing short of incredible," the "best-handling American production car I have ever driven." Hall liked the leather-look instrument panel, calling it "better than fake wood," but voiced the usual complaints about rear seat room, ashtray location and the "crude," two-position "semi-reclining driver's seat." Then he concluded that the reborn Z-28 "lives up to the name of its predecessors, and that is something that the new generation of AMX's, Road Runners and Cobras would be hard-pressed to do."

Road Test's Don Fuller waxed poetic about the new Z in a May driving impression: "I have driven few cars, *damned* few, which are this good. . . . The spring rates, shock absorber valving and power steering all combine to give this car the best subjective feel of any American car I have driven. . . . It has excellent directional stability on the straight and is easily controlled in the corners. . . . The ride is a little firm, but firm in a way that imparts confidence, not in a way that makes it embarrassing to take your mother to dinner in it." Then he came back with a full road test in June, calling the Camaro "the most beautiful shape to emerge from Detroit in a decade" and raving about the handling: "What sets the Z-28 apart from all the rest . . . is that it flat *works*. . . . [It] goes around corners so hard it'll make your ears bleed. . . . You can hang the car right out, and no matter what you do, there'll be no surprises. . . . The cornering attitude is very flat, with very little body lean."

RT's Larry Griffin, after driving one to California from the Daytona press preview, added in a sidebar: "The Z-28 is an excellent GT car. It eats up the miles effortlessly, swallowing great gobs of landscape at a single sitting, a sitting which is also effortless because the seats are such an improvement over previous Camaro designs." Performance figures were 8.0 seconds 0-60, 16.3 seconds at 85 mph in the quarter and 115 mph top speed.

Mark Donohue was tragically killed in a racing practice accident in 1975, but his friend and partner, Bill Mitchell, continued to build and sell very special "Concept Camaros." *Road and Track's* John Lamm drove a '77 Mitchell Camaro on the Lime Rock, Connecticut road course and reported on it in September: "Just the sort of subtle, honest machine that appeals to us. . . . Mitchell rebalances the car to what he believes is the more logical situation for a driver's car: driver only and no luggage. That means working around the car wheel-by-wheel to make sure both front tires support the same weight, and the rears do likewise with the new weight distribution. . . . The ride has not deteriorated appreciably and certainly not to the vision-blurring level of high-performance ponycars. . . . [The] front end bites much better than you'd expect. . . . [It] still has some understeer and prefers to be thrown about in hard corners, but does it with a surprising amount of grace." This latest version wore a slightly toned-down front spoiler and French Kleber GTS radial tires (195/60-14 front, 205/70-14 rear) on Minilite alloy racing wheels.

It was in 1977, a decade after it was introduced, that Chevy's Camaro at last overtook Ford's Mustang in sales—198,755 to 161,-654. Of those, 14,347 were Z-28's, marking the beginning of a big comeback for the performance-image Camaro.

145

CHAPTER EIGHT

Pressing Forward

It was 1978 that brought the third and final facelift to the now eight-year-old body—with the soft, body-colored nose and tail sections at last. The "sugar scoop" front lamp bezels remained, but the grille was now split above and below a rubber-covered bumper whose function was ingeniously disguised. Wide, tri-colored taillamps above a similarly hidden rear bumper made a tremendous improvement at the back. There were now five distinct models: sport coupe, Type LT, Rally Sport, Rally Sport LT and Z-28, the latter getting a fake NACA-duct hood scoop (replacing the '77's decal), real front fender louvers and a new stripe design. New options included a "T-bar" hatch roof with tinted glass lift-out panels, new-design aluminum wheels and an LT interior for the Z-28.

The 4.1-liter six with three-speed manual remained standard, but the 5.0-liter V-8 got an aluminum intake manifold and now came with the four-speed and a 3.08:1 axle ratio. Compression of the Z-28 engine was down slightly, from 8.5 to 8.2:1, but rated horsepower was up from 170 to 185 thanks to a year of diligent development. There was still no manual transmission available in California, and only the two 5.7-liter V-8's with automatic were certified for high-altitude emissions standards. The six-cylinder benefitted from addition of the V-8's electronic ignition and a better-isolated exhaust system, and the evaporative emissions system on all cars improved to collect and re-use fuel vapors from the carburetor as well as the fuel tank. A combination of added front frame reinforcements and redesigned rear spring shackles improved torsional rigidity and rear axle control for better handling. Finally, a charcoal filter was added to the power brake booster vacuum line to absorb corrosive gas fumes, and a nylon brake pressure differential switch replaced the former steel unit for corrosion resistance and a better fuel seal.

Berlinetta Coupe debuts in '79, joining Camaro lineup of Z-28 Sport Coupe, Rally Sport Coupe and Sport Coupe.

The '78 catalog featured a bright yellow Z-28 on its cover. "It'll put butterflies in your stomach, a lump in your throat and a smile on your face," went the pitch. "It's exciting, it's virile, it's a legend. Owning and driving a Z-28 is a rare experience enjoyed most by those who enjoy driving the most." About the Rally Sport, it said: "Driving excitement and then some. Camaro is our way of helping you escape from what too often becomes the routine task of driving." And the LT: "If you think a real car has to look austere, look again." One print ad showed a Z-28 above smaller pictures of its engine, dual exhausts, instrument panel and four-speed shifter, and referred to the car as "His majesty." Another ad used a long-lens frontal shot of a gaggle of IROC racers at speed and Al Unser, that year's series winner, posing with the car that bore his name. "Twelve Champions. Twelve Camaros. Two Winners," it announced. "In four different races a dozen Camaros were pushed to their limit by a dozen men. . . . The winners? Al Unser and Camaro."

"Ladies and gentlemen, let's have a big hand for the car that came back," began a March 1978 *Car and Driver* Z-28 road test, in which engineering editor Don Sherman found much to praise and little to criticize. "This package delivered not only third gear rubber on demand," he enthused, "but also a neat, clean 0-60 time of 7.3 seconds. We found a sixteen-flat quarter-mile ET and enough energy to push it all the way up to 123 mph." He also expressed "general appreciation for one of the few surviving four-speeders in all the land. The ratios are spot-on, there is sparkle to the torque curve and a throaty rumble from the pipes." In the negative column were the Z's rough-pavement ride and more docile at-the-limit cornering power than he felt it should have, and there was some staff disagreement about the abrasive "string-wrapped" steering wheel. "My personal conclusion about the Camaro's handling," he explained, "is that it's perfect for novice Nuvolaris. You can pitch it around and hunt for the apex with ham-hands and club-feet and the worst this car will do is understeer. The best it will do is get you around smoothly and quickly within an 0.77 *g* limit. As a learner's GT, the Z-28 is ideal." In conclusion, Sherman called the Z "practically *the* charter member of America's performance hall of fame. . . . Nineteen seventy-eight brings the best rounded Z-28 ever. The knife edge of acceleration and handling is blunted, but ride, styling and interior comfort are all honed to a new brilliance."

Though Corvette, celebrating its twenty-fifth anniversary, was chosen as the 1978 Indianapolis 500 pace car, some forty-nine specially decked out Z-28's participated as "Official" cars for loan to the race queen, selected press representatives and various VIP's.

Restyled '78 Camaro sported new front and rear. Fresh appearance included body-colored front and rear bumper systems of closed cell plastic.

Rumors flew in the spring that the F-cars (Camaro and Firebird) might be discontinued in '82 or '83 because GM would have too many cars in their general size class by then, and that Chevy was preparing a "Z-29" with stiffer suspension, bigger wheels and tires and possibly a turbocharged engine to compete with Pontiac's more powerful and harder-cornering Trans-Am. It's likely that both possibilities were discussed at one time or another, but neither materialized.

Concept Camaro magic man Bill Mitchell already had been thinking "turbo," and he added a $3000 turbocharging package to his available modifications in 1978. "Mitchell has unleashed his most potent, most well-developed car yet," said writer Glenn Howell in an April 14th *Autoweek* report. "When you climb on it, there's just a nice, gentle thrust that pushes you further and further back in your seat—somewhat the same sensation as taking off in an airliner. . . . Here's a car that seems guided down the road by some invisible force, corners like a go-kart, and gives every sensory cell and neuron in your body a thorough workout." By then Mitchell had become the country's best known builder of custom-modified Chevrolets and was laboring under a backlog of work. Some customers delivered their cars to him for transformation, while others ordered new cars either directly through him or through their own dealers with drop-shipment to his Cheshire, Connecticut shop.

The two-millionth Camaro, a gold sport coupe, was driven off the Van Nuys, California assembly line at 10:15 a.m. on May 11th, 1978

by Chevrolet general manager and GM vice president Bob Lund. "Camaro has consistently been one of the most popular selling sport coupes in the industry," he said on that occasion. "This year's sales are running twenty-seven percent ahead of a year ago nationally, and here in California, sales are up thirty-four percent. Camaro offers a rare combination of value and economy in a car that looks distinctive and is fun to drive." The Norwood, Ohio plant had turned out the first Camaro on August 11th, 1966 and over a million and a half since. Van Nuys had come on-stream in 1967 but had not produced Camaros during the slow sales years between 1971 and 1976.

A new sales record was set in 1978—247,437 cars versus Mustang's 179,039—and a stunning 54,907 of them were Z-28's. By now Camaro also had become one of the most popular U.S. cars in Europe and *the* top American import in West Germany, where one newspaper called it "a lot of car for the money."

There wasn't much new for 1979—why change when you're on a "roll"?—except a new luxury "Berlinetta" model replacing the Type LT, a restyled instrument panel and the usual powertrain revisions and minor engineering improvements. There were a lower (2.56:1) axle ratio with the base six-cylinder, a new "dualjet" carburetor for the 5.0-liter V-8, a semi-flexible plastic front air dam—with extensions that wrapped around to the front wheelhouses—and a redesigned striping scheme for the Z-28. All cars got an improved anti-theft steering column lock and a new exhaust gas recirculation (EGR) and "cold trapped vacuum spark" system for better

Promotional photos and "His Majesty" ad herald arrival of '78 Z-28.

driveability and fuel economy at 1979 emissions levels. New options included an electric rear window defogger, a power antenna and four different stereo entertainment systems.

Also shown at the September 21st press briefing was a very special Camaro, not so much a show car—though it did have a functional cold-air hood scoop, special front spoiler, rear fender flares and Goodyear racing tires on nine-inch-wide wheels—but a development vehicle. Under its hood was an all-aluminum, 10:1 compression, solid-lifter 5.7-liter (350) engine with a special Holley 650 4-bbl. carburetor and aluminized 1⅝ inch exhaust headers. The rumored Z-29? No, just a working platform for the experimental aluminum block, which was "being evaluated for eventual sale to off-road enthusiasts over parts counters of Chevrolet dealers nationally." In other words, a special lightweight racing block for the Can-Am sports car series, and future Indy, sprint, stock, drag cars—whoever wanted and could use it. And maybe a possibility for the smaller, lighter third-generation Camaro now scheduled for '82.

Print ads for 1979 stressed the Berlinetta: "The new Camaro"; "A new way to take your pulse . . . a superb balance between the qualities of a sporty road car and the comfort of a fine touring car." And a Z-28 pitch again used the racy IROC theme as a backdrop for espousing the car's performance-oriented virtues.

Speaking of IROC cars, *Road & Track* tested one for its October 1978 issue. The original stock-based Camaros had been used for three seasons and then sold to amateur and professional road racers;

the latest examples were really little related to a Camaro beyond their engines, transmissions and brightly painted skins. Like many circle-track stock cars, they were built ground-up by the Arden, North Carolina Banjo Mathews shop as balls-out, tube-frame racers. Powered by a 450-hp 350 cubic-inch Traco Chevy, the test car shot to 60 mph in 5.2 seconds, to 100 in 11.0 seconds, and topped out at 152 mph with its 3.91:1 road racing gearing. Though no drag racer, it also turned an impressive 13.3 second quarter-mile at 110.5 mph. It handled, as expected, "like a racer," with heavy steering and mild understeer "until more power was applied. Then the rear end would break loose, but not uncontrollably." The article concluded on a philosophical note: "A few years ago it was rumored that the Camaro would be dropped from the Chevrolet lineup. Customer demand turned the company's head around. Watching those dozen champions battling it out in the race-prepared version leads us to believe that Roger Penske and the International Race of Champions had a lot to do with it."

Another Bill Mitchell Camaro was tested in the November 1978 *Car and Driver*, this one a $15,000 full-house turbocharged job. "The steering response is instantaneous," said author Rich Ceppos, "and the nose whips in toward the apex like a Porsche. Every movement of the steering wheel produces a change in direction; unlike a production car, there is no softness or play anywhere in the steering system. . . . The concept Camaro is the archetype smooth-road screamer. You can blaze along smooth, winding country roads and scorch around onramps, the body staying as level as the horizon.

There is 0.81 *g* of cornering force at your disposal, and mild, controllable understeer is the limiting factor. But if you want to be a wild and crazy kind of guy, a twitch of the wheel and a hard push on the throttle will send you broadsliding like a Saturday-night sprint car." On the other hand, Ceppos pointed out that the car's shortened front springs and super-low Pirelli P7 tires gave away too much ride travel and left the front so low it endangered the car's vital parts; on rough roads it was pretty bad. The turbo motor accelerated it to 60 mph in just 6.3 seconds and through the quarter in 15.0 seconds at 98.9 mph, but there were occasional fuel starvation problems and a tendency toward overheating when driven hard due to insufficient cooling capacity.

The February 1979 *Madison Avenue Magazine* ran an interview of Dr. Thomas Staudt, Chevrolet's marketing director. His comments on the Camaro: "It's clean, handsome and aerodynamically sound, the kind of car that gives you relief from the cares of the world, that frees you from the bounds of your environment. Today, even with all the new entries, it's still one of the hottest cars in Europe." Staudt predicted a best-ever 280,000 sales year for Camaro as well as a record year for the industry as a whole.

And almost no sooner had those words been printed than the small, oil producing country of Iran erupted in revolution and its Shah, a friend of the West, fled for his life. That touched off an overreaction in America's media and, either by coincidence or by someone's design, gasoline shortages appeared almost overnight in such highly visible places as California, New York and Washington.

Opposite (far left): '78 Bill Mitchell turbocharged Camaro and two views of another Mitchell Camaro. Above (right): '79 Rally Sport has "T" top; (below): luxury '79 Berlinetta, with and without "T" roof.

Suddenly it was 1973 all over again. So much for the record year.

But no one then could have known the extent or duration of Fuel Crisis II or the disastrous effect it would have on America's auto industry. For a while, it was pretty much business as usual as the Camaro designers and engineers fine-tuned their '82 third-generation cars and tried to maintain interest in the aging current product. A "Turbo Z" was styled and was seriously considered for a time to counter Pontiac's coming Turbo Trans-Am. A Society of Plastics Engineers award was accepted for the innovative use of chrome plated flexible plastic in the Berlinetta's grille, achieved by a new process called "sputtering" that involved bombarding the part with tiny metal particles inside a vacuum and then coating it with a special clear urethane.

The June 1979 *Popular Mechanics* ran an owners' report on both Camaro and Firebird, in which the GM ponycars scored exceptionally well. Almost three-quarters of the Camaro owners who responded said they had bought the car for its styling, and the same number listed handling as its best attribute. Two-thirds rated their cars' workmanship as good to excellent, nearly sixty percent said they had experienced no mechanical troubles and twenty percent had no complaints whatsoever. Comments included: "Closest thing to a Corvette without the awesome price," "absolutely fun to drive . . . draws girls like a magnet," "last of the factory hot rods," and "sports car handling." Some complained of poor color matches between metal and plastic or rubber parts, or of decals that were beginning to peel off. There also were the usual gripes about poor rear seat and

151

trunk room, though most admitted they had known of such things before buying. "The Camaro has character," one respondent summed up. "It's not like every other car you see on the road. Combine that with excellent roadability, handling, styling, response, value and dependability and you've got one of the best designed U.S.-made cars today." More importantly, more than three-fourths said they would buy another Camaro.

Car and Driver's Rich Ceppos reviewed a new Berlinetta in a September "Short Take" article, wondering about the use of a name that "has graced some of the finest Grand Touring bluebloods Italy ever produced." But he concluded that the luxury Camaro was indeed "a Grand Touring car—albeit one aimed at speed-limited America rather than autostrada-laced Italy." "Above all," he said, "it's a velvety-smooth and soothingly quiet Interstate cocoon." He called its design "a shape that seems to get more attractive as the rest of the automotive world gets boxier."

Camaro sales dipped slightly to 233,802 for model year '79, not a bad performance in light of a buying public that was moving rapidly toward smaller, more fuel efficient models and disastrous U.S. new-car sales in general. Once again most American cars, perceived as gas guzzlers, collected dust on dealer lots while the imports had a field day and Detroit's manufacturers struggled to shift production from big to small, V-8 to V-6 and four-cylinder, and rear drive to front

drive. Interest rates accelerated to staggering levels, and the nation reeled under simultaneous inflation and recession. Plants and businesses, including auto dealerships, closed their doors, and people lost their jobs by the hundreds of thousands. Things were indeed looking bleak for 1980.

Primarily it was the engine lineup that changed for the '80 model year—as always, in the direction of lower weight and better fuel economy. A new, lighter 115 hp (110 in California) 3.8-liter V-6 replaced the old base "straight-six," a 120 hp 4.4-liter V-8 was added, and the optional 5.7-liter V-8 was deleted. On the good news side, the 5.0-liter V-8 was uprated from 130 to 155 hp and the Z-28 5.7-liter engine went from 175 to 190 hp—but from 170 to 165 in California.

New P205/75R-14 steel belted radial tires and color-keyed seat and shoulder belts became standard, and low-friction upper ball joints were added to the front suspension. The Berlinetta got standard wire wheel covers, and the Z-28 got a gimmicky but functional rear-facing cold-air flap (supposedly added to feed the coming turbo-motor) on the hood, operated at full throttle by an electric solenoid. New options were cast aluminum wheels and a heavy-duty cooling system. Hit of the summer "long lead" magazine preview was a stunning turbo 350 concept car called "Ultra Z," complete with a Porsche-like "whale tail" rear spoiler; but there was no sign or mention of a Turbo Z at introduction.

Driving fun and excitement remained the catalog's emphasis, and both the Rally Sport ("Energetic, Electrifying, Economical") and the Z-28 were featured in print ads, the latter appearing with all its engineering features in a highly creative photo montage. "Engineering of a Driving Legend" was the theme; paying homage to the campaigns of earlier, better days, the ad ended with the old nickname, "The Hugger."

Still another Z-28 road test appeared in the April 1980 *Car and Driver*. "A medieval warrior on the path to a rocking chair," lamented the subhead. "The Z-28 before our very eyes has become a museum piece," wrote author Larry Griffin. "Cars like the Z-28 are folding beneath the pressure of more modern methods of combining excitement and transportation. Irrational machines like Z-28's have provided us with wonderful entertainment many times over, but their excesses have only served to hasten their end." It still performed very well and cornered impressively on smooth pavement, "but assault some bumps and the car seems to be playing footsies with a bed of hot coals. . . . Alas, suspension travel remains inadequate, and the shock valving seems equally disappointing." And "the car's lack of efficiency is no longer excusable in the civic sense." With the four-speed and 3.08:1 gearing, the test car covered a quarter-mile in 16.4 seconds at 86 mph, did 0-60 in 8.5 seconds and topped out at an even 120 mph.

The May 1980 *Cars* magazine capped a short Z-28 history with a test of an automatic-equipped '80 version. The authors said they had trouble with the car's cold-engine driveability and complained of "hard jolts and lack of stability" on rough roads due to the suspension's limited travel, but were otherwise optimistic. "On cold mornings," they said, "you just can't turn the key, jam the shifter into drive, and go. The engine will stall if you try it and, even once running, will treat you to all kinds of belches, gasps and hesitations until it warms up. When it's finally warm, though, there's no trace of hesitation. The loose torque converter and 3.42 posi rear launch the car out of the hole with tires frying. . . . Compared to Pontiac's Trans-Am, the Z-28 has a softer ride and a lighter steering effort. Its springs are softer, its shock valving easier, and its sway bars skinnier. And even though the Trans-Am holds the edge in ultimate grit-the-teeth adhesion, the Z does almost the same job with less effort and more comfort. . . .

"As an out-and-out fun car, it's hard to beat the Z. Some of the fancy imports may be more kicks to drive, but their price tags are a whole bunch higher . . . [and] it will do a number on most other '80 models around, with a 0-60 time of 7.3 seconds, and quarter-mile

Above (opposite): '79 Z-28; Turbo Z, proposed for '81, at design center in May 1979. Below: three views of Berlinetta Sport Coupe for '80.

figures of 16.2 seconds at 93 mph. Yes, in a time when macho machines are wasting away into mileage milktoasts, the Z-28 is a throwback to the golden days when you didn't have to stop for a bank loan before visiting your local gas station. And the pure driving pleasure it continues to offer is a welcome reassertion of the human spirit, in the teeth of emission-sniffing pusillanimity."

Car Craft's John Baechtel reviewed an '80 Z in July, and he strongly advised Chevrolet's engineers not to use Pontiac's 4.9-liter turbo V-8 in it—as they had been intending to do at one time. "It seems that they're considering the 301 cubic-inch Pontiac turbo motor as an alternate powerplant for the car," he wrote. "Bad move, guys. It's our considered opinion that Z-28 enthusiasts will not take kindly to a Poncho-powered Z-car. If you thought there was a flap about Olds motors in Firebirds, wait 'till you start putting Pontiac motors in Z-28 Camaros. Z-28 lovers will probably lay siege to Detroit until you take it back."

One of the most striking modified Camaros of recent years was PPG Industries' Z-28 "Cheverra," the official Pace Car at all 1980 CART Indy-car races. Besides its gorgeous two-tone burgundy and beige paint job—in experimental lacquer developed by PPG's Automotive Finishes Group—it featured a huge IROC-look front air dam, a "whale-tail" spoiler, beefed suspension and a 400 hp, 355 cubic-inch V-8 engine for the 100-plus mph speeds required of the Pace Car. It also paced CART's opening 1981 event at Phoenix International Raceway, where it was fitted with special camera mounts to provide an interesting on-track perspective for TV viewers, and then remained in the PPG pace-car lineup through 1981. The name, of course, is a derivation of "Chevrolet" and Porsche's most revered performance label, "Carrera."

After its resurrection and miraculous recovery in the 1970's, Camaro closed out the '80 model year in the dumps again with sales of only 131,066. While it had thrived through the first fuel crisis and the recession that followed—it *was* a small, relatively economical car in those days—it suffered mightily, along with most other "traditional Detroit iron," in the dark days of 1979-80. While there were hopes for a general industry recovery for model year '81 as Detroit's Big Three all launched new state-of-the-art fuel efficient front-wheel-drive cars, there were no such expectations of a strong curtain-call year for the eleven-year-old, too big, too heavy, impractical and fuel-inefficient GM F-cars. They could only try to hold the line as sporty-car enthusiasts eagerly awaited their all-new '82 replacements.

154   There was good news for long-suffering Californians, though,

Three views of the Rally Sport for '80, and same years Z-28 model. Two-page print advertisement stressed the 1980 Z-28's engineering.

AIR INDUCTION

BOLD NEW STRIPING AND HOOD SCOOP DESIGN MAKE Z28 LOOK AS GOOD AS IT PERFORMS.

SOLENOID-OPERATED COLD AIR INTAKE DUCT HELPS ENGINE BREATHE WHEN IT NEEDS IT MOST.

VENTED, POWER-ASSISTED FRONT DISC BRAKES.

Z28 SPRINGS OFFER EXTRA DEFLECTION: 365 LBS./INCH IN FRONT, 130 IN REAR.

SHOCKS PROVIDE THE DAMPING YOU NEED THANKS TO SPECIAL Z28 VALVING. 1" PISTON.

AVAILABLE CAST-ALUMINUM WHEELS WITH WHITE-LETTERED STEEL-BELTED RADIALS IN SIZE P225/70R-15. THEY HELP THE HUGGER HUG. (TIRES SUPPLIED BY VARIOUS MANUFACTURERS.)

FRONT AIR DAM, REAR SPOILER AND FLARED FENDERS GIVE YOU THE GOOD LOOKS YOU EXPECT FROM A "Z".

GOOD/YEAR POLYSTEEL RADIAL

DUAL 12-INCH RESONATORS AND LARGER 2.5" OD TAILPIPES PROVIDE FOR FREE FLOWING EXHAUST AND DISTINCTIVE Z28 SOUND.

THE HEAVIEST STABILIZER BARS ON ANY CAMARO: 1.125" DIA. IN FRONT. .625" IN THE REAR.

DASH WITH TACH, TEMPERATURE GAGE, VOLTMETER AND ELECTRIC CLOCK.

4-SPEED MANUAL TRANSMISSION WITH STICK ON THE FLOOR. (AUTOMATIC REQUIRED IN CALIFORNIA.)

CHEVY CAMARO Z28 FOR 1980.
THE ENGINEERING OF A DRIVING LEGEND.

What you see here is part of the heart of a Camaro Z28...the components that make it very special, extremely capable, a driving legend. It's engineered, from the ground up, with the most sophisticated suspension in the Camaro line, with special shocks, anti-sway bars and springs to help stabilize the ride. It's equipped with steel-belted radials. Bold new cast-aluminum wheels are available in three colors. There's a four-speed gearbox that delivers the power from the smooth 5.7 Liter V8 engine.* A new solenoid-operated air induction scoop helps the engine breathe. The exhaust sings through dual resonators. The Z28 bristles with a good-looking front air dam, fender flares and a rear spoiler.

The Camaro Z28 for 1980. It's your turn to own a driving legend. Buy or lease one today.

*5.0 Liter (305 Cu. In.) V8 with available auto. trans. only in California.

CHEVY CAMARO. THE HUGGER.

Chevrolet

GM

Ultra Z turbocharged idea car shown at '80 model long-lead press preview in July 1979 and its turbo 350 engine. '81 Berlinetta and Z-28; 1980-81 PPG "Cheverra" pace with 400 hp 355 cu.in. engine.

since both the 5.7-liter V-8 and the four-speed manual transmission returned to their state for '81. Unfortunately, they were not available together. Thanks to a sophisticated engine computer system called Computer Command Control, which went into every GM car to meet '81 emissions requirements, all available powertrain combinations were certified for all fifty states. But the 5.7-liter Z-28 engine (now down to a rated 175 hp) came only coupled to a three-speed automatic with a fuel saving, computer controlled lock-up clutch in both second and third gears. Z-28 buyers wishing to shift for themselves had to settle for a 165 hp 5.0-liter/four-speed combination, which came with a 3.42:1 rear axle. Also to improve fuel mileage, the regular 150 hp 5.0-liter/four-speed, non-Z-28 axle ratio was lowered to 2.56:1, the 5.7-liter/automatic Z-28 axle fell to 3.08:1, and non-Z-28 automatic Camaros got a lock-up feature in top gear only. Low-drag power front disc/rear drum brakes, a space-saving compact spare tire and a lighter, more efficient, maintenance-free "Freedom II" battery became standard on all Camaros. There were two useful new options: Halogen headlamps and a wheel cover locking package. The 3.8-liter V-6 (now rated at 110 hp) with three-speed manual remained standard in the base car, and the 4.4-liter V-8 (115 hp) continued as an option with automatic only.

"Personality, plus show-stopping good looks" was the '81 Camaro catalog's theme, "a flair for moving through life with style." And a Z-28 color magazine ad was one of the best and most creative ever. It

featured a red-striped black car photographed against a black background with its doors spread open like the wings of an enormous bird in flight, the triple Z-28 stripe running uninterrupted from door to front spoiler to door—an incredible photograph and an absolutely stunning visual effect. "Spread your wings," exhorts the copy. "The new Z-28 Camaro is for anyone who wants to move up from automotive tedium. It's for those rare drivers who understand the rush of the road and the thrust of finely machined road cars." Once again, the car was called "The Hugger" in the ad's closing line.

As the '81 model year dragged on, most Camaro-loving eyes were firmly fixed on the coming, totally redesigned '82 model. Plenty of "spy" photos already had been published, but *Car and Driver* printed the most comprehensive '82 F-car preview story in November 1980, complete with three big "spy" photos of a sharp-looking red Z-28 prototype being put through its paces at GM's Michigan Proving Ground. "The new F-cars should be better in every respect than the cars they replace," wrote author Rich Ceppos. "In general, the changes center on efficiency—better use of space, lighter curb weights, lower road horsepower [required to overcome wind drag and rolling resistance], advanced aerodynamics. But there will be significant gains in handling and performance as well." Armed with inside information, Ceppos fairly accurately predicted their size, weight, drag coefficients, suspension configuration, powertrains and model variations—"basic, duded-up Berlinetta and hot-dog Z-28," the

same as '81 less the two-toned Rally Sport—and that they would be rear-drive hatchbacks. "Camaros and Firebirds will each have distinct roadgoing personalities, just as they do now," he added, ". . . [and] the Z-28 suspension engineers have been given the mandate to outhandle the Trans-Am. . . . Given what we know about what the engineers assigned to these cars know, we have little doubt that the new Firebird and Camaro will be a step forward for the cause of serious American drivers' cars."

By the spring of 1981 there were some small signs of economic recovery, but the anticipated U.S. industry comeback had not yet materialized. Detroit still was hoping for at least a gradual return to pre-1979 sales and profitability, beginning with the onset of good weather and boosted by a "gentleman's agreement" with the Japanese importers to restrain their U.S. shipments somewhat; but consumers were still balking at sky-high interest rates and new-car prices. GM's small, front-drive J-cars looked like big sellers when they were unveiled in early May, but introduction of the long-overdue F-car sporty coupes would be delayed until November or even December. The smaller Mustangs were outselling Camaros five-to-three.

It's probably safe to say that even as the winter weather was breaking at last, trees and grass greening and flowers finally peeking from their buds, a lot of Chevrolet people in Detroit and elsewhere already were wishing for the next winter's snows to fall.

CHAPTER NINE
Upholding the Tradition

"The '70-½ Camaro was one of the most successful appearance jobs we ever had at General Motors. It will go twelve years. This is two cycles now . . . three cycles in those days. At that time we were running four-year cycles; now we're on six years, and that's still double. It just kept increasing in value and in popularity through the years, getting hotter and hotter.

"We really had a struggle among ourselves over whether the '82 was going to be front-drive or rear-drive. Finally we decided to make it just as small as we possibly could and stay rear-drive—be able to put a V-8 in it and still have good performance, as well as a four-cylinder engine—tighten it up just as tight as we could, get it as light as possible.

"I think we've done a pretty good job on the car. It's got terrific aero and it's terrifically good-looking. It doesn't look as small as it is—but I don't know if that's good or bad any more. It's still in the same context but with a lower hood and a little higher deck, and it's a darned sporty looking car. I think it's going to be extremely successful. And it's going to end up maybe one of our last rear-drive cars. I think it will be a helluva car."

—Elliott M. Estes, retired General Motors president

"We felt we did a damned good car in '70-½, and it lasted a long time. When we started this '82 program, there was a lot of concern about whether we could duplicate that act again. Can we do that one more time, fellas? Well, we kicked it around up here and decided to start that program in Bill Porter's advanced studio. I liked what he had done with the second-generation car when he had the Firebird studio, and so I wanted to try it one more time in Porter's advanced studio. He had an assistant down there by the name of Roger

'82 Camaro Z-28 fiberglass model in its final form, March 1980, showing racer-like side skirts and twin hood scoops.

Hughet—who's now upstairs working with Jerry Palmer on Corvettes and Camaros.

"We'll do a theme in Advanced, look at it, wipe it off the clay, start another, and then settle down and try to create a mood for the production studio when it takes over the problem. But Roger Hughet turned out an illustration, we took one look at it, and that was all I needed. We said, do it in scale, fellas; and they did it in scale. Then we tried it full-size, and it was a success from the very beginning. We moved it outdoors with the current car, and suddenly the current car looked dated.

"We didn't think we could get there because this automobile is considerably shorter and narrower. It has better seating in the back and has a hatch and fold-down rear seats. And we've got one design feature on it that no one else has ever done . . . no one. You talk about the '70-½ not being 'fast' and not being 'notch,' because the roofline pours into the deck very gently . . . and there is a deck, you just never quite see the break. Well, we do the same thing with glass in the new car. We take the backlight glass and form it into a compound curve in two directions and then it flows right into the sheet metal surfaces. Let me tell you the glass people were doing headstands trying to get that for us, and we went through probably thirty-five different samples before we nailed it down. But it's there, and it's beautiful, because it pours out on the sides of the car as well as in silhouette.

"Let me tell you, we were out in Arizona on a test trip recently with a bunch of prototype '82 Camaros and Firebirds. And a group of people in sportscars started chasing us. When we stopped, they came up and asked what our cars were and who built them, because there was no identification on the cars. Of course, we couldn't tell them anything, but one fellow commented that whoever built them, he thought they were better looking than any Ferrari."

—Irvin W. Rybicki, General Motors design vice president

"The '82 project was especially difficult because we had fine-tuned the '70-½ design for so long. The evolution of that car through 1981 was a very carefully done program of improvement in both function and appearance. We like to think that each step we took in the redesign of that car made it better and better-looking, and enhanced its image. Right up to the end, that car has been very exciting and very successful. Even in this sober day and age, it still has some excitement to it.

"When we were faced with designing the third generation Camaro, it was just at the height of excitement over the Z-28's and Trans-

Above (left): GM design director Chuck Jordan; (top, right): Chevrolet design chief Jerry Palmer; Advanced studio chief Bill Porter. Below: Mid-engine Camaro concept from April '75. Page opposite (top): two views of sleek fastback scale model, September '75; (center): full-size October '75 clay model with heritage to second generation design. Bottom: November '75 clay had flared wheel openings, very glassy upper.

Ams. We knew that would be a tough act to follow with a car that was reduced in weight, meaning it would also be reduced in size. We recognized that the Camaro, like the Corvette, is an emotional car . . . not one that you stand up in the rear seat of, or put six milk cans in the trunk. It is an emotional, sporty, personal car, and an important part of that comes from its silhouette, its profile, section and details. The thing had to be exciting to walk up and look at. Doing a new one that was smaller and lighter and more efficiently packaged would be tough, but we were determined to pull it off.

"I think the new one has a great profile. It's not as excessive. You look back on the old Camaro and it's a little more 'cartoon' compared to the new one. Its proportions are a little more exaggerated. The new car's shape has the heritage of the old one, but it's cleaned up and more aerodynamically efficient. I had a chance out at the Proving Ground to take out a prototype '82 and this year's Camaro together on the test track. We followed along behind and had them drive side-by-side; then we got in front and watched. Until you see the two together on the road you really don't appreciate what you've got. You see them come up over a hill, and the one has this big, round, roly-poly look, and the other's got its head down and looks mean. That nose is down, and it's straightforward, not so busy and fussy, and it looks just right. Same thing in the rear, it's got its tail up and it's perky, sassy. It 'reads.' The thing looks clean and clear, no 'foo-foo,' no chrome.

"We all got in and worked on it with dedication. We believed in this car; we loved this car. If there is anything for dessert, it's doing a Camaro design. So we did this with tender, loving care and very, very carefully. I think it's a great looking car. I really believe it's going to be a winner. I think we proved to ourselves that we can capture the same spirit, the same excitement in a car that is somewhat smaller."
—Charles M. Jordan, General Motors director of design

How do you replace a legend? How do you design a new car to supersede one of the best-known, best-loved automotive shapes of all time? One of Bill Mitchell's long-standing rules of good design is that you don't change a car so drastically that you make instant orphans of everything that's gone before it. In other words, there should be a certain continuity of theme, a heritage, carried on from one generation to the next, especially if the one being replaced has been successful. When people see the new Camaro on the street for the first time they should say, "There's the new Camaro," not, "What's that?"

Mitchell also believes that a good design is slightly controversial at

first: "If somebody says it's nice," he says, "that's the end of it. It's no damn good if it's 'nice.' The 70-½ Camaro foundered around a bit at first before it caught on and really went. Look at two movie stars, for example: Lauren Bacall and Clark Gable. She wasn't beautiful but she was different, and so was her voice. Same with Gable. The Errol Flynns were the pretty boys, but he was different."

The '82 Camaro's design evolution began early in 1975 in Jerry Palmer's Chevrolet #3 studio and almost simultaneously in Bill Porter's Advanced #1 studio. Originally intended for the '80 model year, it was seen primarily as a front-wheel-drive sport coupe spun off the new front-wheel-drive compact X-car platform that was being developed for a 1979 introduction. That it should be an X-car derivative was logical since the Camaro/Firebird F-cars always had been sporty cousins to GM's compact family cars. That it should be front-wheel drive was taken almost for granted, at least in the design studios, in light of the worldwide trend toward smaller, more fuel-efficient front-wheel-drive cars . . . not to mention the warm reception given VW's then-new Scirocco, a handsome, quick and agile spin-off of the economical front-wheel-drive Rabbit. There were those, primarily at Chevrolet Engineering, still thinking rear-drive and some who advocated turning the X-car mechanicals around and mounting them in back in a mid-engine configuration, but it was generally assumed that the third generation F-car would be driven by its front wheels.

"We did a package study of a four-place mid-engine configuration," says Palmer, "and at the same time a new front-drive car based on 'X' components. Bill Porter was also playing with some cars downstairs, based along the same lines. Both studios were looking at new F-cars, and I think you can see some degree of the '82 car in some of these early sketches, renderings and models. We were kind of getting the 'F' feel—what is the new Camaro?—without throwing all the existing heritage away."

"At that time," adds Ed Taylor, who was Palmer's immediate boss, "we were playing with the sliding door and the no-glass-drop concepts, looking down the road and thinking aerodynamics, flush glass, weight savings and all. We had a small sliding side window on some of those models. The F-car's long door had been criticized for its lack of parking lot clearance, so there was a lot of resistance against repeating a long door that is heavy and makes the car hard to get into and out of. We had to approach it differently this time, to make it new and different, exciting and lighter in weight. We were downsizing, too, seeing how small we could make the cars."

A substantial number of drawings, scale models and full-size clays were fashioned and evaluated in 1975; some were obvious evolutions of the long-standing Camaro theme and others significant departures in fresh directions. Most had long, low snouts, quad rectangular headlamps and the short dash-to-front-axle dimension characteristic of a transverse engine, front-wheel-drive configuration. By March 1976, several new F-car scale models were on display. Of the two that were Camaros, both had hidden headlamps; one, a sleek, silver beauty with Z-28 identification on its ultra-low nose, looked to be a four-passenger mid-engine concept. More full-size clays followed, several of which were "clownsuit" cars—different on one side than on the other. This technique allows exploration of slightly varying designs, including different lengths, wheelbases and (in this case) driveline configurations, on opposite sides of the same model. Thus an observer can look at a front-drive version, then walk around and see what the same concept would look like as a rear-drive car.

By late 1976, the basic shape of what was still intended to be the '80 F-car seemed fairly well settled. One of Palmer's models had been sent downstairs to Porter's studio so that compromises between the two divisions could be worked out. "Bill was doing the Bird," Palmer explains, "and we were doing the Camaro. We had a common door, and common glass . . . but, I think, different beltlines, different quarter glass, different backlights." By March 1977, with Porter's work complete, the car was back for further development, nearly ready for release—except that the question of front versus rear-drive had yet to be resolved. It still had sliding doors with fixed glass and a "dropped" beltline, and by then it had slipped to an '81-model program. Significantly, Bill Mitchell was about to retire as design vice president.

"We got into a whole different front end," relates Palmer, "a little more contemporary but really not an evolution of the Camaro theme. Then [Bill] Mitchell left, and the whole program was just kind of foundering. No one was taking it too seriously. Irv Rybicki came in [on August 1st, 1977], and he wanted to get updated on everything. We hauled the car out to show it to him, and his statement was: 'I think the basic theme looks good, but I feel very strongly that the F-car should have the single-pane side glass.' Which meant getting back into where we were with the current car. Well, you're always in love with what you're doing at the time, and you don't like somebody coming along and changing it. That was a pretty significant change. But, as it turned out, it *was* a change for the better as far as I'm concerned, and it established a sound foundation for future themes."

In January 1978 Porter's advanced studio was directed to start again on the third-generation F-car, now scheduled for an '82 in-

Above: low nosed, fierce looking mid-engine scale-model Z-28 in March '76; full-size clays for what was still 1980 model program in spring-summer '76.

troduction. "Roger Hughet," Palmer continues, "who was Bill Porter's assistant, did some renderings, and then they did a model from one of them that was pretty significant. It was a gorgeous model, with an all-glass upper. They really did a job of marrying the upper to the lower with sort of a turtle-shell quality and excellent surface development.

"We had been working on the F-body program for some time," explains Porter. "As you know, advanced studios don't often do specific cars, they do body programs, and then the divisional identity is given to the cars at a later stage, depending on what divisions participate. Nominally, the car was a Firebird during its genesis in our studio, but some Camaro versions were drawn and modelled as well. We did a number of proposals on front-wheel-drive packages and a number of rear-drive cars, but we assumed early in the program that it would be front-drive.

"The second generation car was a very hard act to follow, and that was one of the reasons we worked on it for so long. I'm sure I could conservatively say that we tried fifty or more different themes, really left few stones unturned, before we arrived at the one theme that ultimately developed into the car, the wedge-shaped motif with the sort of 'romantic' fender lines and the upper with the 'fiddle-back'-shaped backlight. By 'romantic' I mean fluid, graceful curves that peel off the front like bow waves from a ship. Roger developed this theme in the form of a rendering (which is now hanging on Chuck Jordan's office wall), a full-size rendering, and then a scale model. From that point it was quite clear that this was the direction in which the F-body should go."

By May, Palmer's studio was back into the project in full force. "We started a Camaro based on where they were," he relates. "At that time it was back to rear-wheel drive, and a couple of things were going on. The Firebird had this undulating shoulder going through it, while we had taken more of a wedge look, with a monocoque section and quarter. By then the package had been settled, the wheelbase and the interior dimensions. We had all the dots to connect now, and the more we got into it the better it got. Porter was working on the premise that the reverse-bend backlight was the theme, and we were fighting for a 'faster' windshield, a sixty-two degree windshield. We went through all sorts of configurations on that C-pillar, or 'sail' area. The Pontiac at that time had a very narrow pillar, and they kept painting it black so you couldn't see it too well, but we felt we wanted a wider sail. Then we got into the triangulated sail, and that's the way it ended up.

"By July we had a pretty serious model that was totally a

Above: from 1977, nearly completed car; Z-28 vs. Berlinetta front ends; experiments with new shapes, new window approaches in 1978

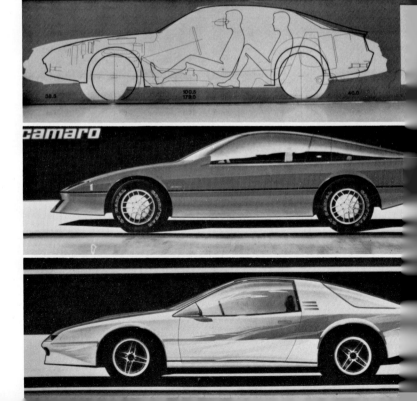

Chevrolet, and we were pretty proud of it. We really felt good about the entire car. We won some battles with it and we lost some. One of the things we lost: Pontiac still wanted the undulating shoulder, but we had a fairly flush section from the glass to the bottom of the door. Also, we had a razor-sharp 'break' along the side, and Pontiac had a softer 'bone' section. Finally the concession was made that we would go with the rolled shoulder on both cars on the door, and Pontiac would have to go with our body break location, only softer. The corporation wanted to do a common rear quarter for both cars, but we were fighting for specific quarters. Eventually we won. While all this was going on, Engineering was getting more input into the car. We were packaging headlamps, air cleaners, all the stuff that has to be packaged, and they were becoming real cars."

One way that such styling disputes between divisions are resolved is for each studio to do a model with its own interpretation on one side and the other division's on the other. "In other words," Ed Taylor explains, "if they had to be like us, this is what their car would look like. If we had to be like them, our other side showed that." This practice facilitated the difficult job of working out a compromise solution to everyone's best advantage.

"As the car got closer to production," Palmer continues, "we took the quarter that Pontiac continues through, and we wrapped it into the leading edge of the sail, providing two separate designs for Chevrolet and Pontiac with one common door. We got too realistic too quick with legalization of the headlamps, and we lost that 'dive,' the wedgy new profile, so we had to work with Chevrolet Engineering to get the headlamps down and figure out a way to make them look 'sneaky.' We were sharing all the front inner sheetmetal with Pontiac, and they had hidden lamps while we had fixed lamps. It was a hell of a compromise, but I think we pulled it off quite well. And having fixed lamps enabled Camaro to have a specific Z-28 front. We wanted a rounder wheel opening, but the corporation wanted Pontiac to have the rounder one. At one point we almost switched, but we ended up with a compromise. Also, we were continually looking at what should be the proper face for the car."

As 1978 turned into 1979 and the deadline for '82 production release approached, many problems remained unsolved. A federal environmental law outlawed lead-soldered joints in assembly plants, but the sail-panel-to-roof joint was thought to be too large to silicon braze. The glass companies said they couldn't form the double bend in the large glass hatch. Production engineers said they couldn't get the headlamps, or for that matter, the car's entire profile, as low as the designers wanted. There was a serious problem with packaging the spare tire. The argument over common rear quarters or specific quarters was still going on. And the search for a specific Z-28 front end had just begun.

The designers wanted specific outside mirrors, mounted on the "patch" at the window's front corner, but a compromise solution used door-mounted mirrors on tall pedestals to bring them up to the patch area. Taylor and then-Chevrolet chief engineer Lloyd Reuss wanted a Z-28 front without upper grille openings, so extra wind-tunnel work had to be done to ensure that enough cooling air would get in through the large opening under the bumper. "We sold ourselves on keeping the graphics below the bumper on the Z," says Palmer, "and I think it looks pretty damned 'snarky.' Who needs hidden lamps?"

As late as mid-1979 some were still promoting the front-drive configuration. Pontiac studio chief John Schinella, for one, who had always thought the new F's should be much smaller in size and weight—and definitely front-wheel drive—was still modelling both front- and rear-drive Firebirds. "The same exact theme," says Palmer, "but changed around to comply to the front drive. I think John was questioning the direction of the program."

Certainly one of the toughest aspects of the '82 F-car design to translate into production was the double-curved rear hatch glass. "The success of that theme," says Porter, "was based on some pretty sophisticated technology that we asked the glass companies to develop. Chuck Jordan, in particular, really leaned on them to exert their finest efforts toward getting some breakthroughs in the forming of glass so that we could achieve that very suave and aerodynamic design. They brought in a number of samples during the course of the program, some of which were a little lumpy and some of which were very beautiful, until finally they were able to achieve it. That was an interesting side issue to the whole thing, because had they not been able to achieve those shapes in glass, that theme would not have been possible. We'd have had to abandon it and do something else.

"I felt very privileged to work on that project," he adds. "I had been in charge of the '70-½ Firebird program when I was Pontiac chief designer, so it was a great thing for me to be able to work on the new body in the advanced studio. Quite a coincidence, but it just worked out that way. One of the reasons you become an automobile designer is to work on programs like that."

Creation of the third-generation F-car interior began in 1977, shortly after Irv Rybicki took over as design vice president. A "concept" interior studio was organized under John Shettler to explore new interior themes or, as he put it, "religions." "We started to study

GUAGE PODS HINGE FOR CORRECT DRIVER POSITION.

COLUMN TILT ADJUSTS GUAGE ANGLE.

Spring '78: separate instrument pods, outer ones adjustable; (below, left): aircraft-like cockpit with "floating" central structure; hooded flat panel look begun in Shettler's studio. Opposite: multi-faced dials and protruding switch panels in August '78; views of colorful interior ideas.

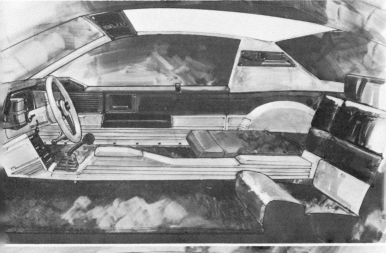

the Lear business jets and the Concorde, which have tremendous aerodynamics," Shettler relates. "Their windshields are pushed down almost flat, and they have these big hoods over the instruments to cut down glare and reflections. We decided to get the feel of those hoods, to bring the controls and the gauges and all the parts that might reflect in the windshield pulled back toward the driver. Jordan liked that quite a bit, and so did Irv. They took that as the direction.

"That was the first job we did under the new system, and it was one of the smoothest interior programs I ever worked on. It was very directed, and it was very simple, because first of all we had a new radio system. We had done the radio concepts for the J-car, and so we knew we had that available. Also we had these new Delco-Remy switches that were smaller, and we were able to bring them closer to the driver and still have a thin look. Another change from the previous times was that we had the project center. The project center worked with us very closely, and we didn't have to involve the divisional engineering groups.

"The human factors were set up because of the exterior religion of the raked windshield, trying to get this close, comfortable feel, to get the driver down into it. The personality was basically set up by the perimeters of reflection. At one time we had the air conditioning right in the hood; we tried to make a rigid foam hood, with all the ducting molded in. But the engineers had a real job trying to make that work because of the heat loading on that big surface, trying to keep it from warping and so on. So that was changed around."

Another interesting facet of the program was the use of foamcore interior mock ups in "stringer bucks." As described by Shettler, foamcore is basically structural foam sandwiched in cardboard, which can be shaped into a fairly accurate representation of a proposed interior layout. A stringer buck is a seating buck made up of bulkheads, or "stringers," simulating the interior dimensions of a given clay model.

"We did a concept simulator, basically," he explains. "We made a stringer buck of the car, the shape that Palmer and Porter were working on, so when their clay model was done we could climb right into this buck and see the interior. It was made out of cardboard, not soft and refined, but as soon as you sat in there, within a week, you'd know if you had a good idea or had to change it. When management came in, Irv could sit there and say, 'well, I like it' or 'I don't like it.' 'Here's what a seventy-degree windshield for example will do to you . . . it'll drive your head way back here.' And we can move those components in and out quickly. It really helped evolve this concept."

Shettler also points out that the interior was designed from the

beginning with serviceability in mind. "That tunnel, the instrument panel and console, and everything is very serviceability oriented," he says. "Everything can be pulled right out. The instrumentation, the cluster, is very easy to take apart. The speakers, at least at the time we turned the car over to the production studio, were also very serviceable. We had the project center people seeing how to service the speakers, how they bounce off the glass when you take them out."

Meanwhile, Bill Scott's Camaro interior studio had been working on some concepts of its own, one of which involved an innovative "floating" central structure that angled down between the upper pad and the floor console, leaving an open, flat floor area underneath. Shettler's concept won out, however, and by October 1978 it was essentially complete. One of its most interesting features was a detailed graphic display in its upper center, just beneath a horizontal row of warning lights. Encompassed in its shrouded instrument cluster were five small, round gauges centrally located between large, circular speedometer and tach faces, and just outboard of it on either side were separate pods housing light and auxiliary switches.

"What John gave me was a beautiful theme," says Scott, "and we tried very hard to keep it intact. But in the process, we went all the way around Robin Hood's barn. We packaged it and re-packaged it and remodelled it and had all kinds of hiccups in the system, but when we really finished the product I think we came very close to maintaining that theme. I think it's an unusual approach and a real breakthrough in doing instrumentation, and I think it's going to set a trend.

"The right side is pared away so there's plenty of room for the passenger. You've seen that in some traditional instrument panels . . . in the X-car, for example; but the 'X' doesn't have a top on it. This one has a hood on top that ties the A-pillars and the door belts together, and it's there for a reason. The windshield is raked at the most severe angle [sixty-two degrees] that we've seen yet, at least in an American production car, and that sets up a whole chain of events in terms of glare and other things. That hood really developed itself to keep all those unwanted reflections and light rays from coming into the windshield. I think it is so right for this car because it really has that aircraft cockpit look about it." Unfortunately, though, the central graphic display did not make it to production.

Scott explains some of the difficulties involved in interior design in today's environment. "Doing interiors," he says, "has become very technical and very challenging. We have to adhere to safety restrictions and all kinds of criteria set up by the government . . . serviceability, sight lines, what can be seen through the opening in the steering wheel. There are standards that say things have to conform to tradition, so certain switches have to be mounted in certain places. And after you get through with all that you can throw in aesthetics."

As Shettler mentions, one element of his initial design that did not survive was the use of integral air conditioning ducts in the hood's downward-angled outboard ends. "We tried very hard to maintain that in the theme," says Scott. "But our management had a problem with that pad breaking at the ends. Although they had liked it at first, they grew tired of it and thought it was a little bit tricky. Also, the engineers couldn't get the air pumped through there. The outlets were kind of long and thin, and I understand that when air is pumped out in a long, thin stream it creates a vortex and pulls hot air off the surface of that big black pad on top. With that much rake in the windshield and that broad, black surface soaking up all kinds of heat, it was actually picking that up and blowing warm air on you instead of cold air. So the air outlets went down lower in the panel and were divided into two pieces. Usually you have an outlet, and then horizontally under the panel you have a lap cooler, but these are two-in-one units with one outlet, which is really the lap cooler, just below the other."

Scott adds that they went through many different steering wheel proposals before one of his designers named Jon Albert came up with a suitable theme. "It had to be sporty, it had to fit the image of the car; and because of the large dials and all the information that you had to see behind the wheel, the horizontal spokes went lower, below the center. And then we put a smaller, third spoke at the bottom for extra structural rigidity. That's the sport wheel, which is also a first for Camaro because it's a real hand-leather-wrapped wheel. The base wheel is also kind of unique. It looks like a one-spoke wheel, but it has two very slim horizontal supports that give it the extra strength and rigidity it needs." Another unique feature, also a Jon Albert idea, is a double-ended speedometer pointer with miles-per-hour on one half of the dial and kilometers on the other. And there's a big, aircraft-looking clock mounted in the console between the seats.

The seats themselves are among the most important elements of the new car's interior. After fourteen years of complaints—too upright, not enough side support, no recliners—the interior designers and engineers were determined to offer at least a standard recliner as well as a "superseat" option for '82. As it turns out, there are three levels of front bucket seats: a base unit (the same as in the current Chevette and Cavalier J-car), which has a good shape, fair lateral support and a standard reclining mechanism; an up-level seat for the Berlinetta with still better lateral support; and a Recaro-type, multi-

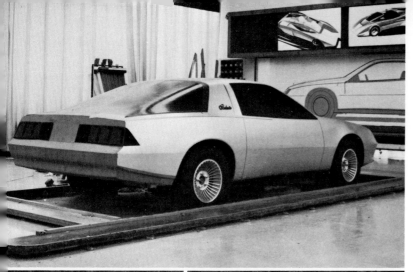

The new shape nearing completion during mid-summer 1978.

adjustable "super-seat," for the driver's side only, standard in the Z-28 but optional in any Camaro.

"It was our first chance to do a real super seat," says Scott. "We worked closely with Lear-Siegler on it, which is something we don't often get to do in the design studio. It was fun to work with them, not only on the aesthetic part but on what we wanted it to do and how we wanted it to adjust. We were able to make quick mock-ups, try them and evaluate them. We had strong leadership and good input from [Camaro chief engineer] Tom Zimmer. He had a strong goal in mind for this articulating Camaro seat, and he didn't want it shared with anyone . . . especially Firebird. He was bound and determined to get that seat in the program, and I think he was primarily responsible for following it through. It has a separate movable headrest, which means it's lower than the integral-headrest passenger seat but matches it as well as possible in appearance. Besides reclining, it has a lumbar support adjustment, thigh support adjustment and adjustable lateral support, with wings that move in and out, and it's soft where it needs to be soft and firm where it needs to be firm.

"Also we wanted to make sure that people knew it was a super seat, sort of hit them over the head with it visually, so we wanted to do something special in the insert to call it out . . . like Recaro does with their "Recaro/Recaro/Recaro" graphics. We ended up using the base seat cloth, which is a tweed cloth with a lot of sporty character, as just an insert in the super seat. That gives it a two-tone effect for the contrast we needed, and it also makes it interchangeable with both luxury and base trims."

About the only negative aspect of the new interior is its unfortunate lack of storage space. "There are engine computers in all the cars now," Scott explains, "and they have to function in a comfortable environment. You can't put them under the hood or in the trunk, and there isn't room under the seat. So they go in the instrument panel . . . and there goes the glove box. We had pockets on the doors, but they went away because of cost. There is a large storage compartment in the console, but that goes away too if passive restraints come in for '83."

On the surface, the engineering assignment was little different from any other involving replacement of an existing product with an all-new version: make it better in every way. But beneath that surface, the '82 program was a whole new ball game. Not only would it be the first Camaro created from the ground up for the new age of fuel consumption consciousness, but it would also be the first conceived and nurtured by a GM Engineering Staff project center instead of by the divisions that would ultimately produce and market it.

Ever since shortly after the oil embargo fuel crisis of 1974, every new family of General Motors automobiles has been generated by the corporation's new and efficient project center system. As described by F-car project manager Bob Knickerbocker, a project center is "a central core group of engineers who attack the program." Initially it may be just a handful of Engineering Staff's Advanced Product Engineering creative types, who are then joined by specialists from Design, Research, and Manufacturing Staffs and from the car divisions involved and GM Assembly Division as the program progresses toward production. The first products to emerge from this system were GM's downsized '77 big cars (conceived early in 1974), followed by new intermediates, front-drive luxury coupes, the transverse engine front-drive X-cars and the slightly smaller J-cars. Next in line came the sporty F-cars.

At Chevrolet Engineering, Tom Zimmer's group had begun formulating the next generation F-car's concept soon after he had taken over as Camaro chief engineer late in 1976. "In gross terms," he remembers, "the objectives were to significantly reduce the weight of the car; try to keep the seating for the front passengers essentially unchanged; improve, or at least maintain, the rear seating; significantly improve the luggage capacity; maintain a specialty-car character, high-styled with a sporty image; and improve the fuel economy.

"We felt we knew going in what the mission of this car ought to be.

It ought to be an extremely good handling car. We looked upon this as a statement of the expertise that resides here in Chevrolet, and in the American automobile industry. As we went along, we used benchmarks like the Lotus Esprit and the Porsche 924. Whenever we wanted to take a ride in our car to find out how we were coming, those are the kinds of cars we took along to compare it to. Everything about the car was designed to suit what we felt the character of the car ought to be, either for the appearance or the performance."

In June 1977, the F-car became an Engineering Staff project. "We started in a very preliminary way putting together the various proposals that would produce a 1982 car in the Camaro and Firebird image," project manager Knickerbocker relates. "At that time we examined the many options that were available—front-wheel drive, rear-wheel drive, two-passenger cars, four-passenger cars, different powertrains and different concepts of fuel economy and performance. That activity, in the financial and engineering analysis stages, went on until about January 1978, when we had our product people on the corporate level and the divisional managements agreeing on a concept. As it turned out, the concept was a rear-wheel drive car with a significant spectrum of powertrains that would provide good fuel economy on one end and reasonable performance, but with improved fuel economy over 1981, on the other. It was decided that the concept should be a four-passenger car because the rear seat in an F-car is still

The Shettler interior design of October 1978 evolves into production version in Scott's studio by January 1979. Note central graphic display.

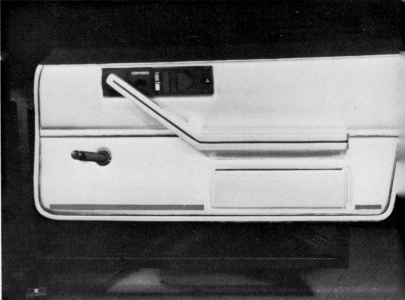

a very usable thing, even though it's been bad-mouthed by a lot of people in the past."

Concept approval came in February 1978, about three-and-a-half years before start of production for a fall 1981 introduction. "Once we had that concept approved," Knickerbocker continues, "we concentrated all of our efforts on putting the program together." From that point, the project began to gather momentum and moved rapidly through program definition approval in July, design (styling) approval in October and release of the final clay model in December 1978. "Then the corporation approved the program specifically, and in that was included all of the financial analysis. They gave us our targets for the monies to be spent, the time situation, which plants were going to produce it and the like." Some fourteen months were devoted to component and pre-prototype testing before the first production prototype was built in February 1980. While pre-prototypes incorporate "all the running gear in some other body," Knickerbocker points out, prototype cars "embody your hardware systems in their [Design Staff's] design concept and your body configuration." After that come "pilot line" and ultimately production cars, each stage progressively tested and developed until (hopefully) every last "bug" is worked out.

Easily the biggest contention point in the early stages was the question of front-wheel drive versus rear-wheel drive. Since the F-cars always had been spin-offs of GM's compact X-cars, it might have been logical to base them on the smaller front-wheel drive X-cars planned for a mid-1979 introduction. This was the approach favored at first by many at Design Staff and in the corporate management because it would result in a significantly lighter, roomier and more fuel-efficient car. Camaro chief engineer Zimmer and others at Chevrolet, however, felt strongly that the new car should retain the character that had made the old one such a favorite among young and youthful thinking buyers for so many years. And that meant a front-mounted V-8 engine driving the rear wheels.

"We went into it looking at predominantly front drive," he explains. "There was about a year when we studied both alternatives. We looked at the pros and cons and the advantages and disadvantages of springing an F-car from X-car components. Piece cost was not an advantage. As a matter of fact, front-wheel drive tends to be a little more expensive when you're talking about vehicle costs. Investment cost would have been much higher because we'd have had to invest in additional capacity to manufacture those components. When you make the decision to go to a body-frame integral car, regardless of whether it's front drive, rear drive, side drive, whatever drive, that automatically requires a total tear-up, clean-out, and rebuild of the assembly plant. We've tried to nail down how much front drive is worth in mass reduction versus rear drive. It's worth a hundred,

Late instrument panel versions; note double-ended speedometer and console clock at left, steering wheel with offset horizontal spoke at right.

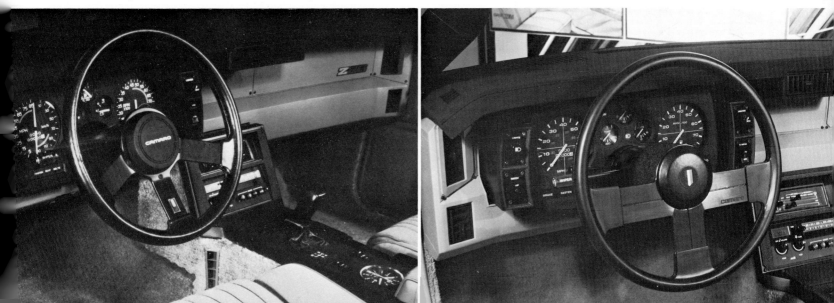

July 1978: Compared to then-current Camaro, smaller '82 has multi-segment taillamps (opposite, left) and integrated rectang

maybe two hundred pounds. The main advantage of front-wheel drive is better interior packaging for a given vehicle size, mainly because of what you can do around the second-seat passenger. You don't have a live axle back there. You can package tighter around a dead axle, and you can handle the gas tank differently.

"In spite of the obvious trend to front-wheel drive, and we're into the forefront of that, when we aligned our priorities and looked at the customer and the market we were trying to serve, the facilities, the packaging, the mass, the fuel economy and all those things, and looked at what kind of physical arrangement would produce the kind of car we wanted, we said we wanted to make it rear-wheel drive. We don't think a Z-28 buyer has the same priorities as somebody buying a J-car or an X-car. We have a slide we use in presentations with a list of cars on it that are real handling cars, front-wheel drive versus rear-wheel drive. And the list goes on and on with front-engine, rear-drive cars. I can only think of one or two, the Scirocco and maybe the Saab, that are front drive. We felt that rear drive was appropriate for this car, and fortunately we would still have the components in place to execute it. We recognize that we're in a transition period, and I would be the first to say that the next time an F-car is done it may become front-wheel drive at that point. But it won't be the same kind of all-out handling, performance-oriented car that an F-car is today. It will probably be more European in character, like a Scirocco or an X1/9."

Like most of today's modern new cars, the '82 Camaro's construction is body-frame integral, or unit body. "The stub frame is no longer there," says Knickerbocker. "In our current environment, the only way you can get a fuel efficient design is, of course, to go to unit body, and this demands a few things. Number one, it demands a lot of high-class structural analysis and design. Generally speaking, it's a

lot more difficult to engineer a structurally sound unit body. It is very complex to manage the plastic deformation of the car to take care of your barrier requirements. It is also much more difficult to take care of the interior noise because you don't have a frame and body mounts to impede vibrations and noises.

"Once you've made the car mass efficient and fuel efficient, all of the tuning items like making it ride nicely, getting the structural feel compatible with what you think it should be and keeping the noise and vibration down are continuing programs. You work with pre-prototypes, prototypes and pilot cars, but you really can't predict what's going to happen until that talented development engineer gets his hands on a prototype car because the modes of vibration and the acoustical characteristics are so discrete. The acoustical treatment in the body, for example, say on the floor pan or the dash . . . it's always surprising to me that you can put a square foot of material in a certain area and the performance might be bad, then you put 1-1/3 square foot on and it could be beautiful. Or you might have something covering the entire floor pan, and you cut off two-thirds of it to save that mass and it might still be good. It's a tremendously complex development process. One important thing is that we have gone from foam headliners to a composite fiberglass, which is built in a mold. It not only looks neat but it's done a helluva job for us there.

"Then you have rubber bushings in your suspension elements, and you have bonded rubber engine mounts, very complicated composite pieces. There again, there is almost an infinite number of rate and damping combinations that you can use. First you concentrate on making the doggone things durable, then you take a look at the niceties. We tried to have different ride packages complement the different models. The sportier it gets, the more roll resistance it has, the higher rates it has, the whole works." Zimmer adds that the car's

...aust tips. Above (center and right): drawings executed during the search for a proper Z-28 front end at the beginning of 1979.

structure and suspension were designed specifically for stiffness, in addition to durability, because stiffness is crucial to a performance car. "Lack of stiffness is compliance," he points out, "and compliance is a rubbery feel."

Instead of the upper and lower A-arms of past Camaros, the front suspension uses a variation of the MacPherson strut design with its coil springs inboard of the struts. "The reason for that," says Knickerbocker, "is that if you put the shock and the spring up on top, you can't get the front sheetmetal down low because the length of travel required by the shock causes it to stick out through the fenders, which is aesthetically kind of poor." Zimmer points out that this was possible because the car did not have front-wheel drive. "We could take the spring off the strut, tuck everything in tighter, bring the hood down and put the spring over on the lower control arm," he explains, "because we didn't have to worry about a driveshaft going through the knuckle." The wishbone-type lower control arm bolts to a crossmember, which in turn is bolted to the body structure. The strut and shock absorber assembly attaches to an underhood shock tower through a slotted mount that provides both camber and caster adjustment. There are specific strut/shock units for the base Camaro, the Berlinetta, the optional F-41 suspension package and the Z-28—the latter with its own special mount—and three different sway bars ranging from 27mm (base) through 29mm (F-41) to a hefty 31mm for the Z-28.

There was serious thought given to independent rear suspension, but the idea was ruled out as not worthy of the tremendous investment it would have required in production tooling and facilities. "If you could start from scratch and tool anything you wanted, I'm sure there would be more cost to an IRS system," Knickerbocker relates, "but the biggest thing in our situation was where in hell would we

produce it? We would have had to build a new plant because it would have been a completely unique system. Early in the program we looked very hard at some of Opel's hardware because they do have some rear-drive independent rears; but the stuff they had was far too heavy, not really mass efficient, and they in no way had the production capacity to take care of us."

Keeping the F-car's traditional rear leaf springs also was considered because, says the project manager, "leaf springs from the standpoint of a handling car are pretty darn good. Unfortunately, they are terrible from a mass efficiency standpoint. So we decided on a torque arm rear suspension somewhat like what we had in the old H-car [Monza]. In doing that, we save considerable mass. We do have a conventional 'banjo' axle so we can have locking differentials and the like." There are four different rear axle assemblies—to accommodate both drum brakes and optional disc brakes, each with and without limited-slip differential—and five ratios ranging from 2.73:1 to 3.42:1 depending on the powertrain. Stamped sheetmetal lower control arms (with specific bushings for the Z-28 and the F-41 option), a lateral track bar and the fore-aft torque arm locate and control the axle, while tubular shocks damp it and coil springs (extra stiff on the Z-28) support the body. There's no rear sway bar on base and Berlinetta suspensions but a 12mm one on the F-41 and a fat 21mm unit on the Z-28.

"From the steering standpoint," Knickerbocker continues, "we agonized a lot about rack-and-pinion. In my estimation, rack-and-pinion steering is overrated to beat hell. There's nothing inherent in it that makes it a more precise mechanism than some of our others. And when you have rear drive with the engine in front and a propshaft, you have some difficulty trying to figure out where to put a rack-and-pinion anyway. So we have recirculating-ball steering

The new Camaro compared to exposed-lamp Firebird model and new '79 Mustang in August of 1978. Lloyd Reuss, Chevy chief engineer during latter

with standard power assist—not variable ratio but with variable effort depending on what package the car has." Ratios are 15:1 base, 14:1 F-41 and a very quick 12.7:1 in the Z-28.

"We have disc front and drum rear brakes, which is kind of conventional; but we have the low-drag concept in front, which keeps the pads off the rotors, to enhance fuel economy, in combination with a quick-take-up master cylinder to give a good, firm braking feel. The parking brake is operated by a lever in the console now, instead of foot-operated, for those people who want to do a little rallying and use it in that manner." The master cylinder is aluminum with a plastic reservoir and a see-through window to allow easy fluid level checks, and both the four-cylinder base car and the Z-28 have weight-saving aluminum rear drums. A vacuum power booster (with a cam-driven vacuum pump on the four-cylinder engine) is standard, and rear disc brakes are optional.

Wheels on the base '82 Camaro are the same 14x6's as on the standard '81 car, painted body color with hubcaps but black when optional wheel covers are ordered. The Berlinetta gets new 14x7 cast aluminum wheels, painted gold, while the Z-28 comes with modified 14x7 steel "rally" wheels in silver, charcoal or gold. When the new dual TBI (throttle-body injection) 5.0 liter engine is ordered in the Z-28, the package includes new 15x7 five-spoke cast aluminum wheels in one of the same three colors. Base tires are P195/75R14 high pressure metric radials, glass-belted with the four-cylinder engine,

steel-belted otherwise. Steel P205/70R14's (blackwall or white-letter) come with the 14x7 rally and aluminum wheels, and white letter P215/65R15's are standard on the 15x7 Z-28 alloy rims. "The tires are somewhat downsized compared to what we have today in keeping with the lighter, smaller automobile," Knickerbocker explains, "but our performance tire is the same relative size. In other words we have a big performance tire for our handling cars, which is kind of unique today when everybody wants you to get the minimum rolling resistance. We still have a very fine tire." The spare is a compact, lightweight, high-pressure temporary unit stored upright in the right rear of the trunk, but an inflatable "stowaway" spare is optional—and mandatory with a limited-slip differential. "It was a real hustle to get the damned thing stashed over there in the rear quarter," Zimmer adds. "You can find them like that in station wagons and some others, but not in small cars like this one."

"Powertrain-wise, we've got a whole range," says Knickerbocker. "We start with a 2.5-liter four-cylinder, which happens to have TBI. We've got a 2.8-liter V-6, and that's a regular varajet carburetor job. It's a version of the Chevrolet sixty-degree X-car engine adapted for longitudinal mounting with rear drive. So you get all the advantages of its high specific output, which is better than the older-design engines, and also much better smoothness. That was a major consideration because our engine-carrying crossmember is bolted rigidly to the car with no rubber to worry about in-between. Then we have a

'2's development, and (right) Tom Zimmer, '82 Camaro chief engineer.

five-liter 4 bbl. V-8 and, for the Z-28, a five-liter dual TBI. The turbo has been abandoned; when you look at the packaging difficulties and the mass, you just can't make it. One of these days somebody might put a turbo on the V-6 or maybe on the four—but the TBI makes a considerable difference. The difference between a carbureted four-cylinder and the TBI job is really impressive. So if you're interested in maximum fuel economy, you can get a really exciting, keen-looking car with a very respectable four-cylinder. You will be able to get a sophisticated V-6 that hopefully will attack markets like that of the BMW with better performance. And if you want to be a hot dog, you can go to one of the V-8's." A mid-range 4.4-liter V-8 also was in the original lineup but was dropped as part of Chevrolet's general deproliferation program.

An aluminum-case, three-speed automatic transmission, with console-mounted shifter and converter clutch lock-up in third gear, can be teamed with any of the engines. A light-duty Muncie four-speed manual is standard with the four-cylinder and V-6, while a heavy-duty, aluminum-case Borg Warner unit comes with the TBI V-8. Asked why there's no five-speed manual available, Knicker-bocker says one is "in the works" for '83. "It just could not be accomplished [for '82] within the time frame we had." Zimmer points out also that the five-speed coming for the '83 model will be from an outside source. "Frankly," he says, "when we're spending $40 billion for all our new-car programs, we have to economize in certain places.

We just could not afford to tool up a new transmission."

The steel fuel tank is mounted between the rear axle and the cargo compartment floor. "We were extremely interested in fuel system integrity," says Knickerbocker, "and we have a very unusual arrangement where the fuel tank is what we call 'semi-over-axle.' It's above and forward of the axle, and it gives us a rather unusual rear compartment space. But it's given us the volume we want, it's very snugly packaged, and its performance seems to be unusually good."

The new Camaro exhaust system uses a single catalytic converter and a transverse, rear-mounted muffler with an integral tailpipe, and the muffler's size and length is tuned to each specific engine. The Z-28 has dual exhausts from the converter back, ending with twin transversely-mounted resonators for a mellow tone. "We have tried to package these things much more efficiently than in the past," Knickerbocker explains. "We used to have a helluva time keeping the exhaust system out of the body, and we sometimes had rattles here and there. Hopefully, we have solved that problem with the new car."

Radiators are crossflow type, with thin aluminum cores and nylon plastic end tanks—except for the heavy-duty V-8 unit, which is a copper and brass design. Bumpers are body-color molded urethane facias over flexible honeycomb enersorbers on rigid impact bars. On the base four-cylinder and the base Z-28, the front impact bar is weight-saving aluminum, but it's steel on all other versions. Rear impact bars on all models are high-strength, lightweight steel. There's an aerodynamic front air deflector below the front bumper, and on the Z-28 an aggressive-looking lower air dam and side "skirts" along the rockers. Jacking is accomplished at designated jack points on the body sides.

"For both appearance and aerodynamics," Knickerbocker continues, "we went to a sixty-two-degree windshield, which is a very 'fast' windshield. For the rear of the car, rather than a conventional trunk, we have a full glass liftback; and that piece of glass is the largest and most sophisticated ever used in a high-volume car. It has a lot of advantages in enhancing the interior compartment, because a lot of glass really improves the perceived roominess. From a dimensional standpoint, the interior is better than the old car. In other words, the seating comfort and roominess in all positions is better than, or at least comparable to, what we had before even though the car is downsized and 500 pounds lighter.

Also, we've increased the front seat track dimension. We always did accommodate the long, tall person in F-cars, but some shorter people could not get the seat far enough forward to reach the pedals comfortably. As I recall, we now have something like 192 millimeters

TBI SCHEMATIC

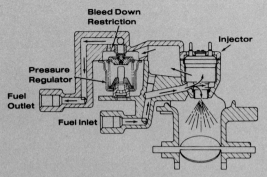

- **Contains Integral 11 PSI Fuel Pressure Regulator**
- **Fuel Sprayed In Finely Dispersed Cone Shape Above Throttle Blade**

SYSTEM OVERVIEW

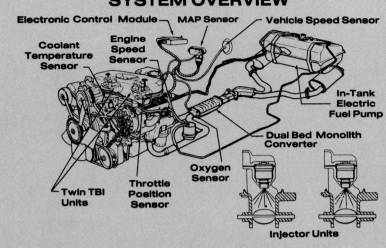

Dual electronic throttle-body fuel injection units on cross-fire manifold power the 5.0 liter Z-28 V-8 engine.

THROTTLE BODY INJECTION
(CLOSED LOOP CONTROL)

ELECTRONIC CONTROL MODULE

SPEED DENSITY

CLOSED LOOP

VEHICLE SPEED

DISTRIBUTOR PULSES

THROTTLE BODY INJECTORS

THROTTLE POSITION

ENGINE SENSORS

EXHAUST SENSOR

CATALYTIC CONVERTER

COOLANT TEMP

MANIFOLD ABSOLUTE PRESSURE (MAP)

IN-TANK ELECTRIC FUEL PUMP

Splash Cup Liquid Vapor Separator

Return Tube

Fuel Tube

Rubber Coupler and Sound Isolator

Fuel Level Sender

Electric Fuel Pump

Filter Strainer

- **Features Separately Serviceable Pump, Sender, and Strainer**

of seat travel, and almost anyone can jump in there and have good comfort and pedal control. We also have recliner seats so the very tall person can get more headroom in that direction. For the first time in an F-car, we have an optional six-way power seat. And, with the rear seat folded down, we can get a full complement of luggage and two golf bags in the back."

Asked whether the base weight (about 2800 pounds) wasn't a bit hefty for a downsized, 1980's car, the project manager replies: "We expect it to be a performance car, as well as a family car, and we expect it to be as rugged as any of our F-cars ever were. That V-8's pretty heavy, you know, and requires a lot of structure around it. Another thing that increases the mass over some other cars is the fact that our option load is tremendous. As we were engineering and developing the car, we kept looking at this. Should we, for instance,

be putting an aluminum hood on it for .01 miles per gallon? In some models, we already have considerable premium material to get us down into a lower EPA weight class. What we have with this program is terrific flexibility. Sometime in the next few years we might not have any market for V-8 engines, and then we'll have a tremendous test bed for applying some of the new, lightweight materials that we have on the shelf. If we go to some things like plastic fenders and plastic T-hatch panels, for example, we'll be able to get this car down substantially."

Camaro chief engineer Zimmer discusses some of the problems that cropped up in bringing the car from drawing board to reality: "There were a lot of little things, and one was the sixty-two-degree windshield angle. The corporation has an internal law, an in-house standard, that says: Thou Shalt Not Go Above Fifty-Nine Degrees because of potential reflections off the instrument cluster. We had to sell that, and it was a tough sell. It seems like a little thing, but it took us quite a while to get everyone convinced. And the backlight, that big lift-up piece of glass that nobody knew how to make because it has a double bend. Not only did the glass manufacturers not know how to make it, but Fisher Body even said they didn't know how to put on the 'beavertail,' that piece of metal on the back end, so that it would be the way we wanted it.

"Another tough battle was the fully-adjustable seat. We had never produced one in the corporation, nor had one ever been offered. Fisher body was bound and determined that that was not an appropriate seat for us to be making. So we contacted some outside suppliers, and when Fisher saw that we were serious about it, they decided they had better get interested. It is now being supplied by an outside company [Lear-Siegler] and Fisher in combination, because Fisher is ultimately responsible for the safety certification. This is the reclining seat with adjustable lateral restraint, adjustable lumbar support and thigh support, adjustable headrest, and, on top of all that, an optional six-way power adjustment. It's better than a Recaro seat, and it's unique to Chevrolet. That was a tough nut. It also poses all kinds of problems with the assembly plant. Normally, they fabricate the seats, but now they have to provide warehouse space for seats that are shipped in fully assembled."

Asked if cost restraints had been as much of a problem as in the past, Zimmer replies: "Nobody came up and told us we had *carte blanche* to do whatever we wanted; but, on the other hand, I never got any resistance to spending money to make the car in the character we wanted it. We were constrained on tool monies and investment monies, but we still had latitude to do the things we felt were essential

to do. We're competing in a little different price range now, and that has caused us to change our thinking. We have taken more of the attitude, well, we're in that price range so let's equip the car to compete in that range rather than being so concerned about the base price. Let's try to make it a single-image car and equip it that way. In that regard it was a very pleasing program for an engineer. It was a fun project for a lot of reasons, but mostly because it was an opportunity to do a car that few people ever have a chance to do.

"I think if there is any market in the future for a sporty car," Zimmer adds, "there's going to be a helluva market for this car. I think it is a tremendous automobile. It's still an American more than a European sports car, but I think its performance and its sophistication are going to be a cut above everything we've seen before from a domestic maker. In many ways the Camaros and Trans-Ams of the past have been pretty hamfisted cars. If you closed your eyes to how much they weighed and how big and cumbersome-looking they were, they handled pretty well. But this is a much more sophisticated car, and I think it's going to re-stimulate a lot of youthful enthusiasts in this country."

Proving Ground development was overseen by assistant staff engineer Fred Schaafsma, who approached the job by breaking it down into logical segments. "We asked ourselves early on, what are the tasks we're going to have a rough time with, if any?" he relates. "Specifically, they were the Z-28 handling, the Berlinetta ride and the Berlinetta acoustics, in that order. From a handling standpoint, we did things differently—we didn't just slap on a bunch of springs, stabilizer bars and struts. We looked at it as a compliance management program, and once that was under control, one of friction management. We did a lot of work both analytically, with measurements, and with subjective evaluations—starting with a front suspension component car—to learn where the compliances were.

"In the pre-prototype stage we were able to refine the system, and we did a lot of stiffness work on the struts and the steering knuckles to handle the lateral [cornering] loads. We had already worked on the front crossmember, and once we got pre-prototype parts we ended up tying it down at an additional point to get rid of any compliance. Of course, we did the standard things that you do in any new car program: optimize the geometry, the swing-arm angles and lengths, to control dive as well as roll. We also did a lot of spring and stabilizer bar development, and we worked on where the roll center height ought to be. We looked at the steering gear and its mounting stiffness. And we found that because there's a large hatch in back, and you can have a T-top, the whole body wanted to twist during roll.

So we ended up doing structural work to get the front and rear sheet-metal stiff enough to keep that down."

A neat trick was used in selecting the front suspension lower control arm bushings. "Because there's a lot of separation between the bushings," Schaafsma explains, "about eighty percent of the lateral load is taken by the front bushing and only twenty percent by the rear bushing. That meant we could use the rear one mostly for impact. We made the front bushing very hard so we wouldn't have a compliance problem with lateral loads; but we kept a large, soft rear bushing for impact compliance, which didn't hurt our handling at all and gave us a helluva lot of ride improvement."

Obviously, Schaafsma is proud of his group's work. Asked what makes the '82 Z-28 so special and unique, he replies without hesitation: "Number one is the on-center handling. I think there's no other car around with the on-center handling of this car. You get a response if you even think about turning. It wants to move immediately. It responds almost to a mental input, with no compliance in the system at all. Second is its degree of refinement as you perceive it on the road. It's not a brutal type of machine, but it has a lot of handling capability. There were no tradeoffs made for ride, yet it's very respectable because we were able to tune the car to have a very good ride quality."

Interestingly, the '82 Camaro evolved under three different Chevrolet chief engineers, all of them strongly performance- and product-oriented. Conception and initial planning took place under Bob Stemple, who then (in November 1978) was promoted to Pontiac Division as general manager and a GM vice president. Stemple was replaced by Lloyd Reuss, who had held a number of top engineering assignments at Chevrolet before moving to Buick Division as chief engineer. Reuss held the position for about two years until December 1980, when the corporation sent him back to Buick as general manager and a GM vice president. At that point, chief passenger-car engineer Paul King moved up to fill the slot.

"I got there after the basic configuration of the car had been decided," Reuss relates. "But then we had to look at what kind of personality it was going to have. What would be the styling details? What would its image be? A month or so after I was there, we had a half-day session to talk about what we were trying to accomplish with it. We decided that probably the biggest personality change should be in the Z-28, and we sort of focused on that. We wanted to revert back to the original '67 Z-28, which had major emphasis on the powertrain, the chassis, the mechanical items that weren't visible just sitting in the showroom. As you'll recall, that car was actually a bit

'82 Camaro Berlinetta fiberglass model in final form, fall 1980.

understated from an appearance standpoint.

"So we decided to design the entire product line, not only the Z-28, to have a much cleaner, more efficient look than the Camaro of the last several years. We wanted to develop two personalities: the Z-28; and then the Berlinetta and the regular base Camaro. For the Z-28 we planned to develop a unique powertrain and a unique suspension and handling system. We were not going to have bold striping schemes, big fender flares and that sort of thing. The new Z-28 was supposed to be more of a gymnast compared to the old one, which was more of a boxer. That was the analogy we used in getting the whole organization thinking that way."

Was this program successful? In the words of Paul King, who helped direct it from the beginning as Chevrolet's chief passenger-car engineer, then as chief engineer after replacing Reuss late in 1980, "It really grabs you in appearance. The styling is outstanding, makes you feel good to be in it, near it and looking at it. The car is more solid, has a better feel. Its general efficiency—what we get out of a given amount of engine or a given amount of fuel—is better. The new

'82 Camaro Z-28 fiberglass model in its final form, March 1980.

engine program makes me particularly happy, both the new Z-28 and the dual TBI, and we'll be able to build on that for a long time. Down the road, we'll have some new things coming on top of that. Driving the car adds to all these impressions . . . it just makes you want to go. It isn't a different kind of car; it's really the same kind as before, the same direction, only better. It's still got the hairy feel, the impressive looks, but it's slicker, with better aero, better structure, better packaging—just a better car all the way around."

Dimensionally, the new Camaro is well over a foot shorter than the '81 at 184 inches overall, and it sits on a seven-inch-shorter 101-inch wheelbase. Both tread widths are 59.3 inches, two inches narrower in front but only 0.7 inches less in back. Overall height is little changed, but the new car is nearly three inches narrower. Nevertheless, interior dimensions are comparable or better in front and (except for hiproom) substantially better in the rear. Cargo volume under the big glass hatch measures 11.7 cubic feet (below window level) compared to the previous 7.1 cubic-foot trunk.

While a lot of desirable equipment such as dual sport mirrors, side window defogger outlets and interior console are standard, the substantial option list includes lift-off T-roof panels, remote hatch release, power windows and door locks, electrically adjustable outside mirrors, electric rear window defogger, rear window washer and wiper, pulse wipers, air conditioning, four-wheel disc brakes, and cruise control (manual or automatic transmission) with resume feature. Other options include tilt steering wheel, rally wheels, limited-slip differential, halogen headlamps, gauge package (standard on Berlinetta and Z-28), power antenna and a selection of new-design radios ranging from AM to AM/FM stereo with eight-track or cassette tape.

As this book goes to press in mid-summer 1981, there is some question about the '82 F-cars' launch time. Originally planned for the normal fall introduction, final development of the new car and an extended "build-out" of the '81 model have delayed the official launch until mid-January 1982.

Whenever it finally hits the street, the '82 Camaro represents a quantum leap forward in specialty-car design and engineering sophistication. We have seen the car and believe it's going to be a new classic. It sits low, lean, mean and hungry . . . looks fast even at rest. Walking up to it, especially the Z-28, you feel the same sort of excitement you would get from a Ferrari or some other rare and expensive exotic. We also were allowed a brief but exhilarating test drive at the Milford, Michigan Proving Ground, and we can't remember a more willing, precise and agile-handling American car.

With a more reasonable, less hostile administration in Washington and a new era of exciting but responsible automotive development on the horizon, we see evidence everywhere that the word "fun" is being restored to the domestic auto industry's vocabulary. A growing number of people are fed up with boring cars, "appliance" cars, designed for little more than transportation from one place to another. They want quality, reliability and, yes, reasonable fuel economy, but they don't want to give up style and driving excitement. We think there's a reborn market for exciting and distinctive automobiles in America, and we think the new Camaro will be at the forefront of that market. It will be an American exotic of sorts, one of the few remaining performance cars with the drive wheels in back where they belong. It will be more expensive than ever before, but a lot more car as well . . . and a lot *less* expensive than anything with comparable design, features and handling.

As Chevrolet general manager and GM vice president Bob Lund succinctly puts it: "This new car, the '82, won't take a back seat to anything."

Camaro:
A Color Portfolio

Color Portraits by Roy Query:
1967/ RS/SS Indy Pace Car, 1967 396 SS,
1967 Z-28, 1968 Base Model, 1968 SS Convertible,
1968 Z-28, 1969 350 SS, 1969 Yenko 427 Coupe
1969 ZL-1, 1970½ RS, 1971 Base Model,
1973 Z-28, 1974 Z-28, 1977 RS, 1978 Mitchell Coupe,
1980 IROC Z-28, 1980 Z-28 Cheverra, 1980 Z-28,
1981 Z-28, 1982 Berlinetta, 1982 Z-28.

Color Portraits by Rick Lenz:
1967 RS, 1967 350 SS, 1969 350 SS, 1969 Z-28,
1970½ Z-28 RS, 1973 Type LT, 1978 Base Model,
1979 Berlinetta.

Car Portraits Courtesy of General Motors Corporation:
1966-67 Prototype Camaro; 1969 RS.

1966-67 Prototype Camaro, Owner: General Motors Corporation

Above: 1967 RS/SS Convertible Indy 500 Pace Car, Owner: Dan Young ● *Below: 1967 RS, Owner: W.H. Heinrich*

Above: 1967 RS/SS 350 Convertible, Owner: Dan Erickson • Below: 1967 RS/SS 396 Turbo-Jet, Owner: Richard Buxbaum

1967 Z-28, Owner: Fred Bartling

1968 Base Model, Owner: William Lear

Above: 1968 SS-350 Convertible, Owner: George Oleskiewicz • Below: 1968 Z-28, Owner: Carl Richardson

Above: 1969 SS 396, Owner: Bill Stephenson ● Below: 1969 SS 350, Owner: Ed Koehler

1969 Yenko 427 SC, Owner: Daniel Mamsen

1969 Z-28, Owner: Bill Orndorff

Above: 1969 RS, Owner: General Motors • Below: 1969 ZL-1, Owner: Bill Porterfield • Right: 1970-½ RS, Owner: Gary Witzenburg

1970-½ Z-28 RS, Owner: Scott Owens

1971 350 Coupe, Owner: Gary Kline

1973 Z-28, Owner: Scott J. Kinder ● Below: 1973 Type LT, Owner: Harrison Reno Honda ● Right: 1974 Z-28, Owner: Jim Murauskis

1977 Type LT RS, Owner: Richard C. Cupp

1978 Base Model, Owner: Debbie Layman

Left: 1978 Mitchell Coupe, Owner: Jon Albert • Above: 1979 Berlinetta, Owner: Ken Brown • 1980 IROC Z-28, Owner: Buck Baker Driving School

1980 Z-28 Cheverra, Owner: PPG Industries

1980 Z-28, Owner: Cameron W. McGill

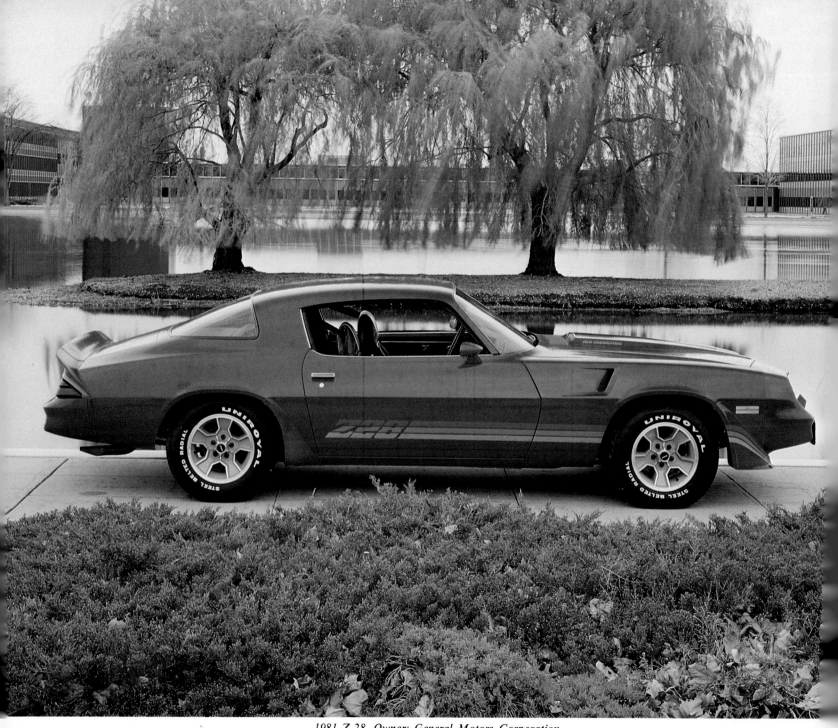

1981 Z-28, Owner: General Motors Corporation

1982 Berlinetta, Owner: General Motors Corporation

1982 Z-28, Owner: General Motors Corporation

Bibliography

Advertising Age, various articles. December 12th, 1966; May 17th, 1967.

"Americans Put the Car in Its Place." *Business Week*, September 18th, 1971.

"A New Way of Putting the Shine On." *Friends*, May 1979.

Applegate, Howard and Shelby, "On Paper." *Car Exchange*, April 1981.

Automotive News, various articles, September 19th, 1966; September 26th, 1966; November 14th, 1966; January 30th, 1967; May 1st, 1967; August 14th, 1967; February 16th, 1970; March 16th, 1970; May 25th, 1970; September 6th, 1971; September 16th, 1974; January 3rd, 1977; January 17th, 1977.

Autoweek, various articles. December 13th, 1975; December 20th, 1975; April 14th, 1978.

Baechtel, John, "Arrogant Acts." *Car Craft*, Petersen Publishing Company, Los Angeles, California, July 1980.

Calvin, Jean, "Chevy's GT Machine." *The Complete Chevrolet Book*, Los Angeles, California: Petersen Publishing Company, 1972.

"Camaro." *The Complete Chevrolet Book*, Los Angeles, California: Petersen Publishing Company, 1973.

Car and Driver, Camaro tests and articles. November 1966, March 1967, May 1967, September 1967, July 1968, August 1969, March 1970, May 1970, May 1971, September 1973, August 1975, September 1979, March 1978, November 1978, April 1980, November 1980.

Car Life, Camaro tests and articles. March 1966, March 1967, September 1968, May 1969, August 1969, March 1970, May 1970.

Cars, Camaro tests and articles. April 1969, May 1980.

Chapin, Kim, "A Win for Cougar, a Wild Ride for Camaro." *Sports Illustrated*, August 14th, 1967.

Chapman, Patricia, "How Youth Has Changed the Look of the '68 Models." *Parade*, October 1st, 1967.

"Chevrolet Division of General Motors." *Madison Avenue Magazine*, February 1979.

"Chevy's Camaro Passes 100,000th Milestone." *Southern Automotive Journal*, May 1967.

Dammann, George H., *Sixty Years of Chevrolet*. Glen Ellyn, Illinois: Crestline Publishing, 1972.

"Detroit Bulletin." *Hot Rod Industry News*, Los Angeles, California: Petersen Publishing Company, January 1967.

Detroit News, various articles. April 8th, 1965; September 13th, 1966; January 24th, 1967; February 25th, 1967; March 7th, 1967; March 25th, 1970; September 15th, 1970; November 26th, 1972.

Gardner, Ev, "About Autos and Racing." *Washington Daily News*, Washington, D.C., January 16th, 1967.

"GMRE Camaro." *Ward's Auto World*, January 1973.

Gutts, Joe, "Joe Gutts Tests the New Camaro." *Science & Mechanics*, December 1966.

Hearst, John Jr., "Camaro Moving Up in Competition Fast." *World Journal Tribune*, New York, New York, January 15th, 1967.

Hot Rod, Camaro tests and articles. January 1967, January 1969, March 1970, June 1972, April 1977.

Lamm, Michael, *The Great Camaro*. Stockton, California: Lamm-Morada Publishing Company, 1978.

Martin, Gordon, "Camaro Takes on Ford, Mercury." *San Francisco Chronicle*, San Francisco, California, September 7th, 1967.

McPherson, Donald H.; Rubly, Charles M.; Valade, Victor D., *The Chevrolet Camaro*. SAE Technical Paper #670016, Warrendale, Pennsylvania: Society of Automotive Engineers, Inc., 1967.

Mechanix Illustrated, Camaro articles. June 1966, November 1966.

Motor Trend, Camaro tests and articles. July 1966, October 1966, November 1966, December 1966, July 1967, February 1969, January 1970, March 1970, February 1973, May 1977, February 1978.

Popular Mechanics, Camaro articles. October 1966, November 1966, July 1967, March 1970.

Popular Science, Camaro articles. December 1965, October 1966.

Road & Track, Camaro tests and articles. March 1967, June 1968, March 1970, May 1970, August 1971, April 1972, May 1975, September 1977, October 1978.

Road Test, Camaro tests and articles. August 1969, April 1970, June 1970, August 1970, June 1973, May 1977, June 1977.

Schorr, Martyn L., *Z-28 Camaro, the Number One Team's Cafe Racer*. Baldwin, Long Island, New York: Performance Publications, 1978.

Shafer, Ronald G., "What's in a Name? Soul Searching, Agony and Woe, Says Detroit." *Wall Street Journal*, June 30th, 1966.

Sports Car Graphic, Camaro Tests and Articles. March 1967, October 1968, March 1970, May 1970, June 1970.

Thomas, Bob, "Chevrolet Edging Back Into Racing With Z-28." *Los Angeles Times*, Los Angeles, California.

Time, various articles. June 17th, 1966; September 9th, 1966; April 5th, 1968.

Tolbert, Frank X., "Chevy's Camaro Proves a Joy." *Dallas Morning News,* Dallas, Texas.

Ward's Automotive Reports, various articles. February 3rd, 1969; May 18th, 1970.

"Wilder Paint Jobs." *Super Service Station*, August 1967.

Williams, Mardo, "Camaro Could Hurt '67 Mustang Sales." *Columbus Dispatch*, Columbus, Ohio, September 25th, 1966.

Yarbrough, Charles, "Camaro, A Hearty Answer." *Washington Star*, Washington, D.C., October 7th, 1966.

Appendices

CAMARO ENGINES

Cyl.	Cu.In.	Bore & Stroke	Carb.	C.R.	BHP & RPM
1967					
6	230	3.875 x 3.25	1 bbl.	8.5	140 @ 4400
6	250	3.875 x 3.53	1 bbl.	8.5	155 @ 4200
V8	302	4.002 x 3.005	4 bbl.	11.0	290 @ 5800
V8	327	4.00 x 3.25	2 bbl.	8.75	210 @ 4600
V8	327	4.00 x 3.25	4 bbl.	10.0	275 @ 4800
V8	350*	4.00 x 3.48	4 bbl.	10.25	295 @ 4800
V8	396	4.094 x 3.76	4 bbl.	10.25	325 @ 4800
V8	396	4.094 x 3.76	4 bbl.	11.0	375 @ 5600

*available only as part of SS option

Cyl.	Cu.In.	Bore & Stroke	Carb.	C.R.	BHP & RPM
1968					
6	230	3.875 x 3.25	1 bbl.	8.5	140 @ 4400
6	250	3.875 x 3.53	1 bbl.	8.5	155 @ 4200
V8	302	4.002 x 3.005	4 bbl.	11.0	290 @ 5800
V8	327	4.001 x 3.25	2 bbl.	8.75	210 @ 4600
V8	327	4.001 x 3.25	4 bbl.	10.0	275 @ 4800
V8	350	4.00 x 3.48	4 bbl.	10.25	295 @ 4000
V8	396	4.094 x 3.76	4 bbl.	10.25	325 @ 4800
V8	396	4.094 x 3.76	4 bbl.	10.25	350 @ 5200
V8	396	4.094 x 3.76	4 bbl.	11.0	375 @ 5600

Cyl.	Cu.In.	Bore & Stroke	Carb.	C.R.	BHP & RPM
1969					
6	230	3.875 x 3.25	1 bbl.	8.5	140 @ 4400
6	250	3.875 x 3.53	1 bbl.	8.5	155 @ 4200
V8	302	4.002 x 3.005	4 bbl.	11.0	290 @ 5800
V8	307	3.875 x 3.25	2 bbl.	9.0	200 @ 4600
V8	327	4.00 x 3.25	2 bbl.	8.75	210 @ 4600
V8	350	4.00 x 3.48	4 bbl.	9.0	255 @ 4800
V8	350*	4.00 x 3.48	4 bbl.	10.25	300 @ 4800
V8	396*	4.094 x 3.76	4 bbl.	10.25	325 @ 4800
V8	396	4.094 x 3.76	4 bbl.	10.25	350 @ 5200
V8	396	4.094 x 3.76	4 bbl.	11.0	375 @ 5600

*available only as part of SS option

Cyl.	Cu.In.	Bore & Stroke	Carb.	C.R.	BHP @ RPM
1970					
6	250	3.875 x 3.53	1 bbl.	8.5	155 @ 4200
V8	307	3.875 x 3.25	2 bbl.	9.0	200 @ 4600
V8	350	4.00 x 3.48	2 bbl.	9.0	250 @ 4800
V8	350*	4.00 x 3.48	4 bbl.	10.25	300 @ 4800
V8	350**	4.00 x 3.48	4 bbl.	11.0	360 @ 5800
V8	396***	4.126 x 3.76 (402 c.i.)	4 bbl.	10.25	350 @ 5200
V8	396	4.126 x 3.76 (402 c.i.)	4 bbl.	11.0	375 @ 5600

* included with Camaro SS option   ** included with Z-28 option
***available only as part of SS option

Cyl.	Cu.In.	Bore & Stroke	Carb.	C.R.	BHP @ RPM
1971					
L6	250	3.875 x 3.53	1 bbl.	8.5	110 @ 3800
V8	307	3.875 x 3.25	2 bbl.	8.5	140 @ 4400
V8	350	4.00 x 3.48	2 bbl.	8.5	165 @ 4000
V8	350	4.00 x 3.48	4 bbl.	8.5	210 @ 4400
V8	396*	4.126 x 3.76 (402 c.i.)	4 bbl.	8.5	260 @ 4400
V8	350**	4.00 x 3.48	4 bbl.	9.0	275 @ 5600

*available only as part of SS option
**included with Z-28 option

Cyl.	Cu.In.	Bore & Stroke	Carb.	C.R.	BHP @ RPM
1972					
L6	250	3.875 x 3.53	1 bbl.	8.5	110 @ 3800
V8	307*	3.875 x 3.25	2 bbl.	8.5	130 @ 4000
V8	350	4.00 x 3.48	2 bbl.	8.5	165 @ 4000
V8	350**	4.00 x 3.48	4 bbl.	8.5	200 @ 4400
V8	396*	4.126 x 3.76 (402 c.i.)	4 bbl.	8.5	240 @ 4400
V8	350***	4.00 x 3.48	4 bbl.	9.0	255 @ 5600

*not available in California   **available only as part of SS option
***included with Z-28 option

Cyl.	Cu.In.	Bore & Stroke	Carb.	C.R.	BHP @ RPM
1973					
L6	250	3.875 x 3.53	1 bbl.	8.25	100 @ 3600
V8	307	3.875 x 3.25	2 bbl.	8.5	115 @ 3600
V8	350	4.00 x 3.48	2 bbl.	8.5	145 @ 4000
V8	350	4.00 x 3.48	4 bbl.	8.5	175 @ 4000
V8	350*	4.00 x 3.48	4 bbl.	9.0	245 @ 5200

*included with Z-28 option

1974

Cyl.	Cu.In.	Bore & Stroke	Carb.	C.R.	BHP & RPM
L6	250	3.875 x 3.53	1 bbl.	8.25	100 @ 3600
V8	350	4.00 x 3.48	2 bbl.	8.5	145 @ 3800
V8	350	4.00 x 3.48	4 bbl.	8.5	160 @ 3800
V8	350	4.00 x 3.48	4 bbl.	8.5	185 @ 4000
V8	350*	4.00 x 3.48	4 bbl.	9.0	245 @ 5200

*included with Z-28 option

1975

Cyl.	Cu.In.	Bore & Stroke	Carb.	C.R.	BHP & RPM
L6	250	3.875 x 3.53	1 bbl.	8.25	105 @ 3800
V8	350	4.00 x 3.48	2 bbl.	8.5	145 @ 3800
V8	350	4.00 x 3.48.	4 bbl.	8.5	155 @ 3800

1976

Cyl.	Cu.In.	Bore & Stroke	Carb.	C.R.	BHP & RPM
L6	250	3.875 x 3.53	1 bbl.	8.25	105 @ 3800
V8	305 (5.0 liter)	3.736 x 3.48	2 bbl.	8.5	140 @ 3800
V8	350 (5.7 liter)	4.00 x 3.48	4 bbl.	8.5	165 @ 3800

1977

Cyl.	Cu.In.	Bore & Stroke	Carb.	C.R.	BHP & RPM
L6	250 (4.1 liter)	3.875 x 3.53	1 bbl.	8.3	110 @ 3800** / 90 @ 3600***
V8	305 (5.0 liter)	3.736 x 3.48	2 bbl.	8.5	145 @ 3800** / 135 @ 3800***
V8	350 (5.7 liter)	4.00 x 3.48	4 bbl.	8.2	170 @ 3800** / 160 @ 3800***
'77½ V8	350* (5.7 liter)	4.00 x 3.48	4 bbl.	8.5	170 @ 3800

*reintroduction of Z-28 option **available in 49 states
***available in California

1978

Cyl.	Cu.In.	Bore & Stroke	Carb.	C.R.	BHP & RPM
L6	250 (4.1 liter)	3.875 x 3.53	1 bbl.	8.1	110 @ 3800** / 90 @ 3600***
V8	305 (5.0 liter)	3.736 x 3.48	2 bbl.	8.4	145 @ 3800** / 136 @ 3800***
V8	350 (5.7 liter)	4.00 x 3.48	4 bbl.	8.2	170 @ 3800** / 160 @ 3800***
V8	350* (5.7 liter)	4.00 x 3.48	4 bbl.	8.2	185 @ 4000** / 175 @ 3800***

*included with Z-28 option ** available in 49 states
***available in California

1979

Cyl.	Cu.In.	Bore & Stroke	Carb.	C.R.	BHP & RPM
L6	250 (4.1 liter)	3.875 x 3.53	1 bbl.	8.0	115 @ 3800**
				8.2	90 @ 3600***
V8	305 (5.0 liter)	3.736 x 3.48	2 bbl.	8.4	130 @ 3200**
					125 @ 3200***
V8	350 (5.7 liter)	4.00 x 3.48	4 bbl.	8.2	170 @ 3800**
					165 @ 3800***
V8	350* (5.7 liter)	4.00 x 3.48	4 bbl.	8.2	175 @ 4000**
					170 @ 4000***

*included with Z-28 option
**available in 49 states
***available in California

1980

Cyl.	Cu.In.	Bore & Stroke	Carb.	C.R.	BHP & RPM
V6	229 (3.8 liter)	3.736 x 3.48	2 bbl.	8.6	115 @ 4000
V6	231 (3.8 liter)	3.80 x 3.40	2 bbl.	8.0	110 @ 3800***
V8	267 (4.4 liter)	3.50 x 3.48	2 bbl.	8.3	120 @ 3600
V8	305 (5.0 liter)	3.736 x 3.48	4 bbl.	8.6	155 @ 4000**
					155 @ 4000***
V8	350* (5.7 liter)	4.00 x 3.48	4 bbl.	8.2	190 @ 4200**
					165 @ 4000***

*included with Z-28 option
**available in 49 states
***available in California

1981

Cyl.	Cu.In.	Bore & Stroke	Carb.	C.R.	BHP & RPM
V6	229 (3.8 liter)	3.736 x 3.48	2 bbl.	8.6	110 @ 4200
V6	231 (3.8 liter)	3.80 x 3.40	2 bbl.	8.0	110 @ 3800***
V8	267 (4.4 liter)	3.50 x 3.48	2 bbl.	8.3	115 @ 4000
V8	305 (5.0 liter)	3.736 x 3.48	4 bbl.	8.6	150 @ 3800
					165 @ 4000*
V8	350** (5.7 liter)	4.00 x 3.48	4 bbl.	8.2	175 @ 4000

*with RPO Z-28
**includedwith Z-28 option
***available in California

CAMARO RACING RECORD

Sports Car Club of America: National Championships

Class A Sedan: Dick Lang, 1968
Bill Petree, 1969
Warren Agor, 1972
Carl Shafer, 1973
Joe Chamberlain, 1974
Jim Crittenden, 1975
Randy Blessing, 1976
Randy Blessing, 1977
Randy Blessing, 1978

GT-1: Jerry Dunbar, 1980

Sports Car Club of America: Trans-Am Sedan Championship Victories

1967: 3 wins
Mark Donohue/Craig Fisher, Marlboro, Maryland
Mark Donohue, Las Vegas, Nevada
Mark Donohue, Kent, Washington

1968: 10 wins, Series Champion
Mark Donohue/Craig Fisher, Sebring, Florida
Mark Donohue, New Mannford, Oklahoma
Mark Donohue, Lime Rock, Connecticut
Mark Donohue, Mid-Ohio, Lexington, Ohio
Mark Donohue, Bridgehampton, New York
Mark Donohue, Carpentersville, Illinois
Mark Donohue, St. Jovite, Quebec
Mark Donohue, Loudon, New Hampshire
Mark Donohue, Castle Rock, Colorado
Mark Donohue, Kent, Washington

1969: 8 wins, Series Champion
Mark Donohue, Loudon, New Hampshire
Mark Donohue, St. Jovite, Quebec
Mark Donohue, Watkins Glen, New York
Mark Donohue, Monterey, California
Mark Donohue, Sonoma, California
Mark Donohue, Riverside, California
Ron Bucknum, Lexington, Ohio
Ron Bucknum, Kent, Washington

1970: 2 wins
Milt Minter, Brainerd, Minnesota
Vic Elford, Watkins Glen, New York

1973: 2 wins
Warren Agor, St. Pie, Quebec
Maurice Carter, Watkins Glen, New York

1976: 1 win
Joe Chamberlain, Portland, Oregon

1979: 1 win
Miguel Muniz, Mexico City, Mexico

1980: 1 win
Roy Woods, Trois-Rivieres, Quebec

CAMARO COLORS

Company Code		DuPont Lucite	Rinished-Mason	Ditzler
1967				
AA	Tuxedo Black	88	A-946	9300
CC	Ermine White	4024L	A-1199	8259
DD	Nantucket Blue	4815L	A-1899	13349
EE	Deepwater Blue	4817L	A-1900	13346
FF	Marina Blue	4850L	A-1920	13364
GG	Granada Gold	4825L	A-1919	22818
HH	Mountain Green	4816L	A-1901	43651
KK	Emerald Turquoise	4818L	A-1903	43661
LL	Tahoe Turquoise	4824L	A-1904-G	43659
MM	Royal Plum	4832L	A-1905	50717
NN	Madeira Maroon	4624LH	A-1711M	50700
RR	Bolero Red	4822LH	A-1907R	71583
SS	Sierra Fawn	4826L	A-1908	22813
TT	Capri Cream	4819L	A-1909	81578
YY	Butternut Yellow	4620L	A-1715	81500
1968				
AA	Tuxedo Black	88	A-946	9300
CC	Ermine White	4024-L	A-1199	8259
DD	Grotto Blue	4892-L	A-1985	13512
EE	Fathom Blue	4899-L	A-1992	13513
FF	Island Teal	4901-L	A-1994	13514
GG	Ash Gold	4896-L	A-1988	22942
HH	Grecian Green	4902-L	A-1995	43775
KK	Tripoli Turquoise	4900-L	A-1993	13516
LL	Teal Blue	4893-L	A-1986	13516
NN	Cordovan Maroon	4915-LH	A-1999M	50775
PP	Seafrost Green	4897-L	A-1989	43774
RR	Matador Red	4948-LH	A-1997R	71634
TT	Palomino Ivory	4895-L	A-1987	81617
VV	Sequoia Green	4898-L	A-1990	43773
YY	Butternut Yellow	4620-L	A-1715	81500
JJ	Rallye Green	5070L	A-2005D	43898
OO	Bronze	4910	A-2010F	43775
UU	LeMans Blue	4908	A-2007	2083
ZZ	British Green	4949	A-2011	43895
1969				
10	Tuxedo Black	88L	A-946	9300
50	Dover White	5033L	A-2080	2058
53	Glacier Blue	5015L	A-2100	2077
51	Dusk Blue	5016L	A-2098	2075
71	LeMans Blue	5030L	A-2109	2083
65	Olympic Gold	5010L	A-2106D	2082
61	Burnished Brown	5011L	A-2104	2081
55	Azure Turquoise	5014L	A-2101	2078

Company Code	
59	Frost Green
67	Burgundy
69	Cortez Silver
52	Garnet Red
63	Champagne
57	Fathom Green
40	Butternut Yellow
72	Hugger Orange
76	Daytona Yellow
79	Rallye Green
1970	
25	Astro Blue
26	Mulsanne Blue
67	Classic Copper
58	Autumn Gold
53	Camaro Gold
17	Shadow Gray
43	Citrus Green
48	Forest Green
45	Green Mist
65	Hugger Orange
75	Cranberry Red
63	Desert Sand
14	Cortez Silver
10	Classic White
51	Daytona Yellow
1971	
19	Tuxedo Black
26	Mulsanne Blue
24	Ascot Blue
67	Classic Copper
53	Placer Gold
43	Lime Green
42	Cottonwood Gre
49	Antique Green
62	Burnt Orange
75	Cranberry Red
78	Rosewood Meta
61	Sandalwood
13	Nevada Silver
11	Antique White
52	Sunflower Yello
1972	
26	Mulsanne Blue
68	Midnight Bronz

Pont :ite	Rinished-Mason	Ditzler
2L	A-2103	2080
3LH	A-2107M	50700
2L	A-2108	2059
9LH	A-2099R	2076
4L	A-2105	22813
3L	A-2102	2079
5L	A-1715	81500
1LM	A-2111R	2084
5LH	A-2119	2094
0L	A-2005D	43898

3L	A-2261	2165
0L	A-2262	2213
L	A-2276G	23215
L	A-2272	2179
L	A-2091F	2174
L	A-1910	32604
L	A2266	2334
L	A-2269	2173
L	A-2268	2171
LM	A-2111R	2084
LH	A-2278F	2189
L	A-2275	2183
L	A-2108	2059
L	A-1802	8631
LH	A-2119	2094

	A-946	9300
L	A-2482	2213
L	A-2439	2328
L	A-2276G	23215
LH	A-2449F	2339
L	A-2445D	2334
L	A-2444G	2333
L	A-2448	2337
L	A-2451G	2340
H	A-2278F	2189
	A-2461	2350
	A-2273	2181
	A-2438	2327
	A-2080	2058
H	A-2422	2338

	A-2482	2213
	A-2565	2451

Company Code		DuPont Lucite	Rinished-Mason	Ditzler
63	Mohave Gold	5434L	A-2562D	2448
53	Placer Gold	5280L	A-2449F	2339
24	Ascot Blue	5270L	A-2439	2328
43	Gulf Green	5428L	A-2548	2435
48	Sequoia Green	5429L	A-2552	2439
36	Spring Green	5436L	A-2546D	2433
65	Orange Flame	5435L	A-2564D	2450
75	Cranberry Red	5339L	A-2278F	2189
14	Pewter Silver	5426L	A-2541	2429
50	Covert Tan	5431L	A-2554	2441
11	Antique White	5338L	A-2080	2058
56	Cream Yellow	5443L	A-2558G	2444
57	Golden Brown	5439L	A-2559	2445

1973

Company Code		DuPont Lucite	Rinished-Mason	Ditzler
64	Silver Metallic	5476L	A-2643	2541
24	Light Blue Metallic	5473L	A-2623	2523
26	Dark Blue Metallic	5478L	A-2624	2524
29	Midnight Blue Metallic	5474L	A-2626	2526
42	Dark Green Metallic	5489L	A-2628	2528
44	Light Green Metallic	5475L	A-2629	2529
46	Green-Gold Metallic	5479L	A-2631D	2530
68	Dark Brown Metallic	5483L	A-2647D	2543
74	Dark Red Metallic	5477L	A-2649F	2545
97	Medium Orange Metallic	5552L	A-2659	2555
60	Light Copper Metallic	5490L	A-2639D	2538
51	Light Yellow	5484L	A-2634G	2533
56	Chamois	5481L	A-2638	2537
48	Midnight Green	5480L	A-2632	2531
75	Medium Red	5485L	A-2650F	2546
11	Antique White	5338L	A-2080	2058

1974

Company Code		DuPont Lucite	Rinished-Mason	Ditzler
11	Antique White	5338L	A-2080	2058
26	Bright Blue Metallic	5478LH	A-2624	2524
29	Midnight Blue Metallic	5474L	A-2626	2526
36	Aqua Blue Metallic	42805L	A-2702	2640
40	Lime-Yellow	42800LH	A-2703	2641
46	Bright Green Metallic	42806	A-2705	2643
49	Medium Dark Green Metallic	42803L	A-2707	2645
50	Cream Beige	42807L	A-2708	2646
51	Bright Yellow	42809LM	A-2709G	2677
53	Light Gold Metallic	42876LM	A-2710G	2649
55	Sandstone	42808L	A-2711	2650
59	Golden Brown Metallic	42875L	A-2480G	2367
64	Silver Metallic	5476L	A-2643	2541
66	Bronze Metallic	42801LH	A-2714G	2653
74	Medium Red Metallic	42810LM	A-2718F	2658
75	Medium Red	5485LM	A-2650F	2546

1975

Company Code		DuPont Lucite	Rinished-Mason	Ditzler
13	Silver Metallic	5338L	A-2080	2518
26	Bright Blue Metallic	43452L	A-2799	2746
29	Dark Blue Metallic	43453L	A-2802	2748
74	Red Metallic	42810LM	A-2718F	2658
11	Antique White	5338L	A-2080	2058
24	Medium Blue	43451L	A-2798	2745
44	Medium Green	42802L	A-2704	2642
49	Dark Green Metallic	43454LH	A-2805	2752
50	Cream Beige	42807L	A-2708	2646
55	Sandstone	43455L	A-2808	2755
58	Dark Sandstone Metallic	43461LH	A-2810	2757
64	Persimmon Metallic	43458LM	A-2813F	2760
63	Light Saddle Metallic	43457LH	A-28112D	2759
75	Red	5485LM	A-2650F	2546
51	Bright Yellow	42809L	A-2709G	2677
15	Light Graystone	43450L	A-2793	2742

1976

Company Code		DuPont Lucite	Rinished-Mason	Ditzler
11	Antique White	5338L	A-2080	2058
19	Black	99L	A-946	9300
36	Firethorn Metallic	43953LH	A-2916F	2811
51	Bright Yellow	44139LH	A-2936D	2094
75	Light Red	5485-LM	A-2650F	2546
13	Silver	43537L	A-2618	2518
28	Light Blue Metallic	44141L	A-2801	2772
35	Dark Blue Metallic	44130LH	A-2930D	2863
37	Mahogany Metallic	44131LM	A-2931G	2864
40	Lime Metallic	44134LH	A-2934G	2816
49	Dark Green Metallic	43454LH	A-2805	2752
50	Cream	44132L	A-2935	2867
65	Buckskin	44159L	A-2939	2829
67	Saddle Brown Metallic	44138L	A-2941	2871
78	Red-Orange	44140LM	A-2942R	2084

1977

Company Code		DuPont Lucite	Rinished-Mason	Ditzler
11	Antique White	5338L	A-2080	2058
13	Silver Metallic	44716L	A-8680	2953
19	Black	99L	A-946	9300
29	Dark Blue Metallic	44718L	A-8645	2959
36	Firethorn Metallic	43953LM	A-2916F	2811
61	Light Buckskin	44713L	A-2999	2869
69	Brown Metallic	44721LH	A-8698F	2972
78	Orange Metallic	44715LM	A-8702F	2976
22	Light Blue Metallic	44171L	A-8682	2955
44	Medium Green Metallic	44719LH	A-8690	2964
63	Buckskin Metallic	44722L	A-86950	2970

CAMARO COLORS (cont.)

Company Code		DuPont Lucite	Rinished-Mason	Ditzler
1977 (cont.)				
51	Bright Yellow	44139LH	A-2936D	2094
38	Dark Aqua Metallic	44714L	A-8687	2961
75	Light Red	5485LM	A-2650F	2546
1978				
11	Antique White	5338	A-2080	2058
15	Silver	45177	A-9369	3076
19	Black	99	A-946	9300
48	Dark Blue-Green Metallic	44718	A-8685	2959
24	Bright Blue Metallic	45185	A-9372D	3079
22	Light Blue Metallic	44717	A-8682	2955
63	Camel Metallic	45181	A-9383D	3090
69	Dark Camel Metallic	45182	A-9385G	3092
77	Carmine Metallic	45184	A-9389F	3096
75	Light Red	45187	—	3095
67	Saffron Metallic	45183	A-9384F	3091
51	Bright Yellow	45186	A-9377F	3084
34	Yellow-Orange	45277*	—	3070*
1979				
11	Antique White	5888	A-2080	2058
15	Silver	45177	A-9369	3076
19	Black	99	A-946	9300
29	Dark Blue Metallic	45801	A-9802G	3121

Company Code		DuPont Lucite	Rinished-Mason	Ditzler
24	Bright Blue Metallic	45807	A-9801	3120
22	Light Blue Metallic	44717	A-8682	2955
40	Light Green	45803	A-9803	3122
44	Medium Green Metallic	45804	A-9805D	3123
51	Bright Yellow	45186	A-93775	3084
61	Beige	45804	A-9809	3124
63	Camel Metallic	45806	A-9811D	3125
69	Dark Brown Metallic	45805	A-9813G	3126
75	Red	45187	A-9388F	3095
77	Carmine Metallic	45184	A-9389F	3096
1980				
11	White	5338	A-2080	2058
15	Silver	45177	A-9369	3076
19	Black	99	A-946	9300
29	Dark Blue Metallic	B-8007	A-11403D	3207
24	Bright Blue Metallic	B-8013	A-11402	3217
80	Bronze Metallic	B-8015	A-11420	3222
67	Dark Brown Metallic	B-8016	A-11413	3226
84	Charcoal Metallic	B-8012	A-11421	3223
76	Dark Claret Metallic	B-8010	A-11417F	3212
57	Gold Metallic	B-8014	A-11410D	3215
40	Lime Green Metallic	B-8011	A-11404	3218
72	Red	44770	A-8699F	2973
79	Red Orange	B-8002	A-11419	3221
51	Bright Yellow	B-8619	A-11409	3219

Company Code	
1981	
11	White
16	Silver Metallic
19	Black
29	Dark Blue Metallic
20	Bright Blue Metallic
21	Light Blue Metallic
67	Dark Brown Metallic
84	Charcoal Metallic
54	Gold Metallic
77	Maroon Metallic
57	Orange Metallic
75	Red
51	Bright Yellow
1982	
11	White
16	Silver Metallic
21	Light Blue Metallic
29	Dark Blue Metallic
45	Light Jadestone Med
55	Gold Wing Metallic
67	Dark Gold Wing Me
75	Spectra Red
84	Charcoal Metallic
78	Dark Claret Metalli
19	Black

CAMARO ROAD TEST PERFORMANCE

Publication	Date	Year/Model	Displ/hp/cyl (cu.in.)	Trans	Axle	0-60 (sec.)	Q-mi/spd (sec/mph)	Top-spd (mph)
Car and Driver	November 1966	'67 SS-350	350/295/V8	4-spd	3.31	7.8	16.1/87	120
Motor Trend	December 1966	'67 RS	327/210/V8	auto	2.73	10.7	18.2/77	—
Hot Rod	January 1967	'67 SS-350	350/295/V8	4-spd	3.55	—	14.9/96	—
Car and Driver	March 1967	'67 Z-28	302/290/V8	4-spd	3.70	6.7	14.9/97	124
Car Life	March 1967	'67 coupe	250/155/6	3-spd	3.31	11.4	18.5/75	104
Car Life	March 1967	'67 SS-350	350/295/V8	4-spd	3.55	7.8	15.8/89	120
Motor Trend	July 1967	'67 Dana 427	427/425/V8	4-spd	3.73	—	12.8/110	—
Car and Driver	July 1967	'67 Nickey 427	427/425/V8	4-spd	3.73	—	13.9/114	—
Car and Driver	July 1968	'68 Z-28	302/290/V8	4-spd	4.10	5.3	13.8/107	132
Hot Rod	January 1969	'69 Z-28	302/290/V8	4-spd	4.88	—	13.1/107	—
Car Life	May 1969	'69 SS-396	396/375/V8	4-spd	3.73	6.8	14.8/99	126
Car Life	August 1969	'69 Z-28	302/290/V8	4-spd	4.10	7.4	15.1/95	133
Car and Driver	August 1969	'69 Z-28	350/370/V8	4-spd	3.73	5.4	13.7/104	129

'ont te	Rinished-Mason	Ditzler
38	2080	2058
8140	12201	3308
	A946/P403	9300
3007	11403D	3207
110	12202F	3309
141	12203	3310
142	12225G	3328
012	11421	3223
116	12219D	3322
109	12231V	3333
113	12222V	3329
115	12229V	3332
019	11409V	3219

8	2080	2058
140	12201	3308
141	1203	3310
007	11403D	3207
403	12215	3318
208	12672	3424
215	12678D	3433
115	12229V	3332
012	11421	3223
213	12685	3440
	A946/P403	9300

CAMARO SALES

	Model Year	Calendar Year
1966	—	46,758
1967	201,134	205,816
1968	217,700	213,980
1969	193,986	171,598
1970	148,301	145,826
1971	116,627	128,106
1972	70,809	45,330
1973	91,678	108,381
1974	135,780	136,404
1975	135,102	145,029
1976	163,653	172,846
1977	198,755	208,511
1978	247,437	260,201
1979	233,802	204,742
1980	131,066	116,824
TOTAL	2,285,830	2,310,352

CAMARO PRODUCTION

	Total Cars (Model Year)	Convertibles (Model Year)	Z-28 (Model Year)	Total Cars (Calendar Year)
1966	—	—	—	94,417
1967	220,906	25,141	602	216,204
1968	235,147	20,440	7,199	229,335
1969	243,085	17,573	19,014	159,201
1970	124,901	—	8,733	143,664
1971	114,643	—	4,863	148,378
1972	68,651	—	2,575	35,943
1973	96,752	—	11,575	117,828
1974	151,008	—	13,802	157,909
1975	145,775	—	—	156,395
1976	182,981	—	—	201,652
1977	218,854	—	14,347	229,647
1978	272,633	—	54,907	281,754
1979	282,582	—	84,879	257,873
1980	152,021	—	45,143	115,574
TOTAL	2,509,939	63,154	267,639	2,545,774

Appendices

Publication	Date	Year/Model	Displ/hp/cyl (cu.in.)	Trans	Axle	0-60 (sec.)	Q-mi/spd (sec/mph)	Top-spd (mph)
Sports Car Graphic	May 1970	'69 T/A Z-28	302/420/V8	4-spd	4.11	5.0	12.8/116	143
Road & Track	May 1970	'70 RS	350/300/V8	auto	3.07	8.8	16.6/86	115
Car and Driver	May 1970	'70 Z-28	350/360/V8	auto	4.10	5.8	14.2/100	118
Sports Car Graphic	June 1970	'70 Z-28	350/360/V8	4-spd	4.10	6.5	14.6/98	120
Car and Driver	May 1971	'71 Z-28	350/330/V8	4-spd	3.73	6.7	15.1/95	130
Road & Track	April 1972	'72 RS	350/165/V8	4-spd	3.08	9.8	17.2/83	—
Car and Driver	September 1973	'73 Z-28/LT	350/245/V8	4-spd	3.42	6.7	15.2/95	123
Car and Driver	August 1975	'75 RS	350/155/V8	auto	3.08	8.5	16.8/82	116
Hot Rod	April 1977	'77 Z-28	350/170/V8	4-spd	3.73	—	15.4/9	110
Motor Trend	May 1977	'77 Z-28	350/170/V8	auto	3.42	8.1	15.4/90	—
Car and Driver	March 1978	'78 Z-28	350/185/V8	4-spd	3.73	7.3	16.0/91	123
Road & Track	October 1978	IROC racer	350/450/V8	4-spd	3.91	5.2	13.3/111	152
Car and Driver	November 1978	Mitchell turbo	350/330/V8	auto	3.42	6.3	15.0/99	—
Car and Driver	April 1980	'80 Z-28	350/190/V8	4-spd	3.08	8.5	16.4/86	120

CAMARO BASIC SPECIFICATIONS: Base Two-Door

	1967	1968	1969	1970	1971	1972	1973	1974	1975	1976	1977	1978	1979	1980	1981	1982
Overall length, inches	184.7	184.6	186.0	188.0	188.0	188.0	195.4	195.4	195.4	195.4	195.4	197.6	197.6	197.6	197.6	187.8
Overall width, inches	72.5	72.3	74.0	74.4	74.4	74.4	74.4	74.4	74.4	74.4	74.4	74.4	74.4	74.4	74.4	72.0
Overall height, inches	51.4	50.9	51.6	50.5	49.1	49.1	49.2	49.2	49.1	49.2	49.2	49.2	49.2	49.2	50.1	49.8
Wheelbase, inches	108.0	108.0	108.0	108.0	108.0	108.0	108.0	108.0	108.0	108.0	108.0	108.0	108.0	108.0	108.0	101.0
Front Tread, inches	59.0	59.6	59.6	61.3	61.3	61.3	61.3	61.3	61.3	61.3	61.3	61.3	61.3	61.3	61.3	60.7
Rear Tread, inches	58.9	59.5	59.5	60.0	60.0	60.0	60.0	60.0	60.0	60.0	60.0	60.0	60.0	60.0	60.0	60.6
Curb weight, pounds	2910	2950	3120	3166	3186	3213	3229	3429	3531	3513	3456	3409	3392	3402	3330	2840
Usable trunk room, cubic feet	8.3	8.3	8.5	7.3	6.4	6.4	6.7	6.3*	6.4*	6.4*	6.4*	6.4*	7.2	7.2	9.2	11.7
Fuel capacity, gallons	18	18	18	19	17	18	18	21	21	21	21	21	21	21	21	17.4**

*7.2 cubic feet with space saver spare tire option, standard in 1979
**16.9 gallons for base four-cylinder and Z-28, which have tank-mounted electric fuel pump

CAMARO OPTIONAL EQUIPMENT INSTALLATION (PERCENTAGE)

	1967	1968	1969	1970	1971	1972	1973	1974	1975	1976	1977	1978	1979	1980
Engine, V-8	73.4	78.3	85.0	89.9	90.2	93.0	96.3	85.3	79.9	79.2	85.7	86.4	92.2	66.4
Engine, Six-Cylinder	26.6	21.7	15.0	10.1	9.8	7.0	3.7	14.7	20.1	20.8	14.3	13.6	7.8	33.6
Transmission, Automatic	56.2	56.4	57.6	73.1	79.4	82.7	82.1	85.0	86.8	87.5	89.8	87.9	88.1	87.3
Transmission, Four-Speed	21.5	20.2	23.9	15.0	9.3	8.5	11.8	7.4	6.0	6.2	6.2	9.7	10.5	8.1
Transmission, Three-Speed	22.3	23.4	18.5	11.9	11.3	8.8	6.1	7.6	7.2	6.3	4.0	2.4	1.4	4.6
Power Brakes	8.3	10.2	6.7	28.5	36.3	78.0	88.4	91.3	85.4	91.7	95.1	96.2	98.2	100.0
Front Disc Brakes	6.7	8.6	29.0	47.7	100.0	100.0	100.0	100.0	100.0	100.0	100.0	100.0	100.0	100.0
Power Steering	41.7	49.0	57.3	74.2	81.3	87.2	100.0	100.0	100.0	100.0	100.0	100.0	100.0	100.0
Limited-Slip Differential	14.4	15.6	21.0	15.8	10.3	11.1	19.4	13.4	6.1	7.0	8.0	12.0	13.7	11.6
Radial-Ply Tires	—	—	—	—	—	—	—	32.9	86.2	91.0	93.5	94.1	97.5	100.0
Power Windows	2.2	1.4	1.4	—	—	—	—	—	7.3	10.4	14.2	18.7	28.8	29.4
Tinted Glass	15.7	27.8	47.2	57.1	58.7	67.6	70.5	78.3	77.6	78.5	83.0	85.5	87.6	85.9
Air Conditioning	12.6	15.3	18.1	30.9	37.1	46.2	51.2	52.4	53.0	60.6	66.1	71.4	78.2	70.5
Cruise Control	0.1	0.1	—	—	—	—	—	—	—	0.5	11.0	17.2	26.5	25.1
Adjustable Steering Column	3.6	2.3	3.0	5.4	7.3	5.4	13.6	15.7	21.6	25.5	35.4	42.9	51.6	52.3
Vinyl Top	23.7	32.8	41.1	34.6	33.4	34.8	32.4	25.2	18.4	13.6	9.0	4.3	1.9	—

Note: A dash indicates the item was not offered.

General Index

Index of Illustrations

Page numbers in bold refer to color photos.

Photo Credits

49, 107, 134 (top, right): courtesy of Car and Driver magazine. (43 top and lower left), 56 (right), 57, 70, 71, 104, 105: photographs by Dave Arnold. 98 (left): photograph by Joe Clark. 150 (top, right), 151 (top, left): photograph by Ken Hill. 56 (left): photograph by Peter Luongo, courtesy of Dan Luginbuhl of Penske Racing. All other photographs and illustrations courtesy of Chevrolet Division and General Motors Design Staff.